HAVENS

for

TRAVELERS

PREFACE

—

Havens for Travelers is dedicated to the Christian auto and RV traveler and their search for overnight accommodations that combine an environment of Christian values with essential amenities at a reasonable cost.

Havens is the result of 11 months of research requiring almost 5000 telephone calls to over 3000 Protestant, Catholic and Orthodox Christian conference centers, retreat centers, camps, monasteries, abbeys and YM/YWCA's across the USA. Of these, 388 covering the 48 contiguous states have qualified for a listing in Havens for Travelers. All provide overnight accommodations to Christian individuals and families "on the road". The remaining 2600 centers restrict themselves either to groups or individuals who are on retreats. Thus, an individual attempting to find an overnight Haven for themselves would, on average, have to contact 7-8 locations before finding one that would be prepared, if space were available, to offer accommodations.

All listings are explicitly Christian, except for three, which have been identified, that are ecumenically spiritual and frequented by Christian groups. By all other measures the variety of listings is enormous.

Accommodations range from bunkrooms to dormitory style (private rooms with shared bath) to motel style (private bath) and cabins, both rustic and fully equipped. Many locations offer deluxe chalets, duplex and efficiency apartments and complete small houses with full kitchen and dining room. Over 40% of all listings offer RV hookups ranging from primitive to full capability. Unless otherwise indicated accommodations are winterized.

Listings are arranged alphabetically by state and similarly within each state by full name. In the table of contents "******" means that location offers RV hookups.

Each location is described by up to 70 items of information in a standard format.

We have also included an Interstate Highway Cross-Index which lists, by page and listing ID number, all those locations which have identified the IS that is closest to them. Most locations are within 40 miles of an IS exit but a few are 80-120 miles.

Prices range from $4/person (bring your own sleeping bag, towels and soap) to over $100 for private room with bath and three meals. Unless otherwise indicated rates are for Sunday through Friday nights, exclude taxes, service charges, and meals.

Reservations are usually not required, but many places fill up rapidly, even weeks ahead, particularly in the summer. They and we recommend strongly that you **CALL AHEAD**, if only one or two days in advance.

If children are part of the travel group, inquire ahead about cribs and high chairs. Most places have children's rates (usually if in the same room as parents); many have family rates. Some large bunkrooms have separate areas for men and women to maximize utilization; others offer one family an entire bunkroom.

Alcohol use is usually prohibited but is sometimes permitted in the RV or in private rooms. Smoking is almost always prohibited inside but usually permitted outside, although sometimes only in designated areas.

There are over 2000 YMCA's and YWCA's in the United States. We have identified and spoken to something over 50 that offer overnight accommodations to transients. These offer rare value for downtown accommodations in urban areas. Many residences include membership in the local "Y" for the duration of your stay as part of the lodging fee. Others charge a nominal fee for use of local facilities which usually include a gym and swimming pool and sometimes a sauna or racquetball court.

We have included a list of amenities for each location. Some locations have more than we could possibly include. The more contemplative retreat centers generally have few recreational activities because their focus is on reflection and quietude. For many people this is exactly what's needed after a long day's drive.

There are many reasons why I undertook to compile this book. The most satisfying is the hope that Christians from across the breadth of the Church will find in *Havens for Travelers* not only places of physical renewal but, perhaps even more importantly, Havens from the spiritual and moral storms raging in our secular culture.

Agape,

Walter W. Lynn
Ridgewood, New Jersey
May, 1999

TABLE OF CONTENTS

** RV Capability

ALABAMA

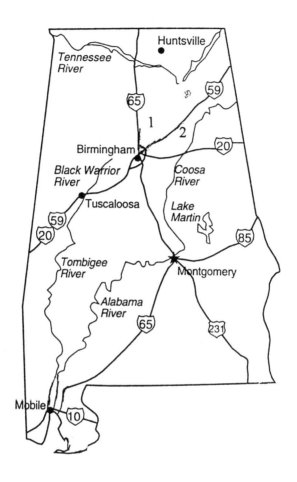

Huntsville

Tennessee River

65

59

1

2

20

Birmingham

Black Warrior River

Coosa River

Tuscaloosa

Lake Martin

59

20

85

Tombigee River

Alabama River

Montgomery

65

231

Mobile

10

NAME OF CENTER: St. Bernard Abbey   Listing ID #: 1

Telephone: 256-734-3946; Fax: 256-734-2925; E-mail:
Address: 1600 Bernard Dr. SE; Cullman; AL; 35055
Nearest Interstate: I-65, Exit 308; 6 miles; Nearest State/US Hwy: US 278.

Restrictions: Age: **None; Pets: Not permitted; Alcohol: Not permitted; Smoking: Outdoors only; Reservation Req'd: 7 days; Max. Adv. Reser.: 6 mo; Seasonal closing: None

RV/Campers overnight hookups: No

ACCOM: Mon. night thru Thurs. night rates for winterized (check if this is critical) rooms w/o meals unless otherwise indicated.

Motel; Max. Pers: 2; Bedding incl ?: Yes; Bath: Private; A/C: Yes:
Rate for: Person; Free will
** Strict behavior required from children.

Main amenities available: Volleyball; Basketball; Hiking
Meals are served in dining room for transients only when other groups are present. Approx. dinner price: Free will donation.
FREE WILL DONATION FOR LODGING AND MEALS

NAME OF CENTER: Sumatanga   Listing ID #: 2

Telephone: 256-538--9860; Fax: 256-538-7488; E-mail: sumatanga@worldnet.att.net
Address: 3616 Sumatanga Rd.; Gallant; AL; 35972
Nearest Interstate: I-59, Nearest State/US Hwy: Rte 31

Restrictions: Age: None; Pets: Not permitted; Alcohol: Not permitted; Smoking: Outdoors only; Reservation Req'd: 1 day; Max. Adv. Reser.: Open; Seasonal closing: None

RV/Campers overnight hookups: Yes; Water: Yes; Electric: Yes; Septic: Yes
Basic Rate/Night: $8.00/ veh

ACCOM: Mon. night thru Thurs. night rates for winterized (check if this is critical) rooms w/o meals unless otherwise indicated.

Motel; Max. Pers: 4; Bedding incl ?: Yes; Bath: Private; A/C: Yes:
Rate for: Person; $36; Rate for #2nd pers: $0; Rate for #3 pers: $5; Child Rate: Free under 6 yrs

Dormitory; Max. Pers: Unk; Bedding incl ?: Unk; Bath: Shared; A/C: Yes
Rate for: Person: $11; Rate for #2nd pers: $11; Rate for #3 pers: $11; Child Rate:

Guest Hse; Max. Pers: 2; Bedding incl ?: Yes; Bath: Private; A/C: Yes:
Rate for: Room: $27

Main amenities available: Canoe/Boat; Tennis; Basketball; Olympic pool; Ping pong; Hiking-1800 acres
Meals are served in dining room for transients. Approx. dinner price: $6; 50% off under 6 yrs; free under 3.

NAME OF CENTER: YMCA - Metro Huntsville Listing ID: 3

Telephone: 256-539-5704   Fax: 256-539-5705
Address: 203 S. Greene St.; Huntsville, AL 35801

Restrictions:
Accommodations offered to (M/F/Families): M. If M/F then must be over 18 yrs.
Pets: Not permitted; Alcohol: Not permitted; Smoking: Bedroom only
Reservation requirements: None
Reservations are accepted up to 0 days in advance. Seasonal closing: None

ACCOMMODATIONS:
Single room: Bedding included ?: Yes; Bath: Shared
Rate for 1 day: not offered; Rate for 1 week: $50+$55 deposit
$6/day for membership in Y

Main amenities: Pool; Gym; Basketball
Meals are not offered in their own cafeteria.

REMEMBER TO CALL AHEAD

ARKANSAS

NAME OF CENTER: Ferncliff Camp & Conference Center   Listing ID #: 4

Telephone: 501-821-3063; Fax: 501-821-3093; E-mail: heatherkilpatrick@ecunet.org
Address: 1720 Ferncliff Rd; Little Rock; AR; 72223
Nearest Interstate: I-430, Exit ; 10 miles; Nearest State/US Hwy: Rte 10; 5 miles.

Restrictions: Age: None; Pets: Not permitted; Alcohol: Not permitted; Smoking: Not permitted in bedroom; Reservation Req'd: 5 days; Max. Adv. Reser.: Open; Seasonal closing: None

RV/Campers overnight hookups: No

ACCOM: Mon. night thru Thurs. night rates for winterized (check if this is critical) rooms w/o meals unless otherwise indicated.

Bunkroom; Max. Pers: Over 5; Bedding incl ?: Yes (w/notice); Bath: Shared; A/C: Yes: Rate for: Person; $15; Rate for #2nd pers: $15; Rate for #3 pers: $15; Child Rate: Free under 5 yrs

Motel; Max. Pers: 4; Bedding incl ?: Yes (w/notice); Bath: Private; A/C: Yes

Main amenities available: Swimming; Volleyball; Basketball; Boating; Ropes course; Hiking
Meals are served in dining room for transients only when other groups are present. Approx. dinner price: $4-$7.00.

NAME OF CENTER: Little Portion Retreat Center   Listing ID #: 5

Telephone: 501-253-7379; Fax: 501-253-2640; E-mail:
Address: 171 Hummingbird Lane; Eureka Springs; AR; 72632
Nearest Interstate: I44, Exit ; 90 miles; Nearest State/US Hwy: Rte 62; 6 miles.

Restrictions: Age: None; Pets: Not permitted; Alcohol: Not permitted; Smoking: Outdoors only; Reservation Req'd: None; Max. Adv. Reser.: Open; Seasonal closing: None

RV/Campers overnight hookups: No

ACCOM: Mon. night thru Thurs. night rates for winterized (check if this is critical) rooms w/o meals unless otherwise indicated.

Motel; Max. Pers: 2; Bedding incl ?: No; Bath: Private; A/C: Yes:
Rate for: Person; $16; Rate for #2nd pers: $10

Main amenities available: Quiet areas
Meals are served in dining room for transients only when other groups are present. Approx. dinner price: $5.00.

NAME OF CENTER: Ozark Conference Center   Listing ID #: 6

Telephone: 501-354-3959; Fax: 501-354-9141; E-mail: Ozark@mev.net
Address: 4 Ozark Mountain Rd.; Solgohachia; AR; 72156
Nearest Interstate: I-40, Exit Morrilton; 7 miles; Nearest State/US Hwy: Rte 9; 2 miles.

Restrictions: Age: None; Pets: Outside only; Alcohol: Not permitted; Smoking: Outdoors only; Reservation Req'd: 2 days; Max. Adv. Reser.: 14 days; Seasonal closing: None

RV/Campers overnight hookups: Yes; Water: Yes; Electric: Yes; Septic: Yes
Basic Rate/Night: $15.00/ veh

ACCOM: Mon. night thru Thurs. night rates for winterized (check if this is critical) rooms w/o meals unless otherwise indicated.

Motel; Max. Pers: 4; Bedding incl ?: Yes; Bath: Private; A/C: Yes:
Rate for: Room; $25

Main amenities available: Swimming pool; Volleyball; Basketball; Horse shoes; Ping pong; Fishing
Meals are not served in dining room for transients . Approx. dinner price: .

ARIZONA

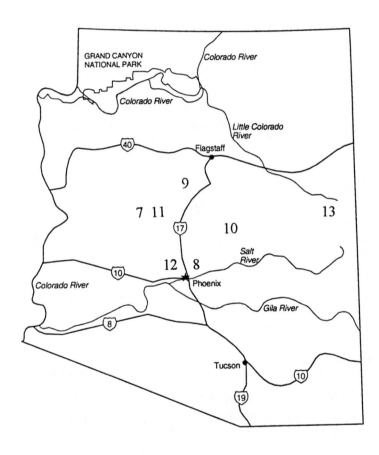

GRAND CANYON
NATIONAL PARK

Colorado River

Colorado River

Little Colorado
River

40   Flagstaff

9

7 11   13

17   10

Salt
River

12   8

10   Colorado River   Phoenix

Gila River

8

Tucson

10

19

NAME OF CENTER: Camp Pinerock   Listing ID #: 7

Telephone: 520-445-8357; Fax: 602-465-5939; E-mail:
Address: 1400 Pine Drive; Prescott; AZ; 86303
Nearest Interstate: I-17; 50 miles; Nearest State/US Hwy: Rte 69; 5 miles.

Restrictions: Age: None; Pets: Not permitted; Alcohol: Not permitted; Smoking: Outdoors only;
Reservation Req'd: 14 days; Max. Adv. Reser.: 1 yr; Seasonal closing: June/Aug

RV/Campers overnight hookups: Yes; Water: Yes; Electric: Yes; Septic: Yes
Basic Rate/Night: $11.00/ veh

ACCOM: Mon. night thru Thurs. night rates for winterized (check if this is critical) rooms w/o
meals unless otherwise indicated.

Bunkroom; Max. Pers: 8; Bedding incl ?: No; Bath: Shared; A/C: No:
Rate for: Room; $25

Cabin; Max. Pers: 10; Bedding incl ?: No; Bath: Shared ; A/C: No
Rate for: Two persons: $35; Rate for #2nd pers: ; Rate for #3 pers: $5; Child Rate: n/a

Motel; Max. Pers: 4; Bedding incl ?: Yes; Bath: Private; A/C: No:
Rate for: Room: $60
Includes fireplace & full kitchen

Main amenities available: Convenience store; Volleyball; Basketball; Horseshoes; Ping-pong; Hiking
Meals are served in dining room for transients only when other groups are present. Approx. dinner price: $4.00.

NAME OF CENTER: Franciscan Renewal Center   Listing ID #: 8

Telephone: 602-948-7460; Fax: 602-948-2325; E-mail: pazybien@aol.com
Address: 5802 E. Lincoln Drive; Scottsdale; AZ; 85253
Nearest Interstate: I-17, 10 miles; Nearest State/US Hwy: Rte 51; 5 miles.

Restrictions: Age: 16 yrs; Pets: Not permitted; Alcohol: Permitted; Smoking: Outdoors only;
Reservation Req'd: Noon of day; Max. Adv. Reser.: Open; Seasonal closing: None

RV/Campers overnight hookups: No

ACCOM: Mon. night thru Thurs. night rates for winterized (check if this is critical) rooms w/o
meals unless otherwise indicated.

Motel; Max. Pers: 2; Bedding incl ?: Yes; Bath: Private; A/C: Yes:
Rate for: Person; $60; Rate for #2nd pers: $60; Rate for #3 pers: n/a; Child Rate: n/a

Main amenities available: Swimming; Hot tub; Bookstore; Hiking
Meals are served in dining room for transients only when other groups are present. Approx. dinner price: $8.00.

7

NAME OF CENTER: **Living Water Worship & Teaching Ctr**   Listing ID #: 9

Telephone: 520-634-4421; Fax: 520-634-0005; E-mail:
Address: PO Box 529; Cornville; AZ; 86325
Nearest Interstate: I-17, Exit; 9 miles; Nearest State/US Hwy: Rte 89A; 3 miles.

Restrictions: Age: None; Pets: Not permitted; Alcohol: Not permitted; Smoking: Outdoors only;
Reservation Req'd: 2 days; Max. Adv. Reser.: Open; Seasonal closing: Christmas & Easter
weekends

RV/Campers overnight hookups: No

ACCOM: Mon. night thru Thurs. night rates for winterized (check if this is critical) rooms w/o
meals unless otherwise indicated.

Motel; Max. Pers: 2; Bedding incl ?: Yes (w/notice); Bath: Private; A/C: Yes:
Rate for: Person; $60; Rate for #2nd pers: $40; Child Rate: n/a

Main amenities available: Swimming; Library; Volleyball; Hiking; Horseshoes; Fishing
Meals are served in dining room for transients only when other groups are present. Approx. dinner price: $7.00.

NAME OF CENTER: **LOMONA**   Listing ID #: 10

Telephone: 520-474-2552; Fax: 520-474-6038; E-mail: mtcross@cybertrails.com
Address: 601 East Highway 260; Payson; AZ; 85541
Nearest Interstate: I-17, Exit 50 miles; Nearest State/US Hwy: Rte 260; 0 miles.

Restrictions: Age: None; Pets: Not permitted; Alcohol: Not permitted; Smoking: Outdoors only;
Reservation Req'd: 3 days; Max. Adv. Reser.: 1 mo; Seasonal closing: None

RV/Campers overnight hookups: No

ACCOM: Mon. night thru Thurs. night rates for winterized (check if this is critical) rooms w/o
meals unless otherwise indicated.

Bunkroom; Max. Pers: 6; Bedding incl ?: No; Bath: Shared; A/C: Yes:
Rate for: Person; $12; Rate for #2 pers: $12; Rate for #3 pers: $12; Child Rate: None;
$8 for second night

Main amenities available: Basketball; Hiking
Meals are not served in dining room for transients only when other groups are present. Dinner price: .
Restaurants very close by

NAME OF CENTER: Prescott Pines Camp & Conf. Ctr.   Listing ID #: 11

Telephone: 520-445-5225; Fax: 602-258-3660; E-mail:
Address: 855 E. Schoolhouse Gulch; Prescott; AZ; 86303
Nearest Interstate: I-17, Exit; 38 miles; Nearest State/US Hwy: Rte 89; 4 miles.

Restrictions: Age: None; Pets: Permitted on leash; Alcohol: Not permitted; Smoking: Nowhere; Reservation Req'd: 2-7 days; Max. Adv. Reser.: Open; Seasonal closing: None

RV/Campers overnight hookups: Yes; Water: Yes; Electric: Yes; Septic: Yes
Basic Rate/Night: $19.00/ veh

ACCOM: Mon. night thru Thurs. night rates for winterized (check if this is critical) rooms w/o meals unless otherwise indicated.

Cabin; Max. Pers: 16; Bedding incl ?: No; Bath: Separate bldg; A/C: No:
Rate for: Person; $20; Rate for #2nd pers: $20; Rate for #3 pers: $20; Child Rate: n/a
Inquire about children's rates

Cabin; Max. Pers: 6-12; Bedding incl ?: No; Bath: In bldg, shared; A/C: No
Rate for: Person: $24; Rate for #2nd pers: $24; Rate for #3 pers: $24; Child Rate: n/a

Motel; Max. Pers: 4; Bedding incl ?: Yes; Bath: Private; A/C: Yes:
Rate for: Person: $33

Main amenities available: Swimming; Volleyball; Basketball; Laundry machine; Bookstore; Hiking
Meals are served in dining room for transients only when other groups are present. Approx. dinner price: $6.00.

NAME OF CENTER: Spirit in the Desert Retreat Center   Listing ID #: 12

Telephone: 602-488-5218; Fax: 602-488-5426; E-mail:
Address: 7415 East Elbow Bend; Carefree; AZ; 85377
Nearest Interstate: I-17, Exit 20 miles; Nearest State/US Hwy: Carefree Hwy; 7 miles.

Restrictions: Age: 18 yrs; Pets: Not permitted; Alcohol: Permitted; Smoking: Outdoors only; Reservation Req'd: None; Max. Adv. Rescr.: 1 yr; Seasonal closing: Dining room closed Easter & Christmas wk; Thanksgiving, New Yr

RV/Campers overnight hookups: No

ACCOM: Mon. night thru Thurs. night rates for winterized (check if this is critical) rooms w/o meals unless otherwise indicated.

Motel; Max. Pers: 2; Bedding incl ?: Yes; Bath: Private; A/C: Yes:
Rate for: Person; $70; Rate for #2nd pers: $20; Child Rate: N/A

Main amenities available: Jacuzzi; Swimming; Hiking
Meals are served in dining room for transients only when other groups are present. Approx. dinner price: $12.00.

NAME OF CENTER: The Love Kitchen, Camp Grace   Listing ID #: 13

Telephone: 520-537-1252; Fax: 520-537-8987; E-mail: scote@cybertails.com
Address: PO Box 1373; Pinetop; AZ; 85935
Nearest Interstate: I-40, Exit 45 miles; Nearest State/US Hwy: Rte 260; 1 miles.

Restrictions: Age: None; Pets: Not permitted; Alcohol: Not permitted; Smoking: Outdoors only; Reservation Req'd: 2 days; Max. Adv. Reser.: 14 days; Seasonal closing: June - Aug 10

RV/Campers overnight hookups: No

ACCOM: Mon. night thru Thurs. night rates for winterized (check if this is critical) rooms w/o meals unless otherwise indicated.

Bunkroom; Max. Pers: Over 5; Bedding incl ?: No; Bath: Separate bldg; A/C: No:
Rate for: Person; $18; Rate for #2nd pers: $18; Rate for #3 pers: $18; Child Rate: $15 under 10 yrs

Dormitory; Max. Pers: 5; Bedding incl ?: No; Bath: Shared; A/C: No
Rate for: Person: $25; Rate for #2nd pers: $18; Rate for #3 pers: $18; Child Rate: $15 under 10 yrs

Motel; Max. Pers: 5; Bedding incl ?: No; Bath: Private; A/C: No:
Rate for: Person: $25; Rate for #2nd pers: $18; Rate for #3 pers: $18; Child Rate: $15 under 10 yrs

Main amenities available: Softball; Volleyball; Basketball; Hiking
Meals are served in dining room for transients only when other groups are present. Approx. dinner price: $5-7.50.

NAME OF CENTER: YMCA - Phoenix Listing ID: 14

Telephone: 602-253-6181   Fax: 602-258-5548
Address: 350 N. 1st Ave.; Phoenix, AZ 85003

Restrictions:
Accommodations offered to (M/F/Families): M&F. If M/F then must be over 18 yrs.
Pets: Not permitted; Alcohol: Not permitted; Smoking: Bedroom only
Reservation requirements: None
Reservations are accepted up to 0 days in advance. Seasonal closing: None

ACCOMMODATIONS:
Single room: Bedding included ?: Yes; Bath: Shared
Rate for 1 day: $23+$10 dep; Rate for 1 week: $90+$10 dep
$2/day or $5/wk for membership in Y

: Bedding included ?: ; Bath:
Rate for 1 day: ; Rate for 1 week:

Main amenities: Laundry machine; Pool; Gym; Sauna; Racquetball; Steam room
Meals are not offered in their own cafeteria.

NAME OF CENTER: YMCA - Bisbee Listing ID: 15

Telephone: 520-432-3542   Fax:
Address: 26 Howell St.; PO Box 968; Bisbee, AZ 85603

Restrictions:
Accommodations offered to (M/F/Families): M&F. If M/F then must be over 18 yrs.
Pets: Not permitted; Alcohol: Not permitted; Smoking: Nowhere
Reservation requirements: None
Reservations are accepted up to 10 days in advance. Seasonal closing: None

ACCOMMODATIONS:
Bunkroom: Bedding included ?: No; Bath: Shared
Rate for 1 day: $10; Rate for 1 week:
Kitchen privilege

Main amenities:
Meals are not offered in their own cafeteria.

REMEMBER TO CALL AHEAD

CALIFORNIA

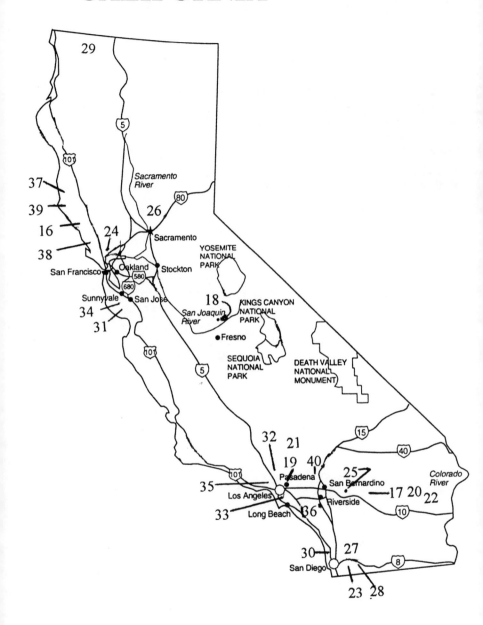

NAME OF CENTER: Alliance Redwoods   Listing ID #: 16

Telephone: 707-874-3507; Fax: 707-874-2509; E-mail: timw@allianceredwoods.com
Address: 6750 Bohemian Hwy; Occidental; CA; 95465
Nearest Interstate: I-80, Exit 40 miles; Nearest State/US Hwy: Rte 101; 40 miles.

Restrictions: Age: None; Pets: Not permitted; Alcohol: Not permitted; Smoking: Not permitted in bedroom; Reservation Req'd: 7 days; Max. Adv. Reser.: Open; Seasonal closing: None

RV/Campers overnight hookups: Yes; Water: Yes; Electric: Yes; Septic: n/a
Basic Rate/Night: $12-15/ veh

ACCOM: Mon. night thru Thurs. night rates for winterized (check if this is critical) rooms w/o meals unless otherwise indicated.

Cabin; Max. Pers: Over 5; Bedding incl ?: Yes; Bath: Shared; A/C: No:
Rate for: Person; $40; Rate for #2nd pers: $40; Rate for #3 pers: $40; Child Rate: n/a

Dormitory; Max. Pers: 5; Bedding incl ?: Yes; Bath: Shared; A/C: No
Rate for: Person: $61; Rate for #2nd pers: $61; Rate for #3 pers: $61; Child Rate: n/a

Motel; Max. Pers: 5; Bedding incl ?: Yes; Bath: Private; A/C: No:
Rate for: Person: $69; Rate for #2nd pers: $69; Rate for #3 pers: $69; Child Rate: n/a

Main amenities available: Swimming; Volleyball; Basketball; Incidentals store; Laundry machine ; Many others
Meals are served in dining room for transients only when other groups are present. Approx. dinner price: .

NAME OF CENTER: Alpine Meadows Camp & Conf. Ctr.   Listing ID #: 17

Telephone: 909-794-3800; Fax: 909-389-1148; E-mail: huber@alpinecamp.com
Address: 42900 Jenks Lake Rd.; Angelus Oaks; CA; 92305
Nearest Interstate: I-10, Exit 30 miles; Nearest State/US Hwy: Rte 38; 1 miles.

Restrictions: Age: None; Pets: Not permitted; Alcohol: Not permitted; Smoking: Not permitted in bedroom; Reservation Req'd: 1 day; Max. Adv. Reser.: 10 days; Seasonal closing: None

RV/Campers overnight hookups: No

ACCOM: Mon. night thru Thurs. night rates for winterized (check if this is critical) rooms w/o meals unless otherwise indicated.

Bunkroom; Max. Pers: Over 5; Bedding incl ?: No; Bath: Shared; A/C: Yes:
Rate for: Person; $26; Rate for #2nd pers: $26; Rate for #3 pers: $26; Child Rate: Free under 5 yrs

Dormitory; Max. Pers: 5; Bedding incl ?: No; Bath: Shared; A/C: Yes
Rate for: Person: $32; Rate for #2nd pers: $32; Rate for #3 pers: $32; Child Rate: Free under 5 yrs

Motel; Max. Pers: 5; Bedding incl ?: No; Bath: Private; A/C: Yes:
Rate for: Person: $46; Rate for #2nd pers: $46; Rate for #3 pers: $46; Child Rate: Free under 5 yrs.

Main amenities available: Swimming; Volleyball; Basketball; Laundry machine; Tennis; VCR-TV
Meals are served in dining room for transients only when other groups are present. Approx. dinner price: $6.00.

13

NAME OF CENTER: **Calvin Crest Conferences**   Listing ID #: 18

Telephone: 559-683-4450; Fax: 559-683-7118; E-mail: calvincr@sierranet.net
Address: 45800 Calvin Crest Rd.; Oakhurst; CA; 93644
Nearest Interstate: I-5, Exit 65 miles; Nearest State/US Hwy: Rte 41; 7 miles.

Restrictions: Age: None; Pets: Not permitted; Alcohol: Not permitted; Smoking: Outdoors only;
Reservation Req'd: 3 days; Max. Adv. Reser.: 2 mo; Seasonal closing: None

RV/Campers overnight hookups: No

ACCOM: Mon. night thru Thurs. night rates for winterized (check if this is critical) rooms w/o
meals unless otherwise indicated.

Motel; Max. Pers: 5; Bedding incl ?: Yes (w/notice); Bath: Private; A/C: Yes:
Up to 4 pers $55 ($75 June - Aug.) $10/additional. Guests make & strip beds

Main amenities available: Swimming; Volleyball; Basketball; Laundry machine; Boating; Hiking
Meals are not served in dining room for transients

NAME OF CENTER: **Camp Arev**   Listing ID #: 19

Telephone: 626-796-0517; Fax: 626-796-1615; E-mail: arevbabe@aol.com
Address: PO Box 70423; Pasadena; CA; 91117
Nearest Interstate: I-5, Exit 10 miles

Restrictions: Age: None; Pets: Not permitted; Alcohol: Not permitted; Smoking: Parking lot
only; Reservation Req'd: 1 day; Max. Adv. Reser.: Open; Seasonal closing: None

RV/Campers overnight hookups: No

ACCOM: Mon. night thru Thurs. night rates for winterized (check if this is critical) rooms w/o
meals unless otherwise indicated.

Bunkroom; Max. Pers: Over 5; Bedding incl ?: No; Bath: Shared; A/C: No:
Rate for: Person; $20; Rate for #2nd pers: $15; Rate for #3 pers: $15; Child Rate: $10

Cabin; Max. Pers: n/a; Bedding incl ?: No; Bath: In bldg; A/C: No
Rate for: Person: $20; Rate for #2nd pers: $15; Rate for #3 pers: $15; Child Rate: $10.00

Main amenities available: Swimming; Volleyball; Basketball; Library; Ball field; Hiking
Meals are served in dining room for transients only when other groups are present. Approx. dinner price: $8.00.

NAME OF CENTER: **Camp Cedar Falls Conference Center**   Listing ID #: 20

Telephone: 909-794-2911; Fax: 909-389-9241; E-mail: cedar_falls@eee.org
Address: 39850 State Hwy 38; Angelus Oaks; CA; 92305
Nearest Interstate: I-10, Exit; 25 miles; Nearest State/US Hwy: Rte 38; 1 miles.

Restrictions: Age: None; Pets: Not permitted; Alcohol: Not permitted; Smoking: Designated outdoor area; Reservation Req'd: None; Max. Adv. Reser.: 1 yr; Seasonal closing: None

RV/Campers overnight hookups: No

ACCOM: Mon. night thru Thurs. night rates for winterized (check if this is critical) rooms w/o meals unless otherwise indicated.

Cabin; Max. Pers: Over 5; Bedding incl ?: No; Bath: Shared; A/C: No:
Rate for: Person; $9; Rate for #2nd pers: $9; Rate for #3 pers: $9; Child Rate: $7 for children 12 yrs; free under 5 yrs

Dormitory; Max. Pers: 5; Bedding incl ?: No; Bath: Shared; A/C: No
Rate for: Person: $9; Rate for #2nd pers: $9; Rate for #3 pers: $9; Child Rate: $7 for children 12 yr; free under 5 yr

Motel; Max. Pers: 5; Bedding incl ?: No; Bath: Private; A/C: No:
Rate for: Person: $21; Rate for #2nd pers: $21; Rate for #3 pers: $21; Child Rate: $11 under 12 yrs; free under 5 yrs

Main amenities available: Ball field; Volleyball; Basketball; Hiking
Meals are served in dining room for transients only when other groups are present. Approx. dinner price: $8.00.

NAME OF CENTER: **Camp Cedar Glen**   Listing ID #: 21

Telephone: 800-244-8622; Fax: ; E-mail:
Address: PO Box 6006; Pasadena; CA; 91102
Nearest Interstate: I-5, Exit; 50 miles; Nearest State/US Hwy: Rte 78; 3 miles.

Restrictions: Age: None; Pets: Not permitted; Alcohol: Not permitted; Smoking: Outdoors only; Reservation Req'd: 1 day; Max. Adv. Reser.: Open; Seasonal closing: June - Sept

RV/Campers overnight hookups: No

ACCOM: Mon. night thru Thurs. night rates for winterized (check if this is critical) rooms w/o meals unless otherwise indicated.

Cabin; Max. Pers: ; Bedding incl ?: No; Bath: In bldg; A/C: No:
Rate for: Cabin; $245
Cabin holds over 8 people.

Main amenities available: Swimming; Volleyball; Basketball; Ball field; Hiking
Meals are not served in dining room for transients .

NAME OF CENTER: **Camp Edwards**   Listing ID #: 22

Telephone: 909-794-1702; Fax: 909-794-3157; E-mail: campen4u@pcinternet.com
Address: 42842 Jenks Lake Rd. E.; Angelus Oaks; CA; 92305
Nearest Interstate: I-10, Exit; 28 miles; Nearest State/US Hwy: Rte 38; 1 miles.

Restrictions: Age: None; Pets: Not permitted; Alcohol: Not permitted; Smoking: Designated
outdoor area; Reservation Req'd: 5 days; Max. Adv. Reser.: 2 mo; Seasonal closing: None

RV/Campers overnight hookups: No

ACCOM: Mon. night thru Thurs. night rates for winterized (check if this is critical) rooms w/o
meals unless otherwise indicated.

Bunkroom; Max. Pers: Over 5; Bedding incl ?: No; Bath: Shared; A/C: No:
Rate for: Person; $8; Rate for #2nd pers: $8; Rate for #3 pers: $8; Child Rate: Free under 3 yrs

Dormitory; Max. Pers: 5; Bedding incl ?: No; Bath: Shared; A/C: No
Rate for: Person: $18; Rate for #2nd pers: $18; Rate for #3 pers: $18; Child Rate: Free under 3
yrs

Main amenities available: Swimming; Volleyball; Sauna; Hiking
Meals are served in dining room for transients only when other groups are present. Approx. dinner price:
$5-7.00.

NAME OF CENTER: **Camp Virginia**   Listing ID #: 23

Telephone: 760-765-0424; Fax: 760-765-1983; E-mail:
Address: 1298 Highway 78; Julian; CA; 92036
Nearest Interstate: I-8, Exit 20 miles; Nearest State/US Hwy: Rte 78; 0 miles.

Restrictions: Age: None; Pets: Not permitted; Alcohol: Not permitted; Smoking: Designated
outdoor area; Reservation Req'd: 2 days; Max. Adv. Reser.: 1 mo; Seasonal closing: None

RV/Campers overnight hookups: Yes Yes; Water: n/a; Electric: Yes; Septic: unk
Basic Rate/Night: $13.00/ veh

ACCOM: Mon. night thru Thurs. night rates for winterized (check if this is critical) rooms w/o
meals unless otherwise indicated.

Cabin; Max. Pers: 10; Bedding incl ?: No; Bath: 2 baths; A/C: No:
Rate for: Person; $26; Rate for #2nd pers: $26; Rate for #3 pers: $26; Child Rate: n/a
3 bedrooms, kitchenette

Main amenities available: Ping pong; Volleyball; Basketball; Library; Hiking
Meals are not served in dining room for transients .

NAME OF CENTER: Christian Bros. Retreat & Conf. Center   Listing ID #: 24

Telephone: 707-252-3810; Fax: 707-252-3818; E-mail: 1bausch@dlsi.org
Address: 4401 Redwood Road; Nappa; CA; 94558
Nearest Interstate: I-680, Exit 15 miles

Restrictions: Age: None; Pets: Permitted w/security dep.; Alcohol: Permitted; Smoking: Outdoors only; Reservation Req'd: 1 day; Max. Adv. Reser.: 1 yr w 30% dep; Seasonal closing: None

RV/Campers overnight hookups: No

ACCOM: Mon. night thru Thurs. night rates for winterized (check if this is critical) rooms w/o meals unless otherwise indicated.

Family Ste; Max. Pers: 4; Bedding incl ?: Yes; Bath: Private; A/C: No:
Rate for: Entire Ste; $135; Rate for #2nd pers: $30; Rate for #3 pers: $0; Child Rate: n/a
$165 for 4 persons

Motel; Max. Pers: 2; Bedding incl ?: Yes; Bath: Private; A/C: No
Rate for: Person: $95; Rate for #2nd pers: $10

Main amenities available: In vineyards; Inside volleyball; Inside basketball; Jacuzzi; Chapel; Hiking
Meals are served in dining room for transients w/48 hours advance notice.. Approx. dinner price: $25+tax/serv chg.

NAME OF CENTER: Church of God Desert Oasis & Ret. Ctr   Listing ID #: 25

Telephone: 760-329-6994; Fax: 760-329-1823; E-mail:
Address: 73200 Dillon Rd.; Desert Hot Springs; CA; 92240
Nearest Interstate: I-10, Exit 8 miles; Nearest State/US Hwy: Palm Drive; 3 miles.

Restrictions: Age: None; Pets: Not permitted; Alcohol: Not permitted; Smoking: Outdoors only; Reservation Req'd: 2 days; Max. Adv. Reser.: 3 mo; Seasonal closing: None

RV/Campers overnight hookups: Yes; Water: Yes; Electric: Yes; Septic: unk
Basic Rate/Night: $10.00/ veh

ACCOM: Mon. night thru Thurs. night rates for winterized (check if this is critical) rooms w/o meals unless otherwise indicated.

Motel; Max. Pers: 9; Bedding incl ?: Yes; Bath: Shared; A/C: Yes:
Rate for: Person; $10; Rate for #2nd pers: $10; Rate for #3 pers: $10; Child Rate: n/a

Main amenities available: Swimming; Volleyball; Basketball; Laundry machine; Bookstore; Library
Meals are served in dining room for transients only when other groups are present. Approx. dinner price: $10.00.

NAME OF CENTER: **Diamond Arrow Christian Conf. Ctr.**   Listing ID #: 26

Telephone: 530-265-3295; Fax: 530-265-6426; E-mail: diamond@oro.net
Address: 15742 North Bloom Field Rd; Nevada City; CA; 95959
Nearest Interstate: I-80, Exit 35 miles; Nearest State/US Hwy: Rte 49; 7 miles.

Restrictions: Age: None; Pets: Not permitted; Alcohol: Not permitted; Smoking: Designated outdoor area; Reservation Req'd: 7 days; Max. Adv. Reser.: 21 days; Seasonal closing: June - Aug.

RV/Campers overnight hookups: Yes; Water: Yes; Electric: Yes; Septic: unk
Basic Rate/Night: $15.00/ veh

ACCOM: Mon. night thru Thurs. night rates for winterized (check if this is critical) rooms w/o meals unless otherwise indicated.

Cabin; Max. Pers: n/a; Bedding incl ?: $5 surcharge; Bath: Shared; A/C: No:
Rate for: Person; $10; Rate for #2nd pers: $10; Rate for #3 pers: $10; Child Rate: $5

Dormitory; Max. Pers: 5; Bedding incl ?: $5 surcharge; Bath: Shared; A/C: No
Rate for: Person: $15; Rate for #2nd pers: $15; Rate for #3 pers: $15; Child Rate: $7.50

Motel; Max. Pers: 2; Bedding incl ?: Yes; Bath: Private; A/C: No:
Rate for: Person: $30; Rate for #2nd pers: $10; ChildRate: $10

Main amenities available: Swimming; Volleyball; Basketball; Horse shoes; Ping pong; Hiking
Meals are served in dining room for transients only when other groups are present. Approx. dinner price: $6.75.

NAME OF CENTER: **Indian Hills Camp**   Listing ID #: 27

Telephone: 619-669-6498; Fax: 619-669-6497; E-mail:
Address: 15763 Lyons Valley Rd.; Jamul; CA; 91935
Nearest Interstate: I-805, Exit 10 miles; Nearest State/US Hwy: Rte 94; 5 miles.

Restrictions: Age: None; Pets: Permitted; Alcohol: Not permitted; Smoking: Outdoors only; Reservation Req'd: Noon of day; Max. Adv. Reser.: No; Seasonal closing: April - May

RV/Campers overnight hookups: Yes; Water: Yes; Electric: Yes; Septic: unk
Basic Rate/Night: $22.00/ veh

ACCOM: Mon. night thru Thurs. night rates for winterized (check if this is critical) rooms w/o meals unless otherwise indicated.

Main amenities available: Volleyball; Basketball; Hiking
Meals are not served in dining room for transients .

NAME OF CENTER: Madre Grande Monastery   Listing ID #: 28

Telephone: 619-468-3810; Fax: 619-468-3512; E-mail:
Address: 18372 Highway 94; Dulzura; CA; 91917
Nearest Interstate: I-8, Exit 20 miles; Nearest State/US Hwy: Rte 94; 3 miles.

Restrictions: Age: None; Pets: Not permitted; Alcohol: Not permitted; Smoking: Designated outdoor area; Reservation Req'd: 7 days; Max. Adv. Reser.: 2 mo; Seasonal closing: None

RV/Campers overnight hookups: No

ACCOM: Mon. night thru Thurs. night rates for winterized (check if this is critical) rooms w/o meals unless otherwise indicated.

Dormitory; Max. Pers: Over 5; Bedding incl ?: Yes; Bath: Shared; A/C: No:
Rate for: Person; $25; Rate for #2nd pers: $25; Rate for #3 pers: $25; Child Rate: 50% off under 12 yrs
Kitchen privilege

Main amenities available: 250+ acres; Hiking
Meals are not served in dining room for transients.

NAME OF CENTER: Methodist Camp at Mt Shasta   Listing ID #: 29

Telephone: 530-468-5273; Fax: ; E-mail:
Address: 9333 Oro Fino Rd; Fort Jones; CA; 96032
Nearest Interstate: I-5, Exit Shasta Central; 8 miles

Restrictions: Age: None; Pets: Not permitted; Alcohol: Not permitted; Smoking: Nowhere; Reservation Req'd: 7 days; Max. Adv. Reser.: 1 mo; Seasonal closing: None

RV/Campers overnight hookups: No

ACCOM: Mon. night thru Thurs. night rates for winterized (check if this is critical) rooms w/o meals unless otherwise indicated.

Lodge; Max. Pers: Over 8; Bedding incl ?: No; Bath: Shared; A/C: No:
Rate for: Entire Lodge;
Off season $75 for entire lodge. $100 June 15 - Aug 30. 2 bedrooms, kitchen

Main amenities available: Swimming; Volleyball; Horseshoes; Fishing; Badminton; Hiking
Meals are not served in dining room for transients .

NAME OF CENTER: **Mission San Luis Rey Retreat Ctr**   Listing ID #: 30

Telephone: 760-757-3659; Fax: 760-757-8025; E-mail: slretreat@sanluisrey.org
Address: 4050 Mission Ave.; Oceanside; CA; 92057
Nearest Interstate: I-5, Exit 4 miles; Nearest State/US Hwy: Rte 76; 0 miles.

Restrictions: Age: 13; Pets: Not permitted; Alcohol: Not permitted; Smoking: Outdoors only; Reservation Req'd: 7 days; Max. Adv. Reser.: Open; Seasonal closing: None

RV/Campers overnight hookups: No

ACCOM: Mon. night thru Thurs. night rates for winterized (check if this is critical) rooms w/o meals unless otherwise indicated.

Dormitory; Max. Pers: 2; Bedding incl ?: Yes; Bath: Shared; A/C: Yes:
Rate for: Person; $30; Rate for #2nd pers: $10

Main amenities available: Swimming (heated); Volleyball; Basketball; VCR-TV; Bookstore; Library
Meals are served in dining room for transients only when other groups are present. Approx. dinner price: $7.00.

NAME OF CENTER: **Mt. Cross Lutheran Camp**   Listing ID #: 31

Telephone: 831-336-5179; Fax: 831-336-2548; E-mail: ruth@mtcross.org
Address: PO Box 387; 7795 Hwy 9; Felton; CA; 95018
Nearest State/US Hwy: Rte 9; 2 miles.

Restrictions: Age: None; Pets: Not permitted; Alcohol: Not permitted; Smoking: Designated outdoor area; Reservation Req'd: 5 days; Max. Adv. Reser.: Open; Seasonal closing: None

RV/Campers overnight hookups: Yes; Water: Yes; Electric: Yes; Septic: unk
Basic Rate/Night: $18.00/ veh

ACCOM: Mon. night thru Thurs. night rates for winterized (check if this is critical) rooms w/o meals unless otherwise indicated.

Bunkroom; Max. Pers: Over 5; Bedding incl ?: $5 surcharge; Bath: Shared; A/C: No:
Rate for: Person; $19; Rate for #2nd pers: $19; Rate for #3 pers: $19; Child Rate: 50% off under 12 yrs, free under 6

Cabin; Max. Pers: n/a; Bedding incl ?: $5 surcharge; Bath: In bldg, shared; A/C: No
Rate for: Person: $19; Rate for #2nd pers: $19; Rate for #3 pers: $19; Child Rate: Same discount as bunkroom

Dormitory; Max. Pers: 5; Bedding incl ?: $5 surcharge; Bath: Shared; A/C: No:
Rate for: Person: $25; Rate for #2nd pers: $25; Rate for #3 pers: $25; Child Rate: Same as bunkroom

Main amenities available: Swimming; Volleyball; Basketball; Laundry machine; Hiking; Ball field
Meals are served in dining room for transients only when other groups are present. Approx. dinner price: $5-6.

NAME OF CENTER: Mountain Home   Listing ID #: 32

Telephone: 805-269-1948; Fax: 805-269-0868; E-mail:
Address: 6221 W. Sierra Highway; PO Box 838; Acton; CA; 93510
Nearest Interstate: I-5, Exit 1 mile; Nearest State/US Hwy: Rte 91; 1 mile

Restrictions: Age: 18; Pets: Not permitted; Alcohol: Not permitted; Smoking: Nowhere; Reservation Req'd: 7 days; Max. Adv. Reser.: 6 mo; Seasonal closing: None

RV/Campers overnight hookups: No

ACCOM: Mon. night thru Thurs. night rates for winterized (check if this is critical) rooms w/o meals unless otherwise indicated.

Bunkroom; Max. Pers: 9; Bedding incl ?: No; Bath: Shared; A/C: No:
Rate for: Person; $10; Rate for #2nd pers: $10; Rate for #3 pers: $10; Child Rate: n/a

Dormitory; Max. Pers: 5; Bedding incl ?: No; Bath: Shared; A/C: No
Rate for: Person: $10; Rate for #2nd pers: $10; Rate for #3 pers: $10; Child Rate: n/a
Kitchen privileges

Main amenities available: Hiking
Meals are not served in dining room for transients .

NAME OF CENTER: Our Lady of Trust Spirituality Ctr   Listing ID #: 33

Telephone: 714-956-1020; Fax: 714-525-8948; E-mail:
Address: 205 S. Pine Dr.; Fullerton; CA; 92833
Nearest Interstate: I-5, Exit 1 miles.

Restrictions: Age: None; Pets: Not permitted; Alcohol: Permitted w/meal; Smoking: Outdoors only; Reservation Req'd: 2 days; Max. Adv. Reser.: 1 mo; Seasonal closing: Fri. thru Sunday night

RV/Campers overnight hookups: No

ACCOM: Mon. night thru Thurs. night rates for winterized (check if this is critical) rooms w/o meals unless otherwise indicated.

Motel; Max. Pers: 2; Bedding incl ?: Yes; Bath: Semi-private (2 rooms); A/C: No:
Rate for: Person; $20-25; Rate for #2nd pers: $20-25; Child Rate: n/a
Close to Disney Land

Main amenities available: Library; Bookstore; Meditation area; VCR-TV
Meals are served in dining room for transients only when other groups are present. Approx. dinner price: $10.00.

NAME OF CENTER: Quaker Center   Listing ID #: 34

Telephone: 408-336-8333; Fax: 831-336-0218; E-mail:
Address: 1000 Hubbard Gulch Rd. PO Box 686; Ben Lomond; CA; 95005
Nearest Interstate: I-880, Exit 17 miles; Nearest State/US Hwy: Rte 17; 15 miles.

Restrictions: Age: None; Pets: Not permitted; Alcohol: Permitted; Smoking: Designated outdoor area; Reservation Req'd: None; Max. Adv. Reser.: 2 mo; Seasonal closing: None

RV/Campers overnight hookups: No

ACCOM: Mon. night thru Thurs. night rates for winterized (check if this is critical) rooms w/o meals unless otherwise indicated.

Bunkroom; Max. Pers: 8; Bedding incl ?: No; Bath: Shared; A/C: No:
Rate for: Person; $13/$18; Rate for #2nd pers: $3/$4; Rate for #3 pers: $3/$4; Child Rate: n/a
Rates are stated as (weekday/weekend).

Cabin; Max. Pers: 4; Bedding incl ?: Yes; Bath: Private; A/C: No
Rate for: Person: $17/$22; Rate for #2nd pers: n/a; Rate for #3 pers: n/a; Child Rate: n/a
Rates (weekday/weekend). Up to 4 persons; total amt ($27/$32. Kitchen priv. See comments at btm

Main amenities available: Hiking; Volleyball
Meals are not served in dining room for transients .
Indicated prices are the minimum. A contribution will be requested.

NAME OF CENTER: Rancho del Rey Christian Center   Listing ID #: 35

Telephone: 805-649-3356; Fax: 805-649-3363; E-mail:
Address: 655 Burnham Rd.; Oak View; CA; 93022
Nearest Interstate: I-5, Exit 60 miles; Nearest State/US Hwy: Rte 101; 10 miles.

Restrictions: Age: None; Pets: Not permitted; Alcohol: Not permitted; Smoking: Designated outdoor area; Reservation Req'd: 4 PM of day; Max. Adv. Reser.: Open; Seasonal closing: None

RV/Campers overnight hookups: Yes; Water: Yes; Electric: Yes; Septic: unk
Basic Rate/Night: $15.00/ veh

ACCOM: Mon. night thru Thurs. night rates for winterized (check if this is critical) rooms w/o meals unless otherwise indicated.

Main amenities available: Playground; Volleyball; Basketball; Horse shoes; Hiking
Meals are served in dining room for transients only when other groups are present. Approx. dinner price: Open.

NAME OF CENTER: Rancho YBarra   Listing ID #: 36

Telephone: 818-353-2423; Fax: n/a; E-mail:
Address: 3150 Big Tujunga Canyon Rd; Tujunga; CA; 91042
Nearest Interstate: I-210, Exit 7 miles; Nearest State/US Hwy: Rte 118; 5 miles.

Restrictions: Age: None; Pets: Not in room; Alcohol: Not permitted; Smoking: Outdoors only; Reservation Req'd: None; Max. Adv. Reser.: 1 mo; Seasonal closing: None

RV/Campers overnight hookups: Yes; Water: n/a; Electric: Yes; Septic: unk
Basic Rate/Night: $20.00/ veh

ACCOM: Mon. night thru Thurs. night rates for winterized (check if this is critical) rooms w/o meals unless otherwise indicated.

Bunkroom; Max. Pers: 8; Bedding incl ?: $5 surcharge; Bath: Shared; A/C: Yes:
Rate for: Person; $18; Rate for #2nd pers: $18; Rate for #3 pers: $18; Child Rate: Free under 5 yrs

Dormitory; Max. Pers: 5; Bedding incl ?: $5 surcharge; Bath: Shared; A/C: Yes
Rate for: Person: $18; Rate for #2nd pers: $18; Rate for #3 pers: $18; Child Rate: Free under 5 yrs

Main amenities available: Swimming; Volleyball; Basketball; hiking
Meals are served in dining room for transients only when other groups are present. Approx. dinner price: $7.00.

NAME OF CENTER: Shenoa Retreat Center   Listing ID #: 37

Telephone: 707-895-3156; Fax: ; E-mail:
Address: PO Box 43; Philo; CA; 95466
Nearest Interstate: I-101, Exit Hwy 128W; 30 miles; Nearest State/US Hwy: Rte 128; 1 miles.

Restrictions: Age: None; Pets: Not permitted; Alcohol: Permitted; Smoking: Designated outdoor area; Reservation Req'd: None; Max. Adv. Reser.: 14 days; Seasonal closing: None

RV/Campers overnight hookups: No

ACCOM: Mon. night thru Thurs. night rates for winterized (check if this is critical) rooms w/o meals unless otherwise indicated.

Cabin; Max. Pers: Over 5; Bedding incl ?: $6 surcharge; Bath: In bldg; A/C: No:
Rate for: Person; $45; Rate for #2nd pers: $45; Rate for #3 pers: $45; Child Rate: Child discount available
Two night minimum.

Cottage; Max. Pers: 2; Bedding incl ?: Yes; Bath: Private; A/C: No
Rate for: Entire bldg: $90
Two night minimum.

Main amenities available: Swimming (stream); Volleyball; Basketball; Tennis; Hiking
Meals are served in dining room for transients only when other groups are present. Approx. dinner price: $9-10.00.

NAME OF CENTER: Silver Penny Farm   Listing ID #: 38

Telephone: 707-762-1498; Fax: n/a; E-mail:
Address: 5215 Old Lakeville Rd. #1; Petulama; CA; 94954
Nearest Interstate: I-101, Exit 4 miles.

Restrictions: Age: 21; Pets: Not permitted; Alcohol: Permitted; Smoking: Designated outdoor area; Reservation Req'd: 14 days w/dep.; Max. Adv. Reser.: Open; Seasonal closing: None

RV/Campers overnight hookups: No

ACCOM: Mon. night thru Thurs. night rates for winterized (check if this is critical) rooms w/o meals unless otherwise indicated.

Dormitory; Max. Pers: 2; Bedding incl ?: Yes (no towel); Bath: Shared; A/C: n/a:
Rate for: Person; $23/$26; Rate for #2nd pers: $13/$20; Child Rate: n/a
Rates (weekday/weekend) Weekend rate requires payment for two nights

Main amenities available: VCR-TV; Kitchenette; Swimming; Hiking
Meals are not served in dining room for transients .

NAME OF CENTER: Wellsring Renewal Center   Listing ID #: 39

Telephone: 707-895-3893; Fax: n/a; E-mail: wellsprg@zapcom.net
Address: 8550 Rays Rd; PO Box 332; Philo; CA; 95466
Nearest Interstate: I-101, Exit Hwy 128W; 30 miles; Nearest State/US Hwy: Rte 128; 1 miles.

Restrictions: Age: None; Pets: Not permitted; Alcohol: Not permitted; Smoking: Outdoors only; Reservation Req'd: None; Max. Adv. Reser.: 1 yr; Seasonal closing: None

RV/Campers overnight hookups: No

ACCOM: Mon. night thru Thurs. night rates for winterized (check if this is critical) rooms w/o meals unless otherwise indicated.

Cabin; Max. Pers: n/a; Bedding incl ?: No; Bath: Separate bldg; A/C: No:
Rate for: Person; $22; Rate for #2nd pers: $22; Rate for #3 pers: $22; Child Rate: $9 under 12 yrs

Cabin; Max. Pers: 5; Bedding incl ?: No; Bath: Private; A/C: No
Rate for: Person: $32; Rate for #2nd pers: $32; Rate for #3 pers: $32; Child Rate: $11 for children under 12 yrs

Lodge; Max. Pers: Over 6; Bedding incl ?: ; Bath: Private; A/C: No:
Rate for: Entire lodge: Minimum chg $89; Rate per adult: $32

Main amenities available: Located on river; Hiking
Meals are served in dining room for transients only when other groups are present. Approx. dinner price: $10; $6 under 12 yrs.
Not specifically Christian. Welcomes all faiths.

NAME OF CENTER: Wrightwood Methodist Camp   Listing ID #: 40

Telephone: 626-568-7333; Fax: 760-249-4113; E-mail:
Address: PO Box 66; 1401 Linnet rd; Wrightwood; CA; 92397
Nearest Interstate: I-15, Exit 15 miles; Nearest State/US Hwy: Rte 2; 1 miles.

Restrictions: Age: None; Pets: Not permitted; Alcohol: Not permitted; Smoking: Nowhere;
Reservation Req'd: None; Max. Adv. Reser.: 7 days; Seasonal closing: Mid-Sept. thru mid-June
from Mon. thru Fri. night

RV/Campers overnight hookups: No

ACCOM: Mon. night thru Thurs. night rates for winterized (check if this is critical) rooms w/o
meals unless otherwise indicated.

Cabin; Max. Pers: 12; Bedding incl ?: ; Bath: Shared; A/C: No:
Rate for: Person; $31; Rate for #2nd pers: $31; Rate for #3 pers: $31; Child Rate: n/a

Main amenities available: Volleyball; Basketball; Hiking
Meals are served in dining room for transients only when other groups are present.

NAME OF CENTER: YMCA - Berkeley Listing ID: 41

Telephone: 510-848-9622   Fax: 510-848-6835
Address: 2001 Allston Way; Berkeley, CA 94704

Restrictions:
Accommodations offered to (M/F/Families): M&F. If M/F then must be over 18 yrs.
Pets: Not permitted; Alcohol: Not permitted; Smoking: Nowhere
Reservation requirements: None
Reservations are accepted up to 14 days in advance. Seasonal closing: None

ACCOMMODATIONS:
Single room: Bedding included ?: Yes; Bath: Shared
Rate for 1 day: $33+$7 dep; Rate for 1 week: not offered
Room fee includes membership in Y

Double room: Bedding included ?: Yes; Bath: Shared
Rate for 1 day: $40+$7/pers dep; Rate for 1 week:

Main amenities: Pool; Gym; Racquetball; Jacuzzi; Laundry machine;
Meals are not offered in their own cafeteria.
Maximum stay is 14 days.

REMEMBER TO CALL AHEAD

NAME OF CENTER: YMCA - Glendale Listing ID: 42

Telephone: 818-240-4130   Fax: 818-500-1737
Address: 140 N. Louise Sr.; Glendale, CA 91206

Restrictions:
Accommodations offered to (M/F/Families): M. If M/F then must be over 18 yrs.
Pets: Not permitted; Alcohol: Not permitted; Smoking: Permitted on one floor
Reservation requirements: None
Reservations are accepted up to 0 days in advance. Seasonal closing: None

ACCOMMODATIONS:
Single room: Bedding included ?: Yes; Bath: Shared
Rate for 1 day: $21+$5 dep; Rate for 1 week: $102+$5 dep
Extra charge of $15 for Y membership

Main amenities: Laundry mach.; Pool **; Gym **; Racquetball **; Steam room **; Jacuzzi **
Meals are not offered in their own cafeteria.
** Requires $15 membership in Y.

NAME OF CENTER: YMCA - San Francisco Listing ID: 43

Telephone: 415-885-0460   Fax: 415-885-5439
Address: 220 Golden Gate Ave; San Francisco, CA 94102

Restrictions:
Accommodations offered to (M/F/Families): M&F. If M/F then must be over 16 yrs.
Pets: Not permitted; Alcohol: Not permitted; Smoking: Bedroom only
Reservation requirements: Yes w/credit card
Reservations are accepted up to 1 yr in advance. Seasonal closing: None

ACCOMMODATIONS:
Single room: Bedding included ?: Yes; Bath: Shared
Rate for 1 day: $37+$5 dep; Rate for 1 week: $222+$5 dep
Room fee includes membership in Y

Double room: Bedding included ?: Yes; Bath: Shared
Rate for 1 day: $47+$5/pers dep; Rate for 1 week:

Main amenities: Laundry machine; Pool; Gym
Meals are offered in their own cafeteria.
All accommodations include breakfast

COLORADO

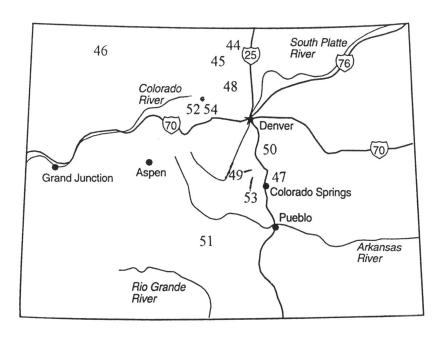

46

44
45
25

South Platte
River

76

Colorado
River

48

52 54

70

Denver

50

70

Grand Junction

Aspen

49

47

53

Colorado Springs

Pueblo

51

Arkansas
River

Rio Grande
River

NAME OF CENTER: Buckhorn United Methodist Camp   Listing ID #: 44

Telephone: 970-484-2508; Fax: ; E-mail: buckhorncamp.org
Address: 2120 County Rd 41; Bellvue; CO; 80512
Nearest Interstate: I-25, Exit Hwy 14; 27 miles; Nearest State/US Hwy: Rte 287; 15 miles.

Restrictions: Age: None; Pets: Not permitted; Alcohol: Not permitted; Smoking: Outdoors only; Reservation Req'd: None; Max. Adv. Reser.: Open; Seasonal closing: None

RV/Campers overnight hookups: Yes; Water: Yes; Electric: $3; Septic: n/a
Basic Rate/Night: $15.00/ veh

ACCOM: Mon. night thru Thurs. night rates for winterized (check if this is critical) rooms w/o meals unless otherwise indicated.

Cabin; Max. Pers: 6; Bedding incl ?: No; Bath: Shared; A/C: No:
Rate for: Person; $15; Rate for #2nd pers: $15; Rate for #3 pers: $15; Child Rate: n/a
Max. $45; Fireplace, some cabins w/kitchenette

Main amenities available: Fishing; Volleyball; Basketball; Horse shoes; Hiking
Meals are served in dining room for transients only when other groups are present. Approx. dinner price: $5.00.
RV's beware. Last 5 miles of road is 12% grade.

NAME OF CENTER: Estes Park Center (YMCA)   Listing ID #: 45

Telephone: 970-586-3341; Fax: 970-586-6078; E-mail: info@ymcarockies.org
Address: 2525 Tunnel Road; Estes Park; CO; 80511
Nearest Interstate: I-25, Exit 33 miles; Nearest State/US Hwy: US 36; 2 miles.

Restrictions: Age: None; Pets: Not permitted; Alcohol: Permitted; Smoking: Outdoors only; Reservation Req'd: None; Max. Adv. Reser.: Open; Seasonal closing: None

RV/Campers overnight hookups: No

ACCOM: Mon. night thru Thurs. night rates for winterized (check if this is critical) rooms w/o meals unless otherwise indicated.

16 different types of bunkroom, cabin, dormitory and motel accommodations.

Almost 1700 beds

Main amenities available: Almost everything
Meals are served in dining room for transients . Approx. dinner price: $8-11.00.

NAME OF CENTER: Euzoa Bible Church & Retreat Center   Listing ID #: 46

Telephone: 970-879-0123; Fax: 970-879-6187; E-mail:
Address: PO Box 770599; Steamboat Springs; CO; 80477
Nearest Interstate: I-70, Exit 90 miles; Nearest State/US Hwy: Rte 40; 2 miles.

Restrictions: Age: None; Pets: Not permitted; Alcohol: Not permitted; Smoking: Outdoors only;
Reservation Req'd: 30 days; Max. Adv. Reser.: Open; Seasonal closing: None

RV/Campers overnight hookups: No

ACCOM: Mon. night thru Thurs. night rates for winterized (check if this is critical) rooms w/o
meals unless otherwise indicated.

Bunkroom; Max. Pers: 6; Bedding incl ?: Yes; Bath: Shared; A/C: No:
Rate for: Person; $18; Rate for #2nd pers: $12; Rate for #3 pers: $12; Child Rate: n/a
Center requests: Strip beds on departure

Dormitory; Max. Pers: 4; Bedding incl ?: Yes; Bath: Shared; A/C: No
Rate for: Person: $20; Rate for #2nd pers: $12; Rate for #3 pers: $12; Child Rate: n/a

Motel; Max. Pers: 5; Bedding incl ?: Yes; Bath: Private; A/C: No:
Rate for: Person: $20; Rate for #2nd pers: $15; Rate for #3 pers: $15; Child Rate: n/a

Main amenities available: Hot tub; Volleyball; Basketball; Boating; Ping pong; Hiking
Meals are not served in dining room for transients .

NAME OF CENTER: Franciscan Center at Mt. St. Francis   Listing ID #: 47

Telephone: 719-598-5486; Fax: 719-260-8044; E-mail:
Address: 7665 Assisi Heights; Colorado Springs; CO; 80919
Nearest Interstate: I-25, Exit 4 miles.

Restrictions: Age: None; Pets: Not permitted; Alcohol: Hard liquor not permitted; Smoking:
Not in bedrooms; Reservation Req'd: 25 days; Max. Adv. Reser.: Open; Seasonal closing: None

RV/Campers overnight hookups: No

ACCOM: Mon. night thru Thurs. night rates for winterized (check if this is critical) rooms w/o
meals unless otherwise indicated.

Motel; Max. Pers: 2; Bedding incl ?: Yes **; Bath: Private; A/C: No:
Rate for: Person; $31; Rate for #2nd pers: $15
** Adv notice required.

Main amenities available: Quiet areas; Hiking; Chapel; Hiking
Meals are served in dining room for transients only when other groups are present. Approx. dinner price: $6.30.

NAME OF CENTER: **Glacier View Ranch**   Listing ID #: 48

Telephone: 303-449-7890; Fax: 303-459-3325; E-mail: cdolensky$compuserve.com
Address: 8748 Overland Rd; Ward; CO; 80481
Nearest Interstate: I-25, Exit 40 miles; Nearest State/US Hwy: Rte 36; 14 miles.

Restrictions: Age: None; Pets: Not permitted; Alcohol: Not permitted; Smoking: Not in bedrooms; Reservation Req'd: 5 days; Max. Adv. Reser.: Open; Seasonal closing: None

RV/Campers overnight hookups: Yes; Water: Yes; Electric: Yes; Septic: n/a
Basic Rate/Night: $12.00/ veh

ACCOM: Mon. night thru Thurs. night rates for winterized (check if this is critical) rooms w/o meals unless otherwise indicated.

Bunkroom; Max. Pers: 9; Bedding incl ?: Yes **; Bath: Shared; A/C: No:
Rate for: Person; $10; Rate for #2nd pers: $10; Rate for #3 pers: $10; Child Rate: n/a
** Adv notice required

Motel; Max. Pers: 4; Bedding incl ?: Yes **; Bath: Private; A/C: No
Rate for: Person: Unk

Main amenities available: Volleyball; Basketball; Hiking
Meals are served in dining room for transients only when other groups are present. Price varies..

NAME OF CENTER: **Lutheran Valley Retreat**   Listing ID #: 49

Telephone: 719-687-3560; Fax: 719-687-3560
E-mail: LutheranValleyRetreat@lvr.org
Address: PO Box 9042; Woodland Park; CO; 80866
Nearest Interstate: I-25, Exit Rte 24; 40 miles; Nearest State/US Hwy: 141; 18 miles.

Restrictions: Age: None; Pets: Camp grounds only; Alcohol: Not permitted; Smoking: Outdoors only; Reservation Req'd: None; Max. Adv. Reser.: Open; Seasonal closing: None

RV/Campers overnight hookups: Yes; Water: No; Electric: Yes; Septic: unk
Basic Rate/Night: $14.00/ veh

ACCOM: Mon. night thru Thurs. night rates for winterized (check if this is critical) rooms w/o meals unless otherwise indicated.

Bunkroom; Max. Pers: 8; Bedding incl ?: No; Bath: Shared; A/C: No:
Rate for: Person; $25; Rate for #2nd pers: $25; Rate for #3 pers: $25; Child Rate: n/a
Room rate incl 3 meals; Sweep & mop before leaving

Main amenities available: Ping pong; Volleyball; Basketball; Hiking
Meals are served in dining room for transients only when other groups are present. Approx. dinner price: $4-6.00.

NAME OF CENTER: Ponderosa Retreat & Conference Ctr   Listing ID #: 50

Telephone: 800-900-0884; Fax: 719-481-6402; E-mail: ponderosa@pcisys.net
Address: 15235 Furrow Rd.; Larkspur; CO; 80118
Nearest Interstate: I-25, Exit 163; 3 miles.

Restrictions: Age: None; Pets: Not permitted; Alcohol: Not permitted; Smoking: Outdoors only;
Reservation Req'd: 5 PM of day; Max. Adv. Reser.: Open; Seasonal closing: None

RV/Campers overnight hookups: Yes; Water: Yes; Electric: Yes; Septic: n/a
Basic Rate/Night: $4/pers/ veh

ACCOM: Mon. night thru Thurs. night rates for winterized (check if this is critical) rooms w/o
meals unless otherwise indicated.

Bunkroom; Max. Pers: 14; Bedding incl ?: $4 surcharge; Bath: Shared; A/C: No:
Rate for: Person; $15; Rate for #2nd pers: $15; Rate for #3 pers: $15; Child Rate: n/a
$35 per family

Dormitory; Max. Pers: 4; Bedding incl ?: $4 surcharge; Bath: Shared; A/C: No
Rate for: Person: $15; Rate for #2nd pers: $15; Rate for #3 pers: $15; Child Rate: n/a
$35 per family

Motel; Max. Pers: 4; Bedding incl ?: $4 surcharge; Bath: Private; A/C: No:
Rate for: Room: $42

Main amenities available: Ping pong; Volleyball; Basketball; VCR-TV; Climbing wall; Hiking
Meals are served in dining room for transients only when other groups are present. Approx. dinner price: $7;
Free under 8 yrs.

NAME OF CENTER: Rainbow Trail Lutheran Camp   Listing ID #: 51

Telephone: 719-942-4220; Fax: 719-942-4000; E-mail:
Address: 3056 County Rd. 198; PO Box T; Hillside; CO; 81232
Nearest Interstate: I-25, Exit 85 miles; Nearest State/US Hwy: Rte 69; 4 miles.

Restrictions: Age: None; Pets: Not permitted; Alcohol: Not permitted; Smoking: Designated
outdoor area, Reservation Req'd: 1 day; Max. Adv. Reser.: 6 mo; Seasonal closing: May - Sept

RV/Campers overnight hookups: No

ACCOM: Mon. night thru Thurs. night rates for winterized (check if this is critical) rooms w/o
meals unless otherwise indicated.

Dormitory; Max. Pers: 5; Bedding incl ?: No; Bath: Shared; A/C: No:
Rate for: Person; $18; Rate for #2nd pers: $18; Rate for #3 pers: $18; Child Rate: 50% off
under 12 yrs, free under 4

Main amenities available: Laundry machine; Volleyball; Library; Ping pong ; Tetherball; Hiking
Meals are served in dining room for transients only when other groups are present. Approx. dinner price: $7;
50% off under 12, free under 4.

NAME OF CENTER: Snow Mountain Ranch   Listing ID #: 52

Telephone: 970-887-2152; Fax: 303-449-6781; E-mail: info@ymcarockies.org
Address: PO Box 169; Winter Park; CO; 80482
Nearest Interstate: I-70, Exit 25 miles; Nearest State/US Hwy: US 40; 2 miles.

Restrictions: Age: None; Pets: Not permitted; Alcohol: Not permitted; Smoking: Outdoors only;
Reservation Req'd: None; Max. Adv. Reser.: Open; Seasonal closing: None

RV/Campers overnight hookups: Yes; Water: Yes; Electric: Yes; Septic: n/a
Basic Rate/Night: $15-19/ veh

ACCOM: Mon. night thru Thurs. night rates for winterized (check if this is critical) rooms w/o
meals unless otherwise indicated.

12 different types of bunkroom, cabin, dormitory and motel accommodations.

Almost 700 beds.

Main amenities available: Almost everything; Volleyball; Basketball; Hiking
Meals are served in dining room for transients only when other groups are present. Approx. dinner price:
$8-11.00 .

NAME OF CENTER: Templed Hills Camp & Retreat Center   Listing ID #: 53

Telephone: 719-687-9038; Fax: ; E-mail: retreatinfo@templedhills.org
Address: 1364 County Rd 75; Woodland Park; CO; 80863
Nearest Interstate: I-25, Exit Rte 24; 30 miles; Nearest State/US Hwy: Rte 24; 2
miles.

Restrictions: Age: None; Pets: Not permitted; Alcohol: Not permitted; Smoking: Outdoors only;
Reservation Req'd: Yes w/$15 dep per rm; Max. Adv. Reser.: 44 days; Seasonal closing: None

RV/Campers overnight hookups: No

ACCOM: Mon. night thru Thurs. night rates for winterized (check if this is critical) rooms w/o
meals unless otherwise indicated.

Motel; Max. Pers: 5; Bedding incl ?: Yes; Bath: Private; A/C: No:
Rate for: Person; $45; Rate for #2nd pers: $32; Rate for #3 pers: $25; Child Rate: Free under
13 yrs

Elevation 8200

Main amenities available: Fishing; Volleyball; Basketball; Hiking
Meals are served in dining room for transients . Approx. dinner price: $7; 50% off under 9 yrs; free under 3.

NAME OF CENTER: **Timberline Lodge Retreat Center**   Listing ID #: 54

Telephone: 970-726-8850; Fax: 970-726-8853; E-mail: timberlinelodge@juno.com
Address: PO Box 3311; Winter Park; CO; 80482
Nearest Interstate: I-25, Exit Rte 24; 40 miles.

Restrictions: Age: None; Pets: Not permitted; Alcohol: Not permitted; Smoking: Nowhere;
Reservation Req'd: Yes w/dep; Max. Adv. Reser.: Open; Seasonal closing: None

RV/Campers overnight hookups: No

ACCOM: Mon. night thru Thurs. night rates for winterized (check if this is critical) rooms w/o
meals unless otherwise indicated.

Motel; Max. Pers: 6; Bedding incl ?: Yes; Bath: Private; A/C: No:
Rate for: Person; ** $50; Rate for #2nd pers: ** $50; Rate for #3 pers: ** $50; Child Rate: $30
under 19 yrs; $20 under 14; free under 4
** Includes 3 meals

Main amenities available: Fishing; X-Ctry skiing; Hot tube; Pool table; Tennis; Hiking
Meals are served in dining room for transients . Approx. dinner price: Included in price of lodging.

NAME OF CENTER: YMCA - Metro Denver Listing ID: 55

Telephone: 303-861-8300   Fax: 303-830-7391
Address: 25 E. 16th Ave.; Denver, CO 80202

Restrictions:
Accommodations offered to (M/F/Families): M&F. If M/F then must be over 18 yrs.
Pets: Not permitted; Alcohol: Not permitted; Smoking: Bedroom only
Reservation requirements: None
Reservations are accepted up to 0 days in advance. Seasonal closing: None

ACCOMMODATIONS:
Single room: Bedding included ?: Yes; Bath: Shared
Rate for 1 day: $29+$12 dep; Rate for 1 week: $116+$12 dep
Room fee includes membership in Y

Single room: Bedding included ?: Yes ; Bath: Semi-private
Rate for 1 day: $32+$12 dep; Rate for 1 week: $129+$12 dep

Main amenities: Laundry machine; Pool; TV viewing room; Gym; ; Hiking
Meals are not offered in their own cafeteria.

CONNECTICUT

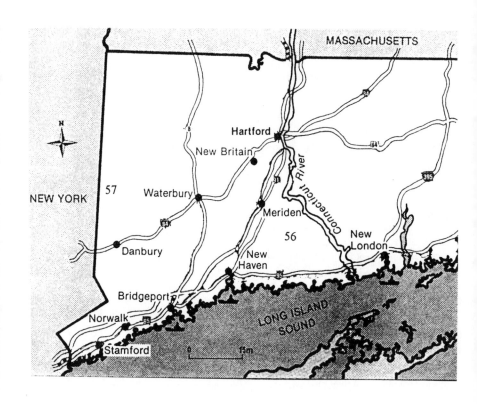

NAME OF CENTER: My Father's House Retreat Center   Listing ID #: 56

Telephone: 860-873-1581; Fax: 860-873-2357; E-mail: my_fathers_house@prodigy.net
Address: PO Box 22, North Moodus Rd.; Moodus; CT; 06469
Nearest Interstate: I-80, Exit 25 miles; Nearest State/US Hwy: Rte 2; 7 miles.

Restrictions: Age: None; Pets: Not permitted; Alcohol: Not permitted; Smoking: Outdoors only; Reservation Req'd: None; Max. Adv. Reser.: Open; Seasonal closing: None

RV/Campers overnight hookups: No

ACCOM: Mon. night thru Thurs. night rates for winterized (check if this is critical) rooms w/o meals unless otherwise indicated.

Bunkroom; Max. Pers: Over 5; Bedding incl ?: $5 surcharge; Bath: Shared; A/C: No:
Rate for: Person; $15; Rate for #2nd pers: $15; Rate for #3 pers: $15; Child Rate: n/a

Dormitory; Max. Pers: 4; Bedding incl ?: $5 surcharge; Bath: Shared; A/C: Yes
Rate for: Person: $15; Rate for #2nd pers: $15; Rate for #3 pers: $15; Child Rate: n/a

Motel; Max. Pers: 5; Bedding incl ?: $5 surcharge; Bath: Private; A/C: Yes:
Rate for: Person: $15; Rate for #2nd pers: $15; Rate for #3 pers: $15; Child Rate: n/a

Main amenities available: Volleyball; Basketball; Hiking
Meals are served in dining room for transients only when other groups are present. Dinner price varies.

NAME OF CENTER: Oratory of the Little Way   Listing ID #: 57

Telephone: 860-354-8294; Fax: 860-354-0574; E-mail: www.cysol.com/oratory
Address: Box 221 South Kent Rd; Gaylordsville; CT; 06755
Nearest Interstate: I-84, Exit 25 miles.

Restrictions: Age: None; Pets: Not permitted; Alcohol: Not permitted; Smoking: Outdoors only; Reservation Req'd: 7 days; Max. Adv. Reser.: 6 mo; Seasonal closing: Christmas, Easter, Thanksgiving

RV/Campers overnight hookups: No

ACCOM: Mon. night thru Thurs. night rates for winterized (check if this is critical) rooms w/o meals unless otherwise indicated.

Dormitory; Max. Pers: 1; Bedding incl ?: Yes; Bath: Shared; A/C: No:
Rate for: Person; $50; Child Rate: Free under 13 yrs.

Main amenities available: Prayer walk; Screened gazebo; Laundry machine; Bookstore; Library; On Housatonic River
Meals are not served in dining room for transients .

NAME OF CENTER: YMCA - Hartford Listing ID: 58

Telephone: 860-522-4180   Fax: 860-724-9858
Address: 160 Jewell St.; Hartford, CT 06103

Restrictions:
Accommodations offered to (M/F/Families): M&F. If M/F then must be over 18 yrs.
Pets: Not permitted; Alcohol: Not permitted; Smoking: Bedroom only
Reservation requirements: None
Reservations are accepted up to 0 days in advance. Seasonal closing: None

ACCOMMODATIONS:
Single room: Bedding included ?: Yes; Bath: Shared
Rate for 1 day: $19; Rate for 1 week: $126

Single room: Bedding included ?: Yes; Bath: Private
Rate for 1 day: $24; Rate for 1 week: $161

Main amenities: Pool Gym; TV lounge; Laundry machine
Meals are offered in their own cafeteria.

NAME OF CENTER: YMCA - Naugatuck Listing ID: 59

Telephone: 203-729-9622   Fax: 203-723-0083
Address: 284 Church St; Naugatuck, CT 06770

Restrictions:
Accommodations offered to (M/F/Families): M. If M/F then must be over 21 yrs.
Pets: Not permitted; Alcohol: Not permitted; Smoking: Outdoors only
Reservation requirements: Application needs 2 days
Reservations are accepted up to 2 wks in advance. Seasonal closing: None

ACCOMMODATIONS:
Single room: Bedding included ?: Yes; Bath: Shared
Rate for 1 day: not offered; Rate for 1 week: $74

Main amenities: Racquet ball; Health ctr; Pool; Gym; Laundry machine; TV lounge
Meals are not offered in their own cafeteria.

NAME OF CENTER: YMCA - New Britian Listing ID: 60

Telephone: 860-229-3788   Fax: 860-225-8063
Address: 50 High St.; New Britian, CT 06051

Restrictions:
Accommodations offered to (M/F/Families): M. If M/F then must be over 21 yrs.
Pets: Not permitted; Alcohol: Not permitted; Smoking: Bedroom only
Reservation requirements: None
Reservations are accepted up to 0 days in advance. Seasonal closing: None

ACCOMMODATIONS:
Single room: Bedding included ?: Yes; Bath: Shared
Rate for 1 day: $13.65+$20 dep; Rate for 1 week: $88.50+$20 dep

Main amenities: Pool; Gym; Fitness ctr; Laundry machine
Meals are not offered in their own cafeteria.

NAME OF CENTER: YMCA - Northern Middlesex Cty Listing ID: 61

Telephone: 860-343-6212   Fax: 860-343-6254
Address: 99 Union St.; Middletown, CT 06459

Restrictions:
Accommodations offered to (M/F/Families): M. If M/F then must be over 18 yrs.
Pets: Not permitted; Alcohol: Not permitted; Smoking: Bedroom only
Reservation requirements: Application needed
Reservations are accepted up to an indefinite time in advance. Seasonal closing: None

ACCOMMODATIONS:
Single room: Bedding included ?: Yes; Bath: Shared
Rate for 1 day: $15+$10 dep; Rate for 1 week: $90+$10 dep

Main amenities: Pool; Gym; Laundry machine; TV lounge
Meals are not offered in their own cafeteria.

NAME OF CENTER: YMCA - Stamford Listing ID: 62

Telephone: 203-357-7000   Fax: 203-425-8060
Address: 909 Washington Blvd; Stamford, CT 06901

Restrictions:
Accommodations offered to (M/F/Families): M&F. If M/F then must be over 18 yrs.
Pets: Not permitted; Alcohol: Not permitted; Smoking: Bedroom only
Reservation requirements: Application w/picture ID
Reservations are accepted up to an indefinite time in advance. Seasonal closing: None

ACCOMMODATIONS:
Single room: Bedding included ?: Yes; Bath: Private
Rate for 1 day: $37; Rate for 1 week: $179

Double room: Bedding included ?: Yes; Bath: Private
Rate for 1 day: $42; Rate for 1 week: $254

Main amenities: Pool; Gym; Library; TV lounge; Laundry machine
Meals are not offered in their own cafeteria.

NAME OF CENTER: **Washington Retreat House**   Listing ID #: 63

Telephone: 202-529-1111; Fax: 202-529-2102; E-mail:
Address: 4000 Harewood Road, NE; Washington; DC; 20017

Restrictions: Age: Adults; Pets: Not permitted; Alcohol: Not permitted; Smoking: Outdoors only; Reservation Req'd: 2 wks w/$20 dep; Max. Adv. Reser.: Open; Seasonal closing: None

RV/Campers overnight hookups: No

ACCOM: Mon. night thru Thurs. night rates for winterized (check if this is critical) rooms w/o meals unless otherwise indicated.

Motel; Max. Pers: over 2; Bedding incl ?: Yes; Bath: Semi-private; A/C: Yes:
Rate for: Person; $35; Rate for #2nd pers: $35; Rate for #3 pers: $35; Child Rate: n/a

Main amenities available: Large library; Video/tape room; Basketball; Chapel; Prayer room;
Meals are served in dining room for transients only when other groups are present. Approx. dinner price: $10.00.

REMEMBER TO CALL AHEAD

NAME OF CENTER: YWCA of New Castle County Listing ID: 64

Telephone: 302-658-7161   Fax: 302-658-7548
Address: 233 King St.; Wilmington, DE 19810

Restrictions:
Accommodations offered to (M/F/Families): F. If M/F then must be over 18 yrs.
Pets: Not permitted; Alcohol: Not permitted; Smoking: Lounge only
Reservation requirements: None
Reservations are accepted up to 2 wks w/dep in advance. Seasonal closing: None

ACCOMMODATIONS:
Single room: Bedding included ?: Yes; Bath: Shared
Rate for 1 day: $15-18.50+$10 dep; Rate for 1 week: $65-75+$10 dep

Main amenities: TV lounge; Kitchen privilege;
Meals are not offered in their own cafeteria.

FLORIDA

76
⑩
Apalachicola
River
Pensacola
Tallahassee ★
68
⑩
Jacksonville
77
95
Suwannee
River
66
St. Johns
River
75
73 ● Daytona Beach
74
Orlando
79
69
● Cape Canaveral
65
78
④
● Melbourne
95
Tampa
67
● Vero Beach
St. Petersburg ●
71
Sarasota
Florida's Tpk
Peace
River
75
75
Lake
Okeechobee
● Palm Beach
70
72
Naples ●
75
● Fort Lauderdale
Hialeah ●
● Miami
EVERGLADES
NATIONAL PARK
Key West ●

NAME OF CENTER: Camp Ithiel   Listing ID #: 65

Telephone: 407-293-3481; Fax: 407-578-2174; E-mail:
Address: 2037 Hempel Ave; mail (PO Box 165); Gotha; FL; 34734
Nearest State/US Hwy: FL Tpke; 2 miles.

Restrictions: Age: None; Pets: Permitted in RV & bedroom; Alcohol: Not permitted; Smoking: Outdoors only; Reservation Req'd: None; Max. Adv. Reser.: 3 mo; Seasonal closing: None

RV/Campers overnight hookups: Yes; Water: Yes; Electric: Yes; Septic: Yes
Basic Rate/Night: $15.00/ veh

ACCOM: Mon. night thru Thurs. night rates for winterized (check if this is critical) rooms w/o meals unless otherwise indicated.

Bunkroom; Max. Pers: 30; Bedding incl ?: No; Bath: Shared; A/C: No:
Rate for: Person; $13; Rate for #2nd pers: $13; Rate for #3 pers: $13; Child Rate: n/a

Eff. apt; Max. Pers: 7; Bedding incl ?: No; Bath: Private; A/C: Yes
Rate for: Person: $10; Rate for #2nd pers: $10; Rate for #3 pers: $10; Child Rate: $5 under 14 yrs
$25 min.; Kitchenette

Main amenities available: Swimming pool; V-ball; Bsk ball; Laundry machine; VCR-TV; Child swings/slide; Hiking/fishing
Meals are served in dining room for transients only when other groups are present. Approx. dinner price: $5.25.

NAME OF CENTER: Camp Kulaqua   Listing ID #: 66

Telephone: 904-454-1351; Fax: 904-454-4748; E-mail:
Address: 700 NW Cheeota Ave.; High Springs; FL; 32643
Nearest Interstate: I-75 S, Exit ; 11 miles; Nearest State/US Hwy: Rte 441; 1 miles.

Restrictions: Age: None; Pets: Not permitted; Alcohol: Not permitted; Smoking: Designated outdoor area; Reservation Req'd: Yes; Max. Adv. Reser.: Open; Seasonal closing: None

RV/Campers overnight hookups: Yes; Water: Yes; Electric: YEs; Septic: Yes
Basic Rate/Night: $12.75/ veh

ACCOM: Mon. night thru Thurs. night rates for winterized (check if this is critical) rooms w/o meals unless otherwise indicated.

Cabin; Max. Pers: 4; Bedding incl ?: $7 surcharge; Bath: Shared; A/C: Yes:
Rate for: 1 side of cabin; $25

Family chalet; Max. Pers: 4-6; Bedding incl ?: Yes; Bath: Private; A/C: Yes
Rate for: Entire Chalet: $66
Includes furnished kitchen

Main amenities available: Swimming; Horseback riding; Basketball; Volleyball; Hiking;
Meals are served in dining room for transients . Approx. dinner price: $6.75; $5.75 under 8 yrs; free under 4.

NAME OF CENTER: Camp Sparta Reg Baptist Camp   Listing ID #: 67

Telephone: 941-382-8696; Fax: 941-382-2669; E-mail: kcr@strato.net
Address: 5055 Camp Sparta Rd.; Sebring; FL; 33872
Nearest Interstate: I-4 , Exit 60 miles; Nearest State/US Hwy: Rte 27; 2 miles.

Restrictions: Age: None; Pets: Not permitted; Alcohol: Not permitted; Smoking: Nowhere;
Reservation Req'd: 5 days; Max. Adv. Reser.: Open; Seasonal closing: June 1 - Sept 1

RV/Campers overnight hookups: Yes

RV camp currently under construction; availability Fall 1999; prices and other information not
yet available.

ACCOM: Mon. night thru Thurs. night rates for winterized (check if this is critical) rooms w/o
meals unless otherwise indicated.

Cabin; Max. Pers: unk; Bedding incl ?: No; Bath: Private; A/C: Yes:
Rate for: Entire cabin; $30

Dormitory; Max. Pers: 5; Bedding incl ?: No; Bath: Shared; A/C: Yes
Rate for: Room: $20

Main amenities available: Swimming; V-ball; Bsk ball; Laundry machine; Tennis; Canoeing; Boating
Meals are served in dining room for transients only when other groups are present. Dinner price: $5-7.00.

NAME OF CENTER: Camp Weed & The Cerveny Conf. Ctr.   Listing ID #: 68

Telephone: 904-364-5250; Fax: 904-362-7557; E-mail: campweed@hankins.com
Address: 11057 Camp Weed Place; Live Oak; FL; 32060
Nearest Interstate: I-10, Exit 8 miles; Nearest State/US Hwy: I-75; 18 miles.

Restrictions: Age: None; Pets: Not permitted; Alcohol: Permitted; Smoking: Smoking rooms &
outside; Reservation Req'd: 4:30 PM of day; Max. Adv. Reser.: Open; Seasonal closing: None

RV/Campers overnight hookups: Yes; Water: Yes; Electric: Yes; Septic: n/a
Basic Rate/Night: $16.00/ veh

ACCOM: Mon. night thru Thurs. night rates for winterized (check if this is critical) rooms w/o
meals unless otherwise indicated.

Motel; Max. Pers: 2; Bedding incl ?: Yes; Bath: Private; A/C: Yes:
Rate for: Person; $45; Rate for #2nd pers: $35; Child Rate: n/a

Bunkroom; Max. Pers: 18; Bedding incl ?: Yes; Bath: Shared; A/C: Ceiling fan
Rate for: Person: $20; Rate for #2nd pers: $20; Rate for #3 pers: $20; Child Rate: n/a

Main amenities available: Lake swimming; V-ball; Bsk-ball; VCR-TV; Ball field; Bookstore; Hiking
Meals are served in dining room for transients only when other groups are present. Approx. dinner price: $9.50.

NAME OF CENTER: Canterbury Retreat & Conference Ctr.   Listing ID #: 69

Telephone: 407-365-5571; Fax: 407-365-9758; E-mail:
Address: 1601 Alfaya Trail; Oviedo; FL; 32765
Nearest State/US Hwy: Rte 417; 1 miles.

Restrictions: Age: None; Pets: Not permitted; Alcohol: Permitted; Smoking: Outdoors only; Reservation Req'd: 1 wk; Max. Adv. Reser.: 1 yr; Seasonal closing: None

RV/Campers overnight hookups: No

ACCOM: Mon. night thru Thurs. night rates for winterized (check if this is critical) rooms w/o meals unless otherwise indicated.

Motel; Max. Pers: 4; Bedding incl ?: Yes; Bath: Private; A/C: Yes:
Rate for: Room; $40

Main amenities available: Boats; Volleyball; Fishing; Horse shoes; Frisebee golf; Hiking
Meals are served in dining room for transients only when other groups are present. Approx. dinner price: $11.00.

NAME OF CENTER: Cenacle Spiritual Life Center   Listing ID #: 70

Telephone: 561-582-2534; Fax: 561-582-8070; E-mail: cenacle2@ix.netcom.com
Address: 1400 S. Dixie Hwy; Lantana; FL; 33462
Nearest Interstate: I-95, Exit 2 miles; Nearest State/US Hwy: US 1; 0 miles.

Restrictions: Age: None; Pets: Not permitted; Alcohol: Not permitted; Smoking: Designated outdoor area; Reservation Req'd: 3 wks; Max. Adv. Reser.: 2 mo; Seasonal closing: Jan - March

RV/Campers overnight hookups: No

ACCOM: Mon. night thru Thurs. night rates for winterized (check if this is critical) rooms w/o meals unless otherwise indicated.

Dormitory; Max. Pers: 1; Bedding incl ?: Yes (w/notice); Bath: Shared; A/C: Yes:
Rate for: Person; ** $50; Child Rate: Adults only
** Includes breakfast & lunch

Main amenities available: Library; Bookstore
Meals are served in dining room for transients only when other groups are present. Approx. dinner price: $5-10.00.

NAME OF CENTER: **Christian Retreat**   Listing ID #: 71

Telephone: 800-782-6414; Fax: 941-748-4793; E-mail: cretreat@gte.net
Address: 1200 Glory Way Blvd; Bradenton; FL; 34202
Nearest Interstate: I-75, Exit 6 miles; Nearest State/US Hwy: Rte 64; 4 miles.

Restrictions: Age: None; Pets: Not permitted; Alcohol: Not permitted; Smoking: Nowhere;
Reservation Req'd: None; Max. Adv. Reser.: Open; Seasonal closing: None

RV/Campers overnight hookups: Yes; Water: Yes; Electric: Yes; Septic: No
Basic Rate/Night: $17.00/ veh

ACCOM: Mon. night thru Thurs. night rates for winterized (check if this is critical) rooms w/o
meals unless otherwise indicated.

Motel; Max. Pers: 4; Bedding incl ?: Yes; Bath: Private; A/C: Yes:
Rate for: Person; ** $44/$58; Rate for #2nd pers: ** $0/$0; Rate for #3 pers: ** $3/$4; Child
Rate: n/a
** Off season rate / in season rate

Main amenities available: Swimming; Volleyball; Basketball; Tennis; Library; Bookstore
Meals are served in dining room for transients only when other groups are present. Approx. dinner price:
$6.75-$7.50.

NAME OF CENTER: **Duncan Conference Center**   Listing ID #: 72

Telephone: 561-496-4130; Fax: 561-496-1726; E-mail:
Address: 15820 S. Military Trail; Delray Beach; FL; 33484
Nearest Interstate: I-95, Exit 3 miles; Nearest State/US Hwy: FL Tpke; 5 miles.

Restrictions: Age: None; Pets: Not permitted; Alcohol: Not permitted; Smoking: Outdoors only;
Reservation Req'd: Noon of day; Max. Adv. Reser.: Open; Seasonal closing: None

RV/Campers overnight hookups: No

ACCOM: Mon. night thru Thurs. night rates for winterized (check if this is critical) rooms w/o
meals unless otherwise indicated.

Motel; Max. Pers: 2; Bedding incl ?: Yes; Bath: Private; A/C: Yes:
Rate for: Person; $45-55; Rate for #2nd pers: $45-55; Child Rate: n/a

Main amenities available: Bookstore; VCR-TV
Meals are served in dining room for transients only when other groups are present. Approx. dinner price:
$13.00.

NAME OF CENTER: El Caribe   Listing ID #: 73

Telephone: 800-445-9889; Fax: 904-254-1940; E-mail: www.elcaribe.com
Address: 2125 South Atlantic Ave.; Daytona Beach; FL; 32118
Nearest Interstate: I-95, Exit 3 miles.

Restrictions: Age: 21; Pets: Not permitted; Alcohol: Permitted; Smoking: Permitted; Reservation Req'd: None; Max. Adv. Reser.: Varies w/season; Seasonal closing: None

RV/Campers overnight hookups: No

ACCOM: Mon. night thru Thurs. night rates for winterized (check if this is critical) rooms w/o meals unless otherwise indicated.

Motel; Max. Pers: 2; Bedding incl ?: Yes; Bath: Private; A/C: Yes:
Rate for: Room; **$42-82; Child Rate: $6 for rollaway bed; Free under 18 yrs w/o add't'l bedding

Apts & Efficiencies; Max. Pers: 4; Bedding incl ?: Yes; Bath: Private; A/C: Yes
Rate for: Entire unit: **$46-92; Child Rate: $6 for rollaway bed; Free under 18 yrs w/o add't'l bedding
** Includes fully equipped kitchen; Apts incl dining rm & lving rm

Main amenities available: Volleyball; Basketball; Hiking
Meals are served in dining room for transients . Approx. dinner price: Wide range of pricing.
Not specifically Christian but caters to many Christian grps

NAME OF CENTER: FL UMC Life Enrichment Center   Listing ID #: 74

Telephone: 352-787-0313; Fax: 352-360-1355; E-mail: sschwartz@flumc.org
Address: 04991 Picciola Rd; Fruitland Park; FL; 34731
Nearest Interstate: I-75; Nearest State/US Hwy: Rte 27; 4 miles.

Restrictions: Age: None; Pets: Not permitted; Alcohol: Not permitted; Smoking: Outdoors only; Reservation Req'd: None; Max. Adv. Reser.: 1 yr; Seasonal closing: None

RV/Campers overnight hookups: Yes; Water: Yes; Electric: Yes; Septic: Yes
Basic Rate/Night: $11 + $2 septic/ vch

ACCOM: Mon. night thru Thurs. night rates for winterized (check if this is critical) rooms w/o meals unless otherwise indicated.

Motel; Max. Pers: 2; Bedding incl ?: Yes (w/notice); Bath: Private; A/C: Yes:
Rate for: Room; $45; Child Rate: n/a

Main amenities available: Library; Bookstore; Volleyball; Laundry machine; Canoeing;
Meals are served in dining room for transients only when other groups are present. Approx. dinner price: $7.50.

NAME OF CENTER: FL UMC South Florida Camp   Listing ID #: 75

Telephone: 941-675-0334; Fax: 941-675-1411; E-mail: sschwartz@flumc.org
Address: 6355 CR 78 West; Alva; FL; 33920
Nearest Interstate: I-75, Exit 17 miles; Nearest State/US Hwy: Rte 27; 23 miles.

Restrictions: Age: None; Pets: Not permitted; Alcohol: Not permitted; Smoking: Nowhere;
Reservation Req'd: None; Max. Adv. Reser.: Open; Seasonal closing: None

RV/Campers overnight hookups: Yes; Water: Yes; Electric: Yes; Septic: Yes
Basic Rate/Night: $11 + $2 septic/ veh

ACCOM: Mon. night thru Thurs. night rates for winterized (check if this is critical) rooms w/o
meals unless otherwise indicated.

Main amenities available: Volleyball; Basketball; Hiking
Meals are not served in dining room for transients .

NAME OF CENTER: Laguna Beach Christian Retreats   Listing ID #: 76

Telephone: 850-234-2502; Fax: 850-234-2576; E-mail: Laguna@panacom.com
Address: 20016 Front Beach Rd; Panama City Beach; FL; 32413
Nearest Interstate: I-10, Exit 60 miles; Nearest State/US Hwy: Rte 79; 3 miles.

Restrictions: Age: None; Pets: Not permitted; Alcohol: Not permitted; Smoking: Outdoors only;
Reservation Req'd: Yes; Max. Adv. Reser.: Varies w/season; Seasonal closing: None

RV/Campers overnight hookups: No

ACCOM: Mon. night thru Thurs. night rates for winterized (check if this is critical) rooms w/o
meals unless otherwise indicated.

Apt; Max. Pers: 4; Bedding incl ?: No; Bath: Private; A/C: Yes;
Rate for: Entire Apt; **$15-40; Child Rate: n/a
** Varies from winter to summer; kitchen, TV

Apt; Max. Pers: 6; Bedding incl ?: No; Bath: Private; A/C: Yes
Rate for: Entire Apt; **$20-50; Child Rate: n/a
** Varies from winter to summer; kitchen, TV

Main amenities available: Laundry machine; Swimming in Gulf; Pools; TV; Chapels; Incidentals store
Meals are served in dining room for transients . Approx. dinner price: Wide range of pricing.
Laguna Beach capacity 1100; On the Gulf

REMEMBER TO CALL AHEAD

NAME OF CENTER: **Montgomery Conference Center**   Listing ID #: 77

Telephone: 352-473-4516; Fax: ; E-mail:
Address: 50 SE 75th St.; Starke; FL; 32091
Nearest Interstate: I-10, Exit 30 miles; Nearest State/US Hwy: I-75; 30 miles.

Restrictions: Age: None; Pets: Not permitted; Alcohol: Not permitted; Smoking: Designated outdoor area; Reservation Req'd: 7 days; Max. Adv. Reser.: 30 days; Seasonal closing: None

RV/Campers overnight hookups: Yes; Water: Yes; Electric: Yes; Septic: Yes
Basic Rate/Night: $8.50/ veh

ACCOM: Mon. night thru Thurs. night rates for winterized (check if this is critical) rooms w/o meals unless otherwise indicated.

Bunkroom; Max. Pers: Over 5; Bedding incl ?: No; Bath: Shared; A/C: Yes:
Rate for: Person; $11; Rate for #2nd pers: $11; Rate for #3 pers: $11; Child Rate: $9 under 11 yrs; free under 6

Cottage; Max. Pers: Over 4; Bedding incl ?: $4 surcharge; Bath: Private; A/C: Yes
Rate for: Person: $17; Rate for #2nd pers: $17; Rate for #3 pers: $17; Child Rate: $12 under 12 yrs; free under 6

Motel; Max. Pers: 4; Bedding incl ?: Yes; Bath: Private; A/C: Yes:
Rate for: Person: $42; Rate for #2nd pers: $0; Rate for #3 pers: $6; Child Rate: n/a
$6 for #4

Main amenities available: VCR-TV; Volleyball; Basketball; Swimming; Canoe/Boat; Hiking
Meals are served in dining room for transients only when other groups are present. Approx. dinner price: $7.50; $6.25 under 12 yrs; free under 6.

NAME OF CENTER: **Tampa Bay Baptist Conference Ctr.**   Listing ID #: 78

Telephone: 813-961-1059; Fax: 813-960-8634; E-mail:
Address: 15601 Lake Magdalene Blvd; Tampa; FL; 33613
Nearest Interstate: I-275, Exit 36; 2 miles.

Restrictions: Age: None; Pets: Not permitted; Alcohol: Not permitted; Smoking: Designated outdoor area; Reservation Req'd: 2 wks; Max. Adv. Reser.: Varies w/season; Seasonal closing: None

RV/Campers overnight hookups: Yes; Water: Yes; Electric: Yes; Septic: Yes
Basic Rate/Night: $16.00/ veh

ACCOM: Mon. night thru Thurs. night rates for winterized (check if this is critical) rooms w/o meals unless otherwise indicated.

Motel; Max. Pers: 4; Bedding incl ?: Yes; Bath: Private; A/C: Yes:
Rate for: Person; $26; Rate for #2nd pers: $14; Rate for #3 pers: $14; Child Rate: n/a

Bunkroom; Max. Pers: 8; Bedding incl ?: No; Bath: Shared; A/C: Yes
Rate for: Person: $16; Rate for #2nd pers: $16; Rate for #3 pers: $16; Child Rate: n/a

Main amenities available: Lake Platt swimming; Fishing/Boating; V-ball; Bsk ball; Child playground; Shuffleboard; Horse shoes
Meals are served in dining room for transients only when other groups are present. Approx. dinner price: $6.00.

NAME OF CENTER: **The Pines Retreat Center**   Listing ID #: 79

Telephone: 352-796-4457; Fax: 352-796-4457; E-mail:
Address: 7029 Cedar Lane; Brooksville; FL; 34601
Nearest Interstate: I-75, Exit 61; 7 miles; Nearest State/US Hwy: 50; 1 miles.

Restrictions: Age: None; Pets: Not permitted; Alcohol: Permitted; Smoking: Outdoors only;
Reservation Req'd: None; Max. Adv. Reser.: 1 mo; Seasonal closing: None

RV/Campers overnight hookups: Yes; Water: Yes; Electric: Yes; Septic: No
Basic Rate/Night: $10.00/ veh

ACCOM: Mon. night thru Thurs. night rates for winterized (check if this is critical) rooms w/o
meals unless otherwise indicated.

Dormitory; Max. Pers: 5; Bedding incl ?: Yes; Bath: Shared; A/C: Yes:
Rate for: Person; $20; Rate for #2nd pers: $20; Rate for #3 pers: $20; Child Rate: Inquire for
family rates
Kitchen privileges

Main amenities available: Cable TV; Hiking; Swimming
Meals are served in dining room for transients only when other groups are present. Approx. dinner price: $6.00.

GEORGIA

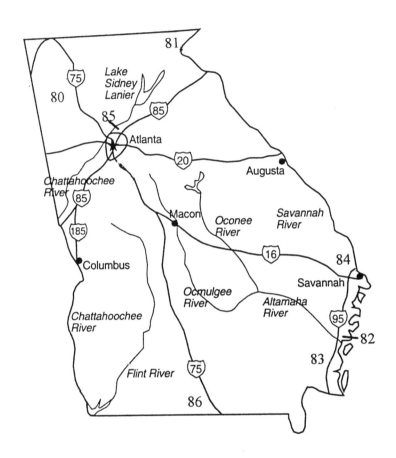

81

75

Lake
Sidney
Lanier

85

85

80

Atlanta

20

Augusta

Chattahoochee
River

85

Macon

Oconee
River

Savannah
River

185

16

84

Columbus

Savannah

Ocmulgee
River

Altamaha
River

95

Chattahoochee
River

82

Flint River

75

83

86

NAME OF CENTER: Cherokee Retreat Center   Listing ID #: 80

Telephone: 770-382-6280; Fax: 770-382-7804; E-mail:
Address: 370 Wilderness Camp Road; White; GA; 30184
Nearest Interstate: I-75, Exit 125; 7 miles; Nearest State/US Hwy: Rte 20; 3 miles.

Restrictions: Age: None; Pets: Not permitted; Alcohol: Not permitted; Smoking: Designated outdoor area; Reservation Req'd: 2 wks; Max. Adv. Reser.: 3 mo; Seasonal closing: June 1 - Aug 15

RV/Campers overnight hookups: Yes; Water: Yes; Electric: Yes; Septic: No
Basic Rate/Night: $14+$2/pers >2 per/ veh

ACCOM: Mon. night thru Thurs. night rates for winterized (check if this is critical) rooms w/o meals unless otherwise indicated.

Cabin; Max. Pers: 14; Bedding incl ?: $4 surcharge; Bath: Separate bldg; A/C: No:
Rate for: Person; $8; Rate for #2nd pers: $8; Rate for #3 pers: $8; Child Rate: n/a
$40 min.; Not heated; Available March 15 - June 1 and Aug 15 - Nov 15

Dormitory; Max. Pers: 4; Bedding incl ?: $4 surcharge; Bath: Shared; A/C: Yes
Rate for: Person: $15; Rate for #2nd pers: $15; Rate for #3 pers: $15; Child Rate: n/a
$27 min.

Main amenities available: Swimming; V-ball; Bsk Ball; Horse shoes; VCR-TV; Ping pong; Hiking
Meals are not served in dining room for transients .

NAME OF CENTER: Covecrest Retreat Center   Listing ID #: 81

Telephone: 706-782-5961; Fax: 706-782-2710; E-mail:
Address: Rt. #1; Box 3117; Tiger; GA; 30576
Nearest Interstate: I-85, Exit 40 miles; Nearest State/US Hwy: Rte 76; 5 miles.

Restrictions: Age: None; Pets: Permitted in RV area; Alcohol: Not permitted; Smoking: Outdoors only; Reservation Req'd: None; Max. Adv. Reser.: Open; Seasonal closing: None

RV/Campers overnight hookups: Yes; Water: Yes; Electric: No; Septic: No
Basic Rate/Night: $20.00/ veh

ACCOM: Mon. night thru Thurs. night rates for winterized (check if this is critical) rooms w/o meals unless otherwise indicated.

Motel; Max. Pers: 4; Bedding incl ?: Yes; Bath: Private; A/C: Yes:
Rate for: Room; $55-80; Child Rate: n/a

Cabin; Max. Pers: Over 4; Bedding incl ?: Yes; Bath: Private; A/C: Y/N
Rate for: Entire cabin: **$70-90; Child Rate: n/a
** Varies from winter to summer; includes kitchen and 2 bedrooms

Main amenities available: Fishing; Volleyball; Basketball; Bookstore
Meals are served in dining room for transients only when other groups are present. Approx. dinner price: $7.25.

NAME OF CENTER: Epworth by the Sea   Listing ID #: 82

Telephone: 912-638-8688; Fax: 912-634-0642; E-mail: epworth@epworthbythesea.org
Address: 100 Arthur Moore Dr. (PO Box 20407); St. Simons Island; GA; 31522
Nearest Interstate: I-95, Exit 12 miles.

Restrictions: Age: None; Pets: Not permitted; Alcohol: Not permitted; Smoking: Smoking rooms & outside; Reservation Req'd: None; Max. Adv. Reser.: Open; Seasonal closing: None

RV/Campers overnight hookups: No

ACCOM: Mon. night thru Thurs. night rates for winterized (check if this is critical) rooms w/o meals unless otherwise indicated.

Motel; Max. Pers: 5; Bedding incl ?: Yes; Bath: Private; A/C: Yes:
Rate for: Room; $42-92; Rate for #2nd pers: $0; Rate for #3 pers: $5; Child Rate: Free under 13 yrs

Main amenities available: Swimming; V-ball; Bsk ball; Tennis; VCR-TV; Bookstore; Hiking
Meals are served in dining room for transients . Approx. dinner price: $8.25; 50% off under 13 yrs.

NAME OF CENTER: Georgia Episcopal Camp & Conf. Ctr   Listing ID #: 83

Telephone: 912-265-9218; Fax: 912-267-6907; E-mail:
Address: 299 Episcopal Conf. Ctr. Rd.; Waverly; GA; 31565
Nearest Interstate: I-95, Exit 5; 5 miles.

Restrictions: Age: None; Pets: Not permitted; Alcohol: Permitted in bedroom; Smoking: Outdoors only; Reservation Req'd: 7 days; Max. Adv. Reser.: 1 yr; Seasonal closing: None

RV/Campers overnight hookups: Yes; Water: Yes; Electric: Yes; Septic: No
Basic Rate/Night: $10.00/ veh

ACCOM: Mon. night thru Thurs. night rates for winterized (check if this is critical) rooms w/o meals unless otherwise indicated.

Dormitory; Max. Pers: Over 5; Bedding incl ?: No; Bath: Shared; A/C: Yes:
Rate for: Person; **$35; Rate for #2nd pers: **$35; Rate for #3 pers: **$35; Child Rate: n/a
** Includes 3 meals

Motel/Hotel; Max. Pers: 2; Bedding incl ?: Yes; Bath: Private; A/C: Yes
Rate for: Room: $39; Rate for #2nd pers: $13; Child Rate: n/a

Main amenities available: Laundry machine; Volleyball; Incidentals store; Child playground; Horse shoes; Ping pong
Meals are served in dining room for transients . Approx. dinner price: $10; free under 5 yrs.

NAME OF CENTER: New Ebenezer Retreat Center   Listing ID #: 84

Telephone: 912-754-9242; Fax: 912-754-7781; E-mail:
Address: 2887 Ebenezer Rd; Rincon; GA; 31326
Nearest Interstate: I-95, Exit 17 miles; Nearest State/US Hwy: Rte 21; 5 miles.

Restrictions: Age: None; Pets: Not permitted; Alcohol: Not permitted; Smoking: Outdoors only; Reservation Req'd: None; Max. Adv. Reser.: 3 wks; Seasonal closing: None

RV/Campers overnight hookups: No

ACCOM: Mon. night thru Thurs. night rates for winterized (check if this is critical) rooms w/o meals unless otherwise indicated.

Cabin/Motel; Max. Pers: 2; Bedding incl ?: Yes; Bath: Private; A/C: Yes:
Rate for: Person; $26; Rate for #2nd pers: $26; Child Rate: Children free w/self provided bedding
4-5 bedrooms/cabin each w/private bath

Main amenities available: Swimming; Volleyball; Shuffleboard; Incidentals store; Paddle boats; Hiking
Meals are served in dining room for transients only when other groups are present. Approx. dinner price: $7.50.

NAME OF CENTER: Simpsonwood Conference Center   Listing ID #: 85

Telephone: 770-441-1111; Fax: 770-416-7976; E-mail: info@simpsonwood.org
Address: 4511 Jones Bridge Circle NW; Norcross; GA; 30092
Nearest Interstate: I-285, Exit 10 miles; Nearest State/US Hwy: Rte 141; 2 miles.

Restrictions: Age: None; Pets: Not permitted; Alcohol: Not permitted; Smoking: Outdoors only; Reservation Req'd: 7 days; Max. Adv. Reser.: 3 mo; Seasonal closing: None

RV/Campers overnight hookups: Yes; Water: Yes; Electric: Yes; Septic: Yes
Basic Rate/Night: $10.00/ veh

ACCOM: Mon. night thru Thurs. night rates for winterized (check if this is critical) rooms w/o meals unless otherwise indicated.

Motel; Max. Pers: 5; Bedding incl ?: Yes; Bath: Private; A/C: Yes:
Rate for: Person; **$55; Rate for #2nd pers: **$55; Rate for #3 pers: **$55; Child Rate: $10 under 17 yrs; free under 3
** Includes 3 meals

Main amenities available: Swimming; V-ball; Bsk ball; Bookstore; Laundry machine; Tennis; Hiking
Meals are served in dining room for transients . Approx. dinner price: $8.00.

NAME OF CENTER: **Tygart Campground**   Listing ID #: 86

Telephone: 912-686-2938; Fax: ; E-mail:
Address: RR #1; Box 3200 Tygart Rd; Ray City; GA; 31645
Nearest Interstate: I-75, Exit 14 miles; Nearest State/US Hwy: Rte 37; 3 miles.

Restrictions: Age: None; Pets: Permitted outside; Alcohol: Not permitted; Smoking: Outdoors only; Reservation Req'd: None; Max. Adv. Reser.: 7 days; Seasonal closing: June - Aug.

RV/Campers overnight hookups: Yes; Water: Yes; Electric: Yes; Septic: Yes
Basic Rate/Night: $15.00/ veh

ACCOM: Mon. night thru Thurs. night rates for winterized (check if this is critical) rooms w/o meals unless otherwise indicated.

House; Max. Pers: 8; Bedding incl ?: No; Bath: Semi-private; A/C: Yes:
Rate for: Entire Hse; $45

House; Max. Pers: 4; Bedding incl ?: No; Bath: Semi-private; A/C: Yes
Rate for: Entire Hse: $40

Main amenities available: VCR-TV; Volleyball; Basketball; Swimming; Hiking
Meals are not served in dining room for transients .

REMEMBER TO CALL AHEAD

IDAHO

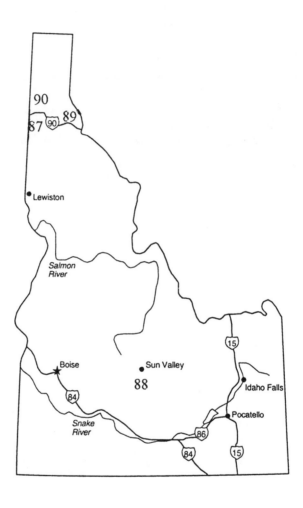

NAME OF CENTER: **Camp Lutherhaven**   Listing ID #: 87

Telephone: 208-667-3459; Fax: 208-765-1713; E-mail:
Address: 3000 W. Lutheranhaven Rd.; Coeur d'Alene; ID; 83814
Nearest Interstate: I-90, Exit 12 miles; Nearest State/US Hwy: Rte 95; 3 miles.

Restrictions: Age: None; Pets: Not in room; Alcohol: With permission; Smoking: Designated outdoor area; Reservation Req'd: 1 day; Max. Adv. Reser.: 2 yrs; Seasonal closing: None

RV/Campers overnight hookups: Yes; Water: Yes; Electric: Yes; Septic: Yes
Basic Rate/Night: $16.00/ veh

ACCOM: Mon. night thru Thurs. night rates for winterized (check if this is critical) rooms w/o meals unless otherwise indicated.

Dormitory; Max. Pers: 5; Bedding incl ?: $5/rm surcharge; Bath: Shared; A/C: No:
Rate for: Person; $14; Rate for #2nd pers: $14; Rate for #3 pers: $14; Child Rate: $9 under 12 yrs; free under 3

Motel; Max. Pers: 5; Bedding incl ?: $5/rm surcharge; Bath: Private; A/C: No
Rate for: Person: $16; Rate for #2nd pers: $16; Rate for #3 pers: $16; Child Rate: $9 under 12 yrs; free under 3

Main amenities available: Laundry machine; Volleyball; Basketball; Swimming; Canoeing; Hiking
Meals are served in dining room for transients only when other groups are present. Approx. dinner price: $7.25; $5 under 12 yrs; free under 3.

NAME OF CENTER: **Cathedral Pines**   Listing ID #: 88

Telephone: 208-726-5007; Fax: 208-726-5007; E-mail:
Address: HC 64; Box 8296; Ketchum; ID; 83340
Nearest Interstate: I-86, Exit 80 miles; Nearest State/US Hwy: Rte 75; 1 miles.

Restrictions: Age: None; Pets: Not permitted; Alcohol: Not permitted; Smoking: Nowhere; Reservation Req'd: 30 days; Max. Adv. Reser.: 6 mo; Seasonal closing: Oct 16 - May 14

RV/Campers overnight hookups: Yes; Water: No; Electric: Yes; Septic: No
Basic Rate/Night: $5/pers/ veh

ACCOM: Mon. night thru Thurs. night rates for winterized (check if this is critical) rooms w/o meals unless otherwise indicated.

Main amenities available: River fishing; Swimming pool **
Meals are served in dining room for transients . Approx. dinner price:Price varies.
** Pool use w/fee

NAME OF CENTER: Sho Shone   Listing ID #: 89

Telephone: 208-667-3459; Fax: 208-765-1713; E-mail:
Address: ; Kellogg; ID; 83837
Nearest Interstate: I-90, Exit 30 miles.

Restrictions: Age: None; Pets: Not in room; Alcohol: With permission; Smoking: Designated outdoor area; Reservation Req'd: 1 day; Max. Adv. Reser.: 2 yrs; Seasonal closing: None

RV/Campers overnight hookups: Yes; Water: Yes; Electric: Yes; Septic: n/a
Basic Rate/Night: $12.00/ veh

ACCOM: Mon. night thru Thurs. night rates for winterized (check if this is critical) rooms w/o meals unless otherwise indicated.

Dormitory; Max. Pers: 5; Bedding incl ?: $5/rm surcharge; Bath: Shared; A/C: No:
Rate for: Person; $13; Rate for #2nd pers: $13; Rate for #3 pers: $13; Child Rate: $8 under 12 yrs; free under 3

Main amenities available: Laundry machine; Volleyball; Basketball; Swimming in river; Canoeing; Hiking
Meals are served in dining room for transients only when other groups are present. Approx. dinner price: $7.25; $5 under 12 yrs; free under 3.

NAME OF CENTER: **Twinlow Camp & Retreat Center**   Listing ID #: 90

Telephone: 208-687-1146; Fax: 208-687-2768; E-mail:
Address: N. 22775 Twinlow Rd.; Rathdrum; ID; 83858
Nearest Interstate: I-90, Exit 15 miles; Nearest State/US Hwy: Rte 41; 0 miles.

Restrictions: Age: None; Pets: Not permitted; Alcohol: Not permitted; Smoking: Designated outdoor area; Reservation Req'd: None; Max. Adv. Reser.: 1 mo; Seasonal closing: Two weeks at Christmas

RV/Campers overnight hookups: No

ACCOM: Mon. night thru Thurs. night rates for winterized (check if this is critical) rooms w/o meals unless otherwise indicated.

Cabin; Max. Pers: 10; Bedding incl ?: No; Bath: Separate bldg; A/C: No:
Rate for: Person; $5; Rate for #2nd pers: $5; Rate for #3 pers: $5; Child Rate: n/a

Motel; Max. Pers: 4; Bedding incl ?: Yes; Bath: Private; A/C: No
Rate for: Room: $50; Rate for #2nd pers: n/a; Rate for #3 pers: n/a; Child Rate: n/a

Main amenities available: Lake swimming; Volleyball; Basketball; Canoeing ; Incidentals store; Hiking
Meals are served in dining room for transients only when other groups are present. Approx. dinner price: $8.00.

ILLINOIS

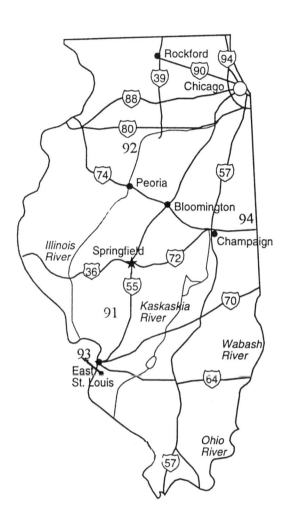

NAME OF CENTER: Lake Williamson Christian Ctr.   Listing ID #: 91

Telephone: 217-854-4824; Fax: 217-854-4840; E-mail:
Address: PO Box 620; Carlinville; IL; 62626
Nearest Interstate: I-55, Exit 8 miles; Nearest State/US Hwy: Rte 4; 0 miles.

Restrictions: Age: None; Pets: Not permitted; Alcohol: Not permitted; Smoking: Outdoors only;
Reservation Req'd: None; Max. Adv. Reser.: Open; Seasonal closing: None

RV/Campers overnight hookups: Yes; Water: Yes; Electric: Yes; Septic: No
Basic Rate/Night: $15.00/ veh

ACCOM: Mon. night thru Thurs. night rates for winterized (check if this is critical) rooms w/o
meals unless otherwise indicated.

Motel; Max. Pers: 6; Bedding incl ?: Yes; Bath: Private; A/C: Yes:
Rate for: Room; $46; Child Rate: n/a

Main amenities available: In-door pool; V-ball; Bsk ball; Hot tub; Racquet ball; Incidentals store; VCR-TV
Meals are served in dining room for transients only when other groups are present. Approx. dinner price: $6.50.

NAME OF CENTER: Menno Haven Camp & Retreat Center   Listing ID #: 92

Telephone: 800-636-6642; Fax: 815-646-4301; E-mail: mennohav@theramp.net
Address: 9301 1575 East St.; Tiskilwa; IL; 61368
Nearest Interstate: I-80, Exit 56; 10 miles; Nearest State/US Hwy: Rte 575E; 0 miles.

Restrictions: Age: None; Pets: Not permitted; Alcohol: Not permitted; Smoking: Outdoors only;
Reservation Req'd: No; Max. Adv. Reser.: Open; Seasonal closing: None

RV/Campers overnight hookups: Yes; Water: Yes; Electric: Yes; Septic: Yes
Basic Rate/Night: $4/per; $20 max/fam/ veh

ACCOM: Mon. night thru Thurs. night rates for winterized (check if this is critical) rooms w/o
meals unless otherwise indicated.

Motel; Max. Pers: 4; Bedding incl ?: Yes; Bath: Private; A/C: No:
Rate for: Person; $50; Rate for #2nd pers: $5; Rate for #3 pers: $10; Child Rate: Free under 4
yrs

Bunkroom; Max. Pers: 18; Bedding incl ?: No; Bath: Shared; A/C: No
Rate for: Person: **$13; Rate for #2nd pers: **$13; Rate for #3 pers: **$13; Child Rate: Free
under 4 yrs
** $65 min.

Main amenities available: Swimming; Volleyball; Canoe/Boat; Shuffleboard; Ping pong; Many others
Meals are served in dining room for transients only when other groups are present. Approx. dinner price: $6.50;
50% off under 9 yrs; free under 4.

NAME OF CENTER: Nat'l Shrine of Our Lady of the Snows Listing ID #: 93

Telephone: 618-397-6700; Fax: 618-398-6549; E-mail: www.oblatesusa.org
Address: 442 S. DeMazenod Dr.; Belleville; IL; 62223
Nearest Interstate: I-255, Exit 17A; 1 miles.

Restrictions: Age: None; Pets: Not permitted; Alcohol: Permitted; Smoking: Smoking &
non-smoking rooms; Reservation Req'd: None; Max. Adv. Reser.: 1 yr; Seasonal closing: None

RV/Campers overnight hookups: No

ACCOM: Mon. night thru Thurs. night rates for winterized (check if this is critical) rooms w/o
meals unless otherwise indicated.

Motel; Max. Pers: 4; Bedding incl ?: Yes; Bath: Priate; A/C: Yes:
Rate for: Person; ** $54; Rate for #2nd pers: ** $3; Rate for #3 pers: ** $5; Child Rate: n/a
** Includes continental breakfast

Main amenities available: Devotional areas; Chapel; Cable TV in room; Children's platground; Hiking on 200
acres
Meals are served in dining room for transients . Approx. dinner price: $7.95; $2.95 under 12 yrs..

NAME OF CENTER: The Woods Retreat Center Listing ID #: 94

Telephone: 217-987-6988; Fax: 217-987-6349; E-mail: dhenslei@prairenet.org
Address: 30624 N500E; Potomac; IL; 61865
Nearest Interstate: I-74, Exit 15 miles.

Restrictions: Age: None; Pets: Not permitted; Alcohol: Not permitted; Smoking: Outdoors only;
Reservation Req'd: Noon of day; Max. Adv. Reser.: Open; Seasonal closing: None

RV/Campers overnight hookups: No

ACCOM: Mon. night thru Thurs. night rates for winterized (check if this is critical) rooms w/o
meals unless otherwise indicated.

Motel; Max. Pers: 5; Bedding incl ?: **$5 surcharge; Bath: Private; A/C: Yes:
Rate for: Person; $15; Rate for #2nd pers: $5; Rate for #3 pers. $5; Child Rate. Free under 8
yrs
** Adv. notice req'd

Dorm; Max. Pers: 5; Bedding incl ?: ** $5 surcharge; Bath: Shared; A/C: No
Rate for: Person: $10; Rate for #2nd pers: $10; Rate for #3 pers: $10; Child Rate: Free unde 8
yrs.
** Adv. notice req'd

Main amenities available: Hiking; Volleyball; Basketball; Ropes course
Meals are not served in dining room for transients .

NAME OF CENTER: YMCA - McGaw (Evanston) Listing ID: 95

Telephone: 847-475-7400   Fax: 847-475-0753
Address: 1000 Grove St.; Evanston, IL 60201

Restrictions:
Accommodations offered to (M/F/Families): M. If M/F then must be over 18 yrs.
Pets: Not permitted; Alcohol: Not permitted; Smoking: Bedroom only
Reservation requirements: 15 days w/credit card
Reservations are accepted up to an indefinite time in advance. Seasonal closing: None

ACCOMMODATIONS:
Single room: Bedding included ?: Yes; Bath: Shared
Rate for 1 day: $36+$3 dep; Rate for 1 week: $101+$3 dep

Main amenities: Pool; Gym; Laundry machine; Sauna; TV lounge; Whirlpool
Meals are not offered in their own cafeteria.
Evanston is all metered parking except 9PM-6AM

NAME OF CENTER: YMCA - Oak Park Listing ID: 96

Telephone: 708-383-5200   Fax: 708-383-0159
Address: 255 S. Marion St.; Oak Park, IL 60302

Restrictions:
Accommodations offered to (M/F/Families): M. If M/F then must be over 18 yrs.
Pets: Not permitted; Alcohol: Not permitted; Smoking: Bedroom only
Reservation requirements: None
Reservations are accepted up to 0 days in advance. Seasonal closing: None

ACCOMMODATIONS:
Single room: Bedding included ?: Yes; Bath: Shared
Rate for 1 day: $40+$10 dep; Rate for 1 week: $108+$10 dep

Main amenities: Pool; Gym; Laundry machine; TV lounge
Meals are not offered in their own cafeteria.
Desire application. Will waive for out-of-towners.

NAME OF CENTER: YWCA - Peoria Listing ID: 97

Telephone: 309-674-1167   Fax:
Address: 301 NE Jefferson St.; Peoria, IL 61602

Restrictions:
Accommodations offered to (M/F/Families): F(M if husb); child. If M/F then must be over None yrs.
Pets: Not permitted; Alcohol: Not permitted; Smoking: Outdoors only
Reservation requirements: No
Reservations are accepted up to 0 days in advance. Seasonal closing: None

ACCOMMODATIONS:
Emer. Shelter: Bedding included ?: Yes; Bath: Shared
Rate for 1 day: Free; Rate for 1 week:

Main amenities:
Meals are not offered in their own cafeteria.

INDIANA

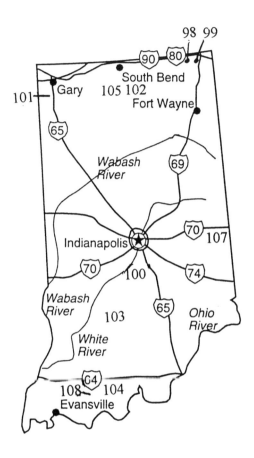

NAME OF CENTER: **Brethren Retreat Center**   Listing ID #: 98

Telephone: 219-768-4519; Fax: 219-768-4615; E-mail: brcship@juno.com
Address: 9095 W 275 N; Shipshewana; IN; 46565
Nearest Interstate: I-80/I-90, Exit 12 miles; Nearest State/US Hwy: US 20; 3 miles.

Restrictions: Age: None; Pets: Not permitted; Alcohol: Not permitted; Smoking: Outdoors only;
Reservation Req'd: 2 days; Max. Adv. Reser.: Open; Seasonal closing: None

RV/Campers overnight hookups: Yes; Water: Yes; Electric: Yes; Septic: n/a
Basic Rate/Night: $12.00/ veh

ACCOM: Mon. night thru Thurs. night rates for winterized (check if this is critical) rooms w/o
meals unless otherwise indicated.

Dormitory; Max. Pers: 4; Bedding incl ?: $5 surcharge; Bath: Shared; A/C: No:
Rate for: Person; $11; Rate for #2nd pers: $11; Rate for #3 pers: $11; Child Rate: 50% under
18 ys; free under 7

Motel; Max. Pers: 4; Bedding incl ?: $5 surcharge; Bath: Private; A/C: No
Rate for: Room: $32; Child Rate: n/a

Main amenities available: Swimming; V-ball; Bsk ball; Ping pong; Canoeing; VCR-TV; Hiking
Meals are served in dining room for transients only when other groups are present. Approx. dinner price:
$5.80-7.50.

NAME OF CENTER: **Camp Lakewood**   Listing ID #: 99

Telephone: 219-351-2331; Fax: 219-351-4552; E-mail:
Address: PO Box 162; S. Milford; IN; 46786
Nearest Interstate: I-80/I-90, Exit 13 miles; Nearest State/US Hwy: I-69; 8 miles.

Restrictions: Age: None; Pets: Not permitted; Alcohol: Not permitted; Smoking: Nowhere;
Reservation Req'd: 7 days; Max. Adv. Reser.: 1 yr; Seasonal closing: None

RV/Campers overnight hookups: No

ACCOM: Mon. night thru Thurs. night rates for winterized (check if this is critical) rooms w/o
meals unless otherwise indicated.

Dormitory; Max. Pers: 8; Bedding incl ?: No; Bath: Shared; A/C: No:
Rate for: Person; $12; Rate for #2nd pers: $12; Rate for #3 pers: $12; Child Rate: n/a

Main amenities available: Volleyball; Basketball; Hiking
Meals are served in dining room for transients only when other groups are present & w/adv notice. Approx.
dinner price: $4.00.

REMEMBER TO CALL AHEAD

NAME OF CENTER: Camp Mone' to   Listing ID #: 100

Telephone: 812-988-7118; Fax: ; E-mail:
Address: 551 N. Camp Mone' to Rd.; Nashville; IN; 47448
Nearest Interstate: I-65, Exit 8 miles; Nearest State/US Hwy: Rte 46; 1 miles.

Restrictions: Age: None; Pets: Permitted outside; Alcohol: Not permitted; Smoking: Outdoors only; Reservation Req'd: None; Max. Adv. Reser.: Open; Seasonal closing: None

RV/Campers overnight hookups: Yes; Water: Yes; Electric: Yes; Septic: n/a
Basic Rate/Night: $8.00/ veh

ACCOM: Mon. night thru Thurs. night rates for winterized (check if this is critical) rooms w/o meals unless otherwise indicated.

Cabin; Max. Pers: Over4; Bedding incl ?: No; Bath: Private; A/C: No:
Rate for: Entire cabin; $24+$4/person; Child Rate: n/a
Includes kitchenette

Half cabin; Max. Pers: 9; Bedding incl ?: No; Bath: Shared; A/C: Yes
Rate for: Half cabin: $40+$4/person; Child Rate: n/a
Includes kitchen

Main amenities available: VCR-TV; Volleyball; Basketball; Swimming; Library; Hiking
Meals are not served in dining room for transients .

NAME OF CENTER: Cedar Lake Bible Conference   Listing ID #: 101

Telephone: 219-374-5941; Fax: 219-374-7830; E-mail: clbcc@mail.ic.congrp.com
Address: PO Box 665; Cedar Lake; IN; 46303
Nearest Interstate: I-80/I-90, Exit 20 miles; Nearest State/US Hwy: Rte 65; 20 miles.

Restrictions: Age: None; Pets: Not permitted; Alcohol: Not permitted; Smoking: Outdoors only; Reservation Req'd: None; Max. Adv. Reser.: 1 mo; Seasonal closing: None

RV/Campers overnight hookups: Yes; Water: Yes; Electric: $21; Septic: n/a
Basic Rate/Night: $18.00/ veh

ACCOM: Mon. night thru Thurs. night rates for winterized (check if this is critical) rooms w/o meals unless otherwise indicated.

Duplex apt; Max. Pers: 6; Bedding incl ?: Yes; Bath: Private; A/C: Yes:
Rate for: Person; **$39
** Family rate: $52-72; includes kitchenette

Main amenities available: Indoor pool; Volleyball; Canoeing; Bookstore; Incidentals store 1/4 mi.; Hiking
Meals are served in dining room for transients only when other groups are present. Approx. dinner price: $8.50; $7 under 12 yrs; $5.50 under 7.

NAME OF CENTER: ****FCA National Conference Center   Listing ID #: 102

Telephone: 800-423-8781; Fax: 765-597-2572; E-mail: ncc@fca.org
Address: Rt 1; Box 81A; Marshall; IN; 47859
Nearest Interstate: I-74, Exit 47 miles; Nearest State/US Hwy: Rte 47; 0 miles.

Restrictions: Age: None; Pets: Not permitted; Alcohol: Not permitted; Smoking: Outdoors only; Reservation Req'd: 10 days; Max. Adv. Reser.: Open; Seasonal closing: None

RV/Campers overnight hookups: No

ACCOM: Mon. night thru Thurs. night rates for winterized (check if this is critical) rooms w/o meals unless otherwise indicated.

Bunkroom; Max. Pers: Over 5; Bedding incl ?: **Surcharge $5 ; Bath: Shared; A/C: Yes: Rate for: Person; $13; Rate for #2nd pers: $13; Rate for #3 pers: $13; Child Rate: 50% off for children
** Adv notice required

Cabin; Max. Pers: Over 4; Bedding incl ?: ** $5 surcharge; Bath: Shared; A/C: Yes
Rate for: Person: $15; Rate for #2nd pers: $15; Rate for #3 pers: $15; Child Rate: 50 % off for children
** Adv notice required

Motel; Max. Pers: 5; Bedding incl ?: $5 surcharge; Bath: Private; A/C: Yes:
Rate for: Person: $19-21; Rate for #2nd pers: $19-21; Rate for #3 pers: $19-21; Child Rate: Children $8.00
** Adv notice required

Main amenities available: V-ball; Bsk ball; VCR-TV; Tennis; Bookstore; Ball field; Hiking
Meals are served in dining room for transients only when other groups are present. Approx. dinner price: $5-8.00.
**** Fellowship of Christian Athletes

NAME OF CENTER: Indian Creek Baptist Camp   Listing ID #: 103

Telephone: 812-279-2161; Fax: 812-277-9790; E-mail:
Address: Rt 12; Box 1000; Bedford; IN; 47421
Nearest Interstate: I-465, Exit 85 miles; Nearest State/US Hwy: Rte 37; 2 miles.

Restrictions: Age: None; Pets: Not permitted; Alcohol: Not permitted; Smoking: Nowhere; Reservation Req'd: None; Max. Adv. Reser.: 2 mo; Seasonal closing: None

RV/Campers overnight hookups: Yes; Water: No; Electric: Yes; Septic: No
Basic Rate/Night: $10.00/ veh

ACCOM: Mon. night thru Thurs. night rates for winterized (check if this is critical) rooms w/o meals unless otherwise indicated.

Cabin; Max. Pers: Over 5; Bedding incl ?: No; Bath: Separate bldg; A/C: No:
Rate for: Person; $9; Rate for #2nd pers: $9; Rate for #3 pers: $9; Child Rate: n/a
Not winterized

Motel; Max. Pers: 2; Bedding incl ?: No; Bath: Private; A/C: Yes
Rate for: Person: $18; Rate for #2nd pers: $18; Child Rate: n/a

Dorm; Max. Pers: 15; Bedding incl ?: No; Bath: shared; A/C: Yes:
Rate for: Person: $16; Rate for #2nd pers: $16; Rate for #3 pers: $16; Child Rate: n/a

Main amenities available: Incidentals store; V-ball; Bsk ball; Laundry machine; VCR-TV; Ping-pong; Tetherball
Meals are served in dining room for transients only when other groups are present. Approx. dinner price: $6.75.

NAME OF CENTER: **Kordes Enrichment Center**   Listing ID #: 104

Telephone: 800-880-2777; Fax: ; E-mail: kordes@thedome.org
Address: 841 E. 14th St.; Ferdinand; IN; 47532
Nearest Interstate: I-64, Exit 1 miles.

Restrictions: Age: None; Pets: Not permitted; Alcohol: Not permitted; Smoking: Outdoors only; Reservation Req'd: 1 day; Max. Adv. Reser.: Open; Seasonal closing: None

RV/Campers overnight hookups: No

ACCOM: Mon. night thru Thurs. night rates for winterized (check if this is critical) rooms w/o meals unless otherwise indicated.

Dormitory; Max. Pers: 5; Bedding incl ?: Yes; Bath: Shared; A/C: Yes:
Rate for: Person; $30; Rate for #2nd pers: $30; Rate for #3 pers: $30; Child Rate: n/a

Main amenities available: Quiet areas
Meals are not served in dining room for transients .

NAME OF CENTER: **Lindenwood Retreat Center**   Listing ID #: 105

Telephone: 219-935-1780; Fax: 219-935-1728; E-mail: lw@lindenwood.org
Address: PO Box 1; 9601 Union Rd.; Donaldson; IN; 46513
Nearest Interstate: US-30, Exit 2 miles; Nearest State/US Hwy: US 31; 8 miles.

Restrictions: Age: 18; Pets: Not permitted; Alcohol: Not permitted; Smoking: Outdoors only; Reservation Req'd: 2 days; Max. Adv. Reser.: 1 mo; Seasonal closing: None

RV/Campers overnight hookups:

ACCOM: Mon. night thru Thurs. night rates for winterized (check if this is critical) rooms w/o meals unless otherwise indicated.

Motel; Max. Pers: 2; Bedding incl ?: Yes; Bath: Private; A/C: Yes:
Rate for: Person; **$48; Rate for #2nd pers: **$48; Child Rate: n/a
** Includes 3 meals. Guests are requested to strip beds at end of stay.

Main amenities available: Library; Bookstore; VCR-TV;
Meals are served in dining room for transients . Price varies.

NAME OF CENTER: Oakwood Park   Listing ID #: 106

Telephone: 219-457-5600; Fax: 219-457-3104; E-mail: www.oakwoodinn.org
Address: 702 East Lake View Rd; Syracuse; IN; 46567
Nearest Interstate: I-80/I-90, Exit ; 25 miles; Nearest State/US Hwy: US 6; 1 miles.

Restrictions: Age: None; Pets: Not permitted; Alcohol: Not permitted; Smoking: Outdoors only;
Reservation Req'd: 1 day; Max. Adv. Reser.: 6 mo; Seasonal closing: None

RV/Campers overnight hookups: Yes; Water: Yes; Electric: Yes; Septic: No
Basic Rate/Night: $12.00/ veh

ACCOM: Mon. night thru Thurs. night rates for winterized (check if this is critical) rooms w/o
meals unless otherwise indicated.

Cabin; Max. Pers: 12; Bedding incl ?: Yes; Bath: Shaared; A/C: Yes:
Rate for: Entire cabin; $120-175

Motel; Max. Pers: 4; Bedding incl ?: Yes; Bath: Private; A/C: Yes
Rate for: Room: $75-105

Main amenities available: Swim 3500 acre lake; V-ball; Bsk ball; Child playground; Laundry machine;
Boat/canoe; Many others
Meals are served in dining room for transients . Approx. dinner price: $8-14.00.

NAME OF CENTER: Quaker Hill Conference Center   Listing ID #: 107

Telephone: 765-962-5741; Fax: ; E-mail:
Address: 10 Quaker Hill Dr.; Richmond; IN; 47374
Nearest Interstate: I-70, Exit 2 miles.

Restrictions: Age: None; Pets: Permitted outside; Alcohol: Not permitted; Smoking: Outdoors
only; Reservation Req'd: Call ahead; Max. Adv. Reser.: 14 days; Seasonal closing: None

RV/Campers overnight hookups: No

ACCOM: Mon. night thru Thurs. night rates for winterized (check if this is critical) rooms w/o
meals unless otherwise indicated.

Motel; Max. Pers: 2; Bedding incl ?: Yes; Bath: Private; A/C: Yes:
Rate for: Person; $25; Rate for #2nd pers: $15; Rate for #3 pers: Child"on floor" $5

Main amenities available: Stream w/waterfall; Volleyball; Basketball; Hiking
Meals are served in dining room for transients only when other groups are present. Approx. dinner price: $8.00.

NAME OF CENTER: St. **Meinrad Archabbey Guest House**   Listing ID #: 108

Telephone: 800-581-6905; Fax: 812-357-6325; E-mail:
Address: St. Meinrad Archabbey Guest House; St. Meinrad; IN; 47577
Nearest Interstate: I-64, Exit 8 miles; Nearest State/US Hwy: Rte 62; 4 miles.

Restrictions: Age: None; Pets: Not permitted; Alcohol: Not permitted; Smoking: Outdoors only;
Reservation Req'd: None; Max. Adv. Reser.: Open w/$20 dep; Seasonal closing: None

RV/Campers overnight hookups: No .

ACCOM: Mon. night thru Thurs. night rates for winterized (check if this is critical) rooms w/o
meals unless otherwise indicated.

Motel; Max. Pers: 3; Bedding incl ?: Yes; Bath: Private; A/C: Yes:
Rate for: Person; $29; Rate for #2nd pers: $6; Rate for #3 pers: $6; Child Rate: n/a

Main amenities available: Chapel; Bookstore; Chapel; Laundry machine; VCR-TV; Hiking
Meals are served in dining room for transients only when other groups are present. Approx. dinner price:
$5-5.48.

NAME OF CENTER: YMCA - Fall Creek Branch (Indianapolis) Listing ID: 109

Telephone: 317-634-2478   Fax: 317-687-3693
Address: 860 W. 10th St.; Indianapolis, IN 46202

Restrictions:
Accommodations offered to (M/F/Families): M&F. If M/F then must be over 18 yrs.
Pets: Not permitted; Alcohol: Not permitted; Smoking: Bedroom only
Reservation requirements: None
Reservations are accepted up to 14 days in advance. Seasonal closing: None

ACCOMMODATIONS:
Single room: Bedding included ?: ; Bath: Shared
Rate for 1 day: $25-35+$5 dep; Rate for 1 week: $77-87+$5 dep

Main amenities: Pool; Gym; TV; Reading room; Laundry machine; Fitness room
Meals are not offered in their own cafeteria.

NAME OF CENTER: YWCA - Muncie Listing ID: 110

Telephone: 765-284-3345   Fax: 765-289-0416
Address: 310 East Charles St.; Muncie, IN 47305

Restrictions:
Accommodations offered to (M/F/Families): F & Babies. If M/F then must be over 18 yrs.
Pets: Not permitted; Alcohol: Not permitted; Smoking: Outdoors only
Reservation requirements: None
Reservations are accepted up to 0 days in advance. Seasonal closing: None

ACCOMMODATIONS:
Emer. Shelter: Bedding included ?: No; Bath: Shared
Rate for 1 day: $5 w/o deposit; Rate for 1 week:

Main amenities: TV; Laundry machine; Basketball
Meals are not offered in their own cafeteria.

IOWA

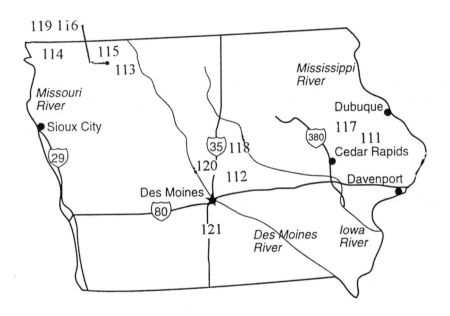

119 116
114   115
      113
Missouri
River
● Sioux City
(29)

Mississippi
River
Dubuque ●
117 111
(380)
Cedar Rapids ●
Davenport ●

(35) 118
120
112
Des Moines ★
(80)
121
Des Moines
River
Iowa
River

NAME OF CENTER: Camp Wyoming   Listing ID #: 111

Telephone: 319-488-3893; Fax: 319-488-3895; E-mail: campwyo@netins.net
Address: 9106 42nd Ave; Wyoming; IA; 52362
Nearest Interstate: I-80, Exit 40 miles; Nearest State/US Hwy: Rte 64; 1 miles.

Restrictions: Age: None; Pets: Permitted in RV area; Alcohol: Not permitted; Smoking: Outdoors only; Reservation Req'd: 7 days; Max. Adv. Reser.: Open; Seasonal closing: None

RV/Campers overnight hookups: Yes; Water: Yes; Electric: Yes; Septic: n/a
Basic Rate/Night: $12.50/ veh

ACCOM: Mon. night thru Thurs. night rates for winterized (check if this is critical) rooms w/o meals unless otherwise indicated.

Bunkrooms; Max. Pers: Over 5; Bedding incl ?: No; Bath: Shared; A/C: No:
Rate for: Person; $14; Rate for #2nd pers: $14; Rate for #3 pers: $14; Child Rate: 50% off under 5 yrs; Free under 2

Main amenities available: Swimming; Volleyball; Basketball; Ping pong; Canoeing; Hiking
Meals are served in dining room for transients only when other groups are present. Approx. dinner price: $6.25.

NAME OF CENTER: Christian Conference Center   Listing ID #: 112

Telephone: 515-792-1266; Fax: 515-791-1266; E-mail:
Address: 5064 Lincoln St.; Newton; IA; 50208
Nearest Interstate: I-80, Exit 168; 5 miles.

Restrictions: Age: None; Pets: Not permitted; Alcohol: Not permitted; Smoking: Designated outdoor area; Reservation Req'd: 1 day; Max. Adv. Reser.: 14 days; Seasonal closing: June - Aug; RV's OK all yr

RV/Campers overnight hookups: Yes; Water: Yes; Electric: Yes; Septic: n/a
Basic Rate/Night: $5.00/ veh

ACCOM: Mon. night thru Thurs. night rates for winterized (check if this is critical) rooms w/o meals unless otherwise indicated.

House ★★; Max. Pers: 18; Bedding incl ?: No; Bath: Shared; A/C: Yes:
Rate for: Person; $15; Rate for #2nd pers: $15; Rate for #3 pers: $15; Child Rate: n/a
★★ 4 bedrooms; 3 baths; Kitchen privileges; Min $50

Main amenities available: Playground area; Volleyball; Basketball; Ball field; Hiking
Meals are served in dining room for transients only when other groups are present. Approx. dinner price: $4-6.50.

NAME OF CENTER: Ingham Lake Lutheran Bible Camp   Listing ID #: 113

Telephone: 712-867-4170; Fax: ; E-mail:
Address: 2258 450th Ave.; Wallingford; IA; 51365
Nearest Interstate: I-90, Exit; 40 miles; Nearest State/US Hwy: Rte 2/9; 11 miles.

Restrictions: Age: None; Pets: Not permitted; Alcohol: Not permitted; Smoking: Nowhere; Reservation Req'd: None; Max. Adv. Reser.: 3 mo; Seasonal closing: None

RV/Campers overnight hookups: Yes; Water: Yes; Electric: Yes; Septic: n/a
Basic Rate/Night: $5.00/ veh

ACCOM: Mon. night thru Thurs. night rates for winterized (check if this is critical) rooms w/o meals unless otherwise indicated.

Cabin; Max. Pers: 9; Bedding incl ?: No; Bath: In bldg; A/C: No:
Rate for: Cabin; $45

Dormitory; Max. Pers: 2; Bedding incl ?: No; Bath: Shared; A/C: Yes
Rate for: Room: $40
Kitchen privileges

Main amenities available: Lake swimming; Volleyball; Basketball; Laundry machine; Ping pong; Pool table
Meals are served in dining room for transients only when other groups are present. Approx. dinner price: $5.50.

NAME OF CENTER: **Inspiration Hills**   Listing ID #: 114

Telephone: 712-986-5193; Fax: 712-986-2301; E-mail: ihills@iw.net
Address: 1242 280th St.; Inwood; IA; 51240
Nearest Interstate: I-29, Exit 10 miles; Nearest State/US Hwy: Rte 18; 8 miles.

Restrictions: Age: None; Pets: Not permitted; Alcohol: Not permitted; Smoking: Outdoors only; Reservation Req'd: 8 days; Max. Adv. Reser.: Open; Seasonal closing: None

RV/Campers overnight hookups: Yes; Water: Yes; Electric: Yes; Septic: n/a
Basic Rate/Night: $10.00/ veh

ACCOM: Mon. night thru Thurs. night rates for winterized (check if this is critical) rooms w/o meals unless otherwise indicated.

Bunkroom; Max. Pers: Over 5; Bedding incl ?: **$3.50 surcharge; Bath: Shared; A/C: No:
Rate for: Person; $13; Rate for #2nd pers: $13; Rate for #3 pers: $13; Child Rate: n/a
** Adv notice required

Motel; Max. Pers: 4; Bedding incl ?: $3.50 surcharge; Bath: Private; A/C: No
Rate for: Person: $13; Rate for #2nd pers: $13; Rate for #3 pers: $13; Child Rate: n/a

Main amenities available: Swimming; Ping pong; Yolleyball; Basketball; Tennis; Hiking
Meals are served in dining room for transients only when other groups are present. Approx. dinner price: $8.50.

NAME OF CENTER: Lake Okoboji Camp & Retreat Ctr   Listing ID #: 115

Telephone: 712-336-2936; Fax: 712-336-1822; E-mail: okoboji@ncn.net
Address: 21413 154th Street Place; Spirit Lake; IA; 51360
Nearest Interstate: I-90, Exit 16 miles; Nearest State/US Hwy: Rte 9; 6 miles.

Restrictions: Age: None; Pets: Permitted; Alcohol: Not permitted; Smoking: Outdoors only; Reservation Req'd: None; Max. Adv. Reser.: Open; Seasonal closing: None

RV/Campers overnight hookups: Yes; Water: No; Electric: Yes; Septic: No
Basic Rate/Night: $5.00/ veh

ACCOM: Mon. night thru Thurs. night rates for winterized (check if this is critical) rooms w/o meals unless otherwise indicated.

Bunkroom; Max. Pers: 8; Bedding incl ?: No; Bath: Shared; A/C: Yes:
Rate for: Person; $10; Rate for #2nd pers: $10; Rate for #3 pers: $10; Child Rate: 50% off under 8 yrs; Free under 4

Dormitory; Max. Pers: 4; Bedding incl ?: No; Bath: Shared; A/C: Yes
Rate for: Person: $13; Rate for #2nd pers: $13; Rate for #3 pers: $13; Child Rate: 50% off under 8 yrs; free under 4

Main amenities available: Swimming; Volleyball; Basketball; VCR-TV; Canoeing; Hiking
Meals are served in dining room for transients only when other groups are present. Approx. dinner price: $4-6.00.

NAME OF CENTER: Okoboji Lutheran Bible Camp   Listing ID #: 116

Telephone: 800-656-2654; Fax: 712-337-3501; E-mail:
Address: 1203 Inwan St.; Milford; IA; 51351
Nearest Interstate: I-90, Exit 15 miles; Nearest State/US Hwy: Rte 86; 0 miles.

Restrictions: Age: None; Pets: Not permitted; Alcohol: Not permitted; Smoking: Outdoors only; Reservation Req'd: None; Max. Adv. Reser.: 3 mo; Seasonal closing: None

RV/Campers overnight hookups: No

ACCOM: Mon. night thru Thurs. night rates for winterized (check if this is critical) rooms w/o meals unless otherwise indicated.

Motel; Max. Pers: 8; Bedding incl ?: $3 surcharge; Bath: Private; A/C: Yes:
Rate for: Room; $52-72; Child Rate: n/a

Main amenities available: Jacuzzi; Volleyball; Basketball; Lake swimming; Gym; Boating
Meals are served in dining room for transients only when other groups are present. Approx. dinner price: $5.00; 50% off under 12 yrs.

REMEMBER TO CALL AHEAD

NAME OF CENTER: **Pictured Rocks**   Listing ID #: 117

Telephone: 319-465-4194; Fax: 319-465-6022; E-mail:
Address: 12004 190th St.; Monticello; IA; 52310
Nearest Interstate: I-80, Exit 60 miles; Nearest State/US Hwy: Rte 38; 1 miles.

Restrictions: Age: None; Pets: Not permitted; Alcohol: Not permitted; Smoking: Outdoors only;
Reservation Req'd: Noon of day; Max. Adv. Reser.: 6 mo; Seasonal closing: Mid June - Aug.;
RV's OK all yr

RV/Campers overnight hookups: Yes; Water: Yes; Electric: Yes; Septic: n/a
Basic Rate/Night: $9.00/ veh

ACCOM: Mon. night thru Thurs. night rates for winterized (check if this is critical) rooms w/o
meals unless otherwise indicated.

Bunkroom; Max. Pers: 10; Bedding incl ?: No; Bath: Shared; A/C: No:
Rate for: Person; $15; Rate for #2nd pers: $15; Rate for #3 pers: $15; Child Rate: n/a

Dormitory; Max. Pers: 4; Bedding incl ?: No; Bath: Shared; A/C: Yes
Rate for: Person; $15; Rate for #2nd pers: $15; Rate for #3 pers: $15; Child Rate: Free under 4
yrs.

Main amenities available: On the river; Volleyball; Basketball; Laundry machine; Canoeing; Hiking
Meals are served in dining room for transients only when other groups are present. Approx. dinner price: $4.50;
Free under 4 yrs.

NAME OF CENTER: **Pine Lake Christian Center**   Listing ID #: 118

Telephone: 515-858-3284; Fax: 515-858-2476; E-mail: plccrev@aol.com
Address: PO Box 535; Eldora; IA; 50627
Nearest Interstate: I-35, Exit 27 miles; Nearest State/US Hwy: Rte 175; 0 miles.

Restrictions: Age: None; Pets: Not permitted; Alcohol: Not permitted; Smoking: Outdoors only;
Reservation Req'd: 4 days; Max. Adv. Reser.: Open; Seasonal closing: None

RV/Campers overnight hookups: Yes; Water: Yes; Electric: Yes; Septic: n/a
Basic Rate/Night: $8.50/ veh

ACCOM: Mon. night thru Thurs. night rates for winterized (check if this is critical) rooms w/o
meals unless otherwise indicated.

Bunkroom; Max. Pers: Over 5; Bedding incl ?: No; Bath: Shared; A/C: No:
Rate for: Person; $8; Rate for #2nd pers: $3; Rate for #3 pers: $3; Child Rate: Free under 3

Motel; Max. Pers: 4; Bedding incl ?: No; Bath: Private; A/C: Yes
Rate for: Person; $9; Rate for #2nd pers: $9; Rate for #3 pers: $9; Child Rate: Free under 3 yrs

Main amenities available: Swimming; Volleyball; Basketball; Canoe/Boating; Ping pong; Hiking
Meals are served in dining room for transients only when other groups are present. Approx. dinner price: $9.00.

NAME OF CENTER: Presbyterian Camp on Okoboji   Listing ID #: 119

Telephone: 712-337-3313; Fax: 712-337-0104; E-mail: prescamp@rconnect.com
Address: 1864 Highway 86; Milford; IA; 51351
Nearest Interstate: I-90, Exit 15 miles; Nearest State/US Hwy: Rte 86; 0 miles.

Restrictions: Age: None; Pets: Not permitted; Alcohol: Not permitted; Smoking: Outdoors only; Reservation Req'd: 7 days; Max. Adv. Reser.: Open; Seasonal closing: None

RV/Campers overnight hookups: No

ACCOM: Mon. night thru Thurs. night rates for winterized (check if this is critical) rooms w/o meals unless otherwise indicated.

Bunkroom; Max. Pers: 18; Bedding incl ?: **$8 surcharge; Bath: Shared; A/C: No:
Rate for: Cabin; $77
** Adv. notice required

Dormitory; Max. Pers: 4; Bedding incl ?: **$8 surcharge; Bath: Shared; A/C: No
Rate for: Cabin: $140
** Adv notice required

Main amenities available: Ping pong; Volleyball; Basketball; Swimming; Boat/canoe; Hiking
Meals are served in dining room for transients only when other groups are present. Prices vary.

NAME OF CENTER: Riverside Lutheran Bible Camp   Listing ID #: 120

Telephone: 515-733-5271; Fax: 515-733-4096; E-mail:
Address: 3001 Riverside Rd.; Story City; IA; 50248
Nearest Interstate: I-35, Exit 2 miles.

Restrictions: Age: None; Pets: Not permitted; Alcohol: Not permitted; Smoking: Outdoors only; Reservation Req'd: 2 days; Max. Adv. Reser.: 10 days; Seasonal closing: Christmas week

RV/Campers overnight hookups: No

ACCOM: Mon. night thru Thurs. night rates for winterized (check if this is critical) rooms w/o meals unless otherwise indicated.

Cabins; Max. Pers: 12; Bedding incl ?: $4 surcharge; Bath: Shared; A/C: No:
Rate for: Cabin; $50-65

Dormitory; Max. Pers: 4; Bedding incl ?: $4 surcharge; Bath: Shared; A/C: Yes
Rate for: Room: $40-55

Main amenities available: VCR-TV; Volleyball; Basketball; Ping pong; Pool table; Hiking
Meals are served in dining room for transients only when other groups are present. Price varies.

NAME OF CENTER: Wesley Woods Camp & Retreat Center   Listing ID #: 121

Telephone: 515-961-4523; Fax: 515-961-4162; E-mail: wwcarc@aol.com
Address: 1086 Nixon; Indianola; IA; 50125
Nearest Interstate: I-35, Exit 14 miles; Nearest State/US Hwy: Rte 92; 4 miles.

Restrictions: Age: None; Pets: Not permitted; Alcohol: Not permitted; Smoking: Outdoors only;
Reservation Req'd: Noon of day; Max. Adv. Reser.: Open; Seasonal closing: None

RV/Campers overnight hookups: Yes; Water: Yes; Electric: Yes; Septic: n/a
Basic Rate/Night: $10.50/ veh

ACCOM: Mon. night thru Thurs. night rates for winterized (check if this is critical) rooms w/o
meals unless otherwise indicated.

Bunkroom; Max. Pers: 12; Bedding incl ?: No; Bath: Shared; A/C: No:
Rate for: Person; $12; Rate for #2nd pers: $12; Rate for #3 pers: $12; Child Rate: n/a
Family rate $35

Dormitory; Max. Pers: 4; Bedding incl ?: No; Bath: Shared; A/C: Yes
Rate for: Person: $15; Rate for #2nd pers: $15; Rate for #3 pers: $15; Child Rate: n/a
Family rate $40

Motel; Max. Pers: 6; Bedding incl ?: No; Bath: Private; A/C: Yes:
Rate for: Person: $15; Rate for #2nd pers: $15; Rate for #3 pers: $15; Child Rate: n/a
Family rate $40

Main amenities available: Swimming; Volleyball; Basketball; Ping pong; Canoeing; Hiking
Meals are served in dining room for transients only when other groups are present. Approx. dinner price:
$6-8.00,50% off under 9 yrs,<3 free.

NAME OF CENTER: YWCA - Des Moines Listing ID: 122

Telephone: 515-244-8961   Fax: 515-244-1118
Address: 717 Grand Ave.; Des Moines, IA 50309

Restrictions:
Accommodations offered to (M/F/Families): F; Child<10. If M/F then must be over yrs.
Pets: Not permitted; Alcohol: Not permitted; Smoking: Bedroom only
Reservation requirements: Strongly advised
Reservations are accepted up to an indefinite time in advance. Seasonal closing: None

ACCOMMODATIONS:
Dormitory: Bedding included ?: Yes; Bath: Shared
Rate for 1 day: Free in emergency; Rate for 1 week:

Main amenities: Laundry machine
Meals are not offered in their own cafeteria.

KANSAS

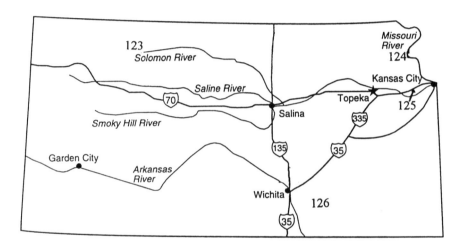

NAME OF CENTER: Camp Pecusa Conference Ctr   Listing ID #: 123

Telephone: 785-839-4292; Fax: ; E-mail:
Address: RR #2; Box 143; Stockton; KS; 67669
Nearest Interstate: I-70, Exit 60 miles; Nearest State/US Hwy: Rte 24; 1 miles.

Restrictions: Age: None; Pets: Not permitted; Alcohol: Not permitted; Smoking: Outdoors only; Reservation Req'd: None; Max. Adv. Reser.: ; Seasonal closing: None

RV/Campers overnight hookups: No

ACCOM: Mon. night thru Thurs. night rates for winterized (check if this is critical) rooms w/o meals unless otherwise indicated.

Bunkroom; Max. Pers: 8; Bedding incl ?: $5 surcharge; Bath: Shared; A/C: No:
Rate for: Person; $15; Rate for #2nd pers: $15; Rate for #3 pers: $15; Child Rate: Free under 5 yrs

Motel; Max. Pers: 4; Bedding incl ?: $5 surcharge; Bath: Private; A/C: Yes
Rate for: Person: $20; Rate for #2nd pers: $20; Rate for #3 pers: $20; Child Rate: n/a
4 bedrooms ea sleep 4; shared living rm, dining rm and kitchen

Main amenities available: Lake Webster swim; Volleyball; Basketball; Ping pong; Horse shoes; Hiking
Meals are served in dining room for transients only when other groups are present. Approx. dinner price: Price variable.

NAME OF CENTER: Sophia Center   Listing ID #: 124

Telephone: 913-367-6110; Fax: 913-367-3866; E-mail: jkputnam@juno.com
Address: 751 South 8th St.; Atchison; KS; 66002
Nearest Interstate: I-29, Exit 23 miles; Nearest State/US Hwy: Rte 273; 4 miles.

Restrictions: Age: 15; Pets: Not permitted; Alcohol: Not permitted; Smoking: Outdoors only; Reservation Req'd: None; Max. Adv. Reser.: Open; Seasonal closing: None

RV/Campers overnight hookups: No

ACCOM: Mon. night thru Thurs. night rates for winterized (check if this is critical) rooms w/o meals unless otherwise indicated.

Dormitory; Max. Pers: 4; Bedding incl ?: Yes (w/notice); Bath: Shared; A/C: Yes:
Rate for: Person **; $40; Rate for #2nd pers: $40; Rate for #3 pers: $40; Child Rate: n/a
** Includes 3 meals

Main amenities available: Bookstore; Library; Quiet areas ; Chapel
Meals are served in dining room for transients . Prices vary.

NAME OF CENTER: Tall Oaks Conference Center   Listing ID #: 125

Telephone: 800-617-1484; Fax: 913-723-3213; E-mail: patti@www.talloaks.org
Address: 12797 189th St; PO Box 116; Linwood; KS; 66052
Nearest Interstate: I-70, Exit 10 miles; Nearest State/US Hwy: Rte K10; 5 miles.

Restrictions: Age: None; Pets: Not permitted; Alcohol: Not permitted; Smoking: Nowhere; Reservation Req'd: 10 days; Max. Adv. Reser.: Open; Seasonal closing: None

RV/Campers overnight hookups: Yes; Water: Yes; Electric: Yes; Septic: No
Basic Rate/Night: $10.00/ veh

ACCOM: Mon. night thru Thurs. night rates for winterized (check if this is critical) rooms w/o meals unless otherwise indicated.

Bunkroom; Max. Pers: Over 5; Bedding incl ?: $6 surcharge; Bath: Shared; A/C: Y/N:
Rate for: Person; $24; Rate for #2nd pers: $24; Rate for #3 pers: $24; Child Rate: Children $19; free under 6 yrs

Dormitory; Max. Pers: 4; Bedding incl ?: $6 surcharge; Bath: Shared; A/C: Yes
Rate for: Person: $24; Rate for #2nd pers: $24; Rate for #3 pers: $24; Child Rate: Children $19; free under 6 yrs

Motel; Max. Pers: 4; Bedding incl ?: $6 surcharge; Bath: Private; A/C: Yes:
Rate for: Person: $35; Rate for #2nd pers: $35; Rate for #3 pers: $35; Child Rate: Free under 6 yrs.

Main amenities available: Swimming; V-ball; Bsk-ball; VCR-TV; Horseback riding; Ropes course; Hiking
Meals are served in dining room for transients only when other groups are present. Approx. dinner price: $5.25-$7.50.

NAME OF CENTER: Westminster Woods Camp & Conf Ctr   Listing ID #: 126

Telephone: 316-692-3695; Fax: 316-692-3695; E-mail:
Address: Route 1; Box 97; Fall River; KS; 67047
Nearest Interstate: I-35, Exit 80 miles; Nearest State/US Hwy: Rte 400; 2 miles.

Restrictions: Age: None; Pets: On leash/not in room; Alcohol: Not permitted; Smoking: Designated outdoor area; Reservation Req'd: 11 AM of day; Max. Adv. Reser.: 1 yr; Seasonal closing: Late May thru 1st wk of Aug.

RV/Campers overnight hookups: Yes; Water: Yes; Electric: Yes; Septic: No
Basic Rate/Night: $6.50/ veh

ACCOM: Mon. night thru Thurs. night rates for winterized (check if this is critical) rooms w/o meals unless otherwise indicated.

Suites; Max. Pers: 10; Bedding incl ?: Yes; Bath: Private; A/C: Yes:
Rate for: **;
** Available starting June '99. Rates not yet set: 2 bedroom; 2 baths; kitchenette

Main amenities available: Lake fishing; V-ball; Bsk-ball; Badminton; Laundry machine; Boat/canoe; Shuffleboard
Meals are served in dining room for transients only when other groups are present. Approx. dinner price: $4.00.

77

KENTUCKY

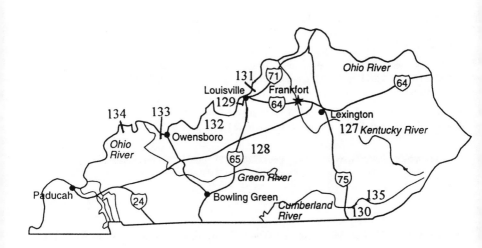

NAME OF CENTER: Aldersgate Camp & Retreat Center   Listing ID #: 127

Telephone: 606-723-2233; Fax: 606-723-5078; E-mail:
Address: 125 Aldersgate Camp Rd.; Ravenna; KY; 40472
Nearest Interstate: I-64, Exit 35 miles; Nearest State/US Hwy: Rte 52; 3 miles.

Restrictions: Age: None; Pets: Not permitted; Alcohol: Not permitted; Smoking: Outdoors only; Reservation Req'd: 2 days; Max. Adv. Reser.: Open; Seasonal closing: May 31 - Aug.7

RV/Campers overnight hookups: No

ACCOM: Mon. night thru Thurs. night rates for winterized (check if this is critical) rooms w/o meals unless otherwise indicated.

Rustic cabins; Max. Pers: 8; Bedding incl ?: No; Bath: Separate bldg; A/C: No:
Rate for: Person; $9; Rate for #2nd pers: $9; Rate for #3 pers: $9; Child Rate: n/a

Smith Dormitory; Max. Pers: 3; Bedding incl ?: No; Bath: Shared; A/C: No
Rate for: Person: $14; Rate for #2nd pers: $14; Rate for #3 pers: $14; Child Rate: $7 under 13 yrs; free under 4
Shared living room w/fireplace.

Dorm Cottage; Max. Pers: 5; Bedding incl ?: No; Bath: Semi-private; A/C: No:
Rate for: Person: $18; Rate for #2nd pers: $18; Rate for #3 pers: $18; Child Rate: $9 under 13 yrs; free under 4
4 bedrooms & 2 baths per cottage; kitchen; "great rm"

Main amenities available: V-ball; Bsk ball; Laundry machine; Swimming; Ping pong; Croquet; Hiking
Meals are served in dining room for transients .Approx. dinner price: $4.50; 50% off under 13 yrs; free under 4.

NAME OF CENTER: Catherine Spalding Center   Listing ID #: 128

Telephone: 502-348-1515; Fax: 502-348-1518; E-mail: pcoulter@scnazarethky.org
Address: CSC; PO Box 24; Nazareth; KY; 40048
Nearest Interstate: I-65, Exit 15 miles; Nearest State/US Hwy: Rte 245; 15 miles.

Restrictions: Age: None; Pets: Not permitted; Alcohol: Hard liquor not permitted; Smoking: Outdoors only; Reservation Req'd: 1 day; Max. Adv. Reser.: Open; Seasonal closing: None

RV/Campers overnight hookups: No

ACCOM: Mon. night thru Thurs. night rates for winterized (check if this is critical) rooms w/o meals unless otherwise indicated.

Dorm; Max. Pers: 2; Bedding incl ?: Yes; Bath: Shared; A/C: Yes:
Rate for: Person; ** $45; Rate for #2nd pers: ** $45;   Child Rate: Free under 5 yrs
** Includes 2 or 3 meals

Motel; Max. Pers: 2; Bedding incl ?: Yes; Bath: Private; A/C: Yes
Rate for: Person: ** $50; Rate for #2nd pers: ** $50; Child Rate: Free under 5 yrs
** Includes 2 or 3 meals

Main amenities available: Laundry machine; Volleyball; VCR-TV; Library; Bookstore; Hiking
Meals are served in dining room for transients . Approx. dinner price: $5 for children who don't pay lodging fee.

NAME OF CENTER: Cedar Ridge Camp   Listing ID #: 129

Telephone: 502-267-5848; Fax: 502-267-0116; E-mail:
Address: 4010 Routt Rd.; Louisville; KY; 40299
Nearest Interstate: I-64, Exit 20 miles; Nearest State/US Hwy: Gene Snyder Freeway;
10 miles.

Restrictions: Age: None; Pets: Not permitted; Alcohol: Not permitted; Smoking: Designated
outdoor area; Reservation Req'd: None; Max. Adv. Reser.: 1 yr; Seasonal closing: None

RV/Campers overnight hookups: No

ACCOM: Mon. night thru Thurs. night rates for winterized (check if this is critical) rooms w/o
meals unless otherwise indicated.

Cabin; Max. Pers: Over 6; Bedding incl ?: No; Bath: Separate bldg; A/C: No:
Rate for: Person; $8; Rate for #2nd pers: $8; Rate for #3 pers: $8; Child Rate: n/a
$50 min.

Main amenities available: Laundry machine; Volleyball; Basketball; Horse shoes; Hiking; Swimming pool
Meals are served in dining room for transients only when other groups are present. Approx. dinner price: $7.00.

NAME OF CENTER: Henderson Settlement   Listing ID #: 130

Telephone: 606-337-3613; Fax: 606-337-2225; E-mail: hendsett@jellico.com
Address: PO Box 205; Frakes; KY; 40940
Nearest Interstate: I-75, Exit 27 miles; Nearest State/US Hwy: Rte 190; 18 miles.

Restrictions: Age: None; Pets: Permitted in RV area; Alcohol: Not permitted; Smoking:
Outdoors only; Reservation Req'd: 2 days; Max. Adv. Reser.: Open; Seasonal closing: None

RV/Campers overnight hookups: Yes; Water: Yes; Electric: Yes; Septic: No
Basic Rate/Night: $3.00/ veh

ACCOM: Mon. night thru Thurs. night rates for winterized (check if this is critical) rooms w/o
meals unless otherwise indicated.

Bunkroom; Max. Pers: 16; Bedding incl ?: No; Bath: Shared; A/C: Yes:
Rate for: Person; $10; Rate for #2nd pers: $10; Rate for #3 pers: $10; Child Rate: n/a
Unavailable May - Aug.

Dormitory; Max. Pers: 16; Bedding incl ?: Yes; Bath: Shared; A/C: Yes
Rate for: Person: $15; Rate for #2nd pers: $15; Rate for #3 pers: $15; Child Rate: $7 under 13
yrs; free under 5

House; Max. Pers: 2; Bedding incl ?: Yes; Bath: Shared; A/C: Yes:
Rate for: Person: $15; Rate for #2nd pers: $15; Rate for #3 pers: $15; Child Rate: $7 under 13
yrs; free under 5
Guests will please strip beds and clean up kitchen. Kitchen available

Main amenities available: V-ball; Bsk ball; Swimming; Incidentals store; Laundry machine; Ping pong; Many
others
Meals are served in dining room for transients only when other groups are present. Approx. dinner price: $8.00;
50% off under 9 yrs; free under 5.

NAME OF CENTER: Kavanaugh Life Enrichment Center   Listing ID #: 131

Telephone: 502-241-9091; Fax: 502-241-1279
E-mail: www.gbgm_umc.org/kavanaugh
Address: 7505 Kavanaugh Rd.; Crestwood; KY; 40014
Nearest Interstate: I-265, Exit 30; 4 miles; Nearest State/US Hwy: ; miles.

Restrictions: Age: None; Pets: Not permitted; Alcohol: Not permitted; Smoking: Outdoors only; Reservation Req'd: None; Max. Adv. Reser.: 1 yr; Seasonal closing: None

RV/Campers overnight hookups: Yes; Water: Yes; Electric: Yes; Septic: No
Basic Rate/Night: $10.00/ veh

ACCOM: Mon. night thru Thurs. night rates for winterized (check if this is critical) rooms w/o meals unless otherwise indicated.

Cottage; Max. Pers: 10; Bedding incl ?: Yes; Bath: Shared; A/C: Yes:
Rate for: Entire Cottage; $99
Includes kitchenette

Motel; Max. Pers: 4; Bedding incl ?: Yes; Bath: Private; A/C: Yes
Rate for: Room: $39; Child Rate: n/a

Main amenities available: Swimming; Volleyball; Basketball; Horseshoes; Ball field; Hiking
Meals are served in dining room for transients only when other groups are present. Approx. dinner price: $6.95; 24 hr notice reqd.

NAME OF CENTER: Loucon   Listing ID #: 132

Telephone: 502-242-7160; Fax: 502-242-7313; E-mail:
Address: 8044 Anneta Rd.; Leitchfield; KY; 42754
Nearest Interstate: Western KY Tpke, Exit 12 miles; Nearest State/US Hwy: Rte 259; 0 miles.

Restrictions: Age: None; Pets: Not permitted; Alcohol: Not permitted; Smoking: Outdoors only; Reservation Req'd: None; Max. Adv. Reser.: 1 yr; Seasonal closing: Christmas - 3rd wk of Jan

RV/Campers overnight hookups: No

ACCOM: Mon. night thru Thurs. night rates for winterized (check if this is critical) rooms w/o meals unless otherwise indicated.

Bunkroom; Max. Pers: 8; Bedding incl ?: No; Bath: Separate bldg; A/C: No:
Rate for: Person; $13; Rate for #2nd pers: $13; Rate for #3 pers: $13; Child Rate: 50% off
5-8th grade; free under 4th grade

Dormitory; Max. Pers: 5; Bedding incl ?: No; Bath: Shared; A/C: Yes
Rate for: Person: $16-24; Rate for #2nd pers: $16-24; Rate for #3 pers: $16-24; Child Rate: Same as bunkroom

Motel; Max. Pers: 5; Bedding incl ?: No; Bath: Private; A/C: Yes:
Rate for: Person: $20-30; Rate for #2nd pers: $20-30; Rate for #3 pers: $20-30; Child Rate: Same as bunkroom

Main amenities available: Laundry machine; Volleyball; Basketball; Hiking
Meals are served in dining room for transients only when other groups are present. Approx. dinner price: $6.00.

NAME OF CENTER: Mount St. Joseph Center   Listing ID #: 133

Telephone: 502-229-0200; Fax: 502-229-0299; E-mail:
Address: 8001 Cummings Rd.; Maple Mount; KY; 42356
Nearest Interstate: Pennyril Pkwy, Exit 11 miles; Nearest State/US Hwy: Rte 56; 1 miles.

Restrictions: Age: None; Pets: Not permitted; Alcohol: Not permitted; Smoking: Outdoors only; Reservation Req'd: 1 day; Max. Adv. Reser.: Open; Seasonal closing: June - July

RV/Campers overnight hookups: No

ACCOM: Mon. night thru Thurs. night rates for winterized (check if this is critical) rooms w/o meals unless otherwise indicated.

Bunkroom; Max. Pers: Over 5; Bedding incl ?: Yes; Bath: Shared; A/C: Yes:
Rate for: Person; ** $17; Rate for #2nd pers: ** $17; Rate for #3 pers: ** $17; Child Rate: ** $15 ** Includes 3 meals

Dormitory; Max. Pers: 5; Bedding incl ?: Yes; Bath: Shared; A/C: Yes
Rate for: Person: ** $25; Rate for #2nd pers: ** $25; Rate for #3 pers: ** $25; Child Rate: ** $19 ** Includes 3 meals

Motel; Max. Pers: 5; Bedding incl ?: Yes; Bath: Private; A/C: Yes:
Rate for: Person: **$25; Rate for #2 pers: **$25; Rate for #3 pers: **$25; Child Rate: ** $19

Main amenities available: Swimming; Volleyball; Laundry; VCR-TV; Bookstore; Hiking
Meals are served in dining room for transients only when other groups are present. Approx. dinner price: $4.50-7.50.

NAME OF CENTER: Potter's Ranch   Listing ID #: 134

Telephone: 606-586-5425; Fax: 606-586-5491; E-mail:
Address: 11500 Victory School House Rd.; Union; KY; 41091
Nearest Interstate: I-75, Exit 15 miles; Nearest State/US Hwy: Rte 338; 1 miles.

Restrictions: Age: None; Pets: Not permitted; Alcohol: Not permitted; Smoking: Nowhere; Reservation Req'd: 3 days; Max. Adv. Reser.: 1 yr; Seasonal closing: None

RV/Campers overnight hookups: No

ACCOM: Mon. night thru Thurs. night rates for winterized (check if this is critical) rooms w/o meals unless otherwise indicated.

Motel; Max. Pers: 2; Bedding incl ?: Yes; Bath: Private; A/C: Yes:
Rate for: Room; $40; Rate for #2 pers: $0; Rate for #3 pers: $10 w/cot; Child Rate: $5 under 18 yrs; $3 under 11; $1 under 6 using own bedding

Main amenities available: Laundry machine; Volleyball; Ball field; Ropes course; Horseback riding; Hiking
Meals are not served in dining room for transients . Approx. dinner price:Varies

REMEMBER TO CALL AHEAD

NAME OF CENTER: Red Bird Mission   Listing ID #: 135

Telephone: 606-598-3155; Fax: 606-598-3151; E-mail: rbmission@kih.net
Address: HC 69; Box 700; Beverly; KY; 40913
Nearest Interstate: I-75, Exit 55 miles; Nearest State/US Hwy: Rte 421 ; 18 miles.

Restrictions: Age: None; Pets: Not permitted; Alcohol: Not permitted; Smoking: Outdoors only;
Reservation Req'd: 1 day; Max. Adv. Reser.: 14 days; Seasonal closing: None

RV/Campers overnight hookups: Yes; Water: Yes; Electric: Yes; Septic: No
Basic Rate/Night: $5.00/ veh

ACCOM: Mon. night thru Thurs. night rates for winterized (check if this is critical) rooms w/o
meals unless otherwise indicated.

Bunkroom; Max. Pers: Over 5; Bedding incl ?: No; Bath: Shared; A/C: Yes:
Rate for: Person; $5; Rate for #2 pers: $5; Rate for #3 pers: $5; Child Rate: Free under 10 yrs

Dormitory; Max. Pers: 5; Bedding incl ?: Yes (w/notice); Bath: Shared; A/C: Yes
Rate for: Person: $10; Rate for #2 pers: $5; Rate for #3 pers: $5; Child Rate: n/a

Motel; Max. Pers: 5; Bedding incl ?: Yes (w/notice); Bath: Private; A/C: No:
Rate for: Person: $10; Rate for #2 pers: $5; Rate for #3 pers: $5; Child Rate: n/a

Main amenities available: Ball field; Volleyball; Basketball; Hiking
Meals are served in dining room for transients only when other groups are present. Approx. dinner price:
$2-5.00.

NAME OF CENTER: YMCA - High St. Br. (Lexington) Listing ID: 136

Telephone: 606-254-9622   Fax: 606-255-5653
Address: 239 E. High St ; Lexington, KY 40507

Restrictions:
Accommodations offered to (M/F/Families): M. If M/F then must be over 18 yrs.
Pets: Not permitted; Alcohol: Not permitted; Smoking: Outdoors only
Reservation requirements: None
Reservations are accepted up to 14 days in advance. Seasonal closing: None

ACCOMMODATIONS:
Single room: Bedding included ?: Yes; Bath: Shared
Rate for 1 day: $20+$40 dep; Rate for 1 week: $85+$40 dep

Main amenities: Pool; Gym; Reading room; TV lounge
Meals are not offered in their own cafeteria.

LOUISIANA

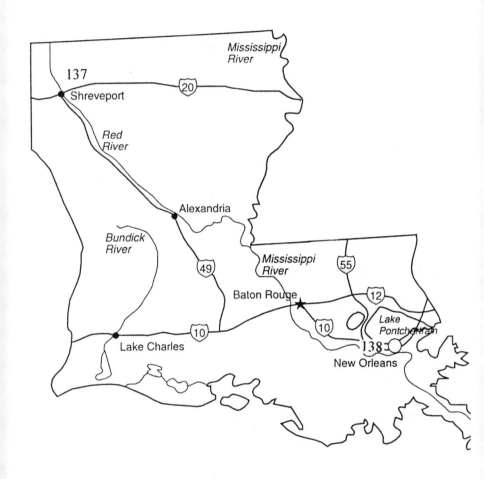

137
Shreveport
Mississippi River
20

Red River

Alexandria

Bundick River

49

Mississippi River
55

Baton Rouge
12

10
10
Lake Pontchartrain

Lake Charles
138
New Orleans

NAME OF CENTER: Caney Conference Center   Listing ID #: 137

Telephone: 318-377-6756; Fax: ; E-mail:
Address: 1175 Methodist Camp Rd; Minden; LA; 71055
Nearest Interstate: I-20, Exit 5 miles; Nearest State/US Hwy: ; miles.

Restrictions: Age: None; Pets: Permitted on leash; Alcohol: Not permitted; Smoking: Outdoors only; Reservation Req'd: 7 days; Max. Adv. Reser.: Within calendar yr; Seasonal closing: None

RV/Campers overnight hookups: Yes; Water: n/a; Electric: Yes; Septic: unk
Basic Rate/Night: n/a/

ACCOM: Mon. night thru Thurs. night rates for winterized (check if this is critical) rooms w/o meals unless otherwise indicated.

Cabin; Max. Pers: 10; Bedding incl ?: No; Bath: Shared; A/C: :
Rate for: ; ; Rate for #2 pers: ; Rate for #3 pers: ; Child Rate:
Center will not give out rates. Must call ahead to determine rates.

Main amenities available: Laundry machine; Volleyball; Basketball; Swimming; Lake boating; Hiking
Meals are served in dining room for transients only when other groups are present. Approx. dinner price: Call ahead for rates.

NAME OF CENTER: YMCA - International Hotel New Orleans Listing ID: 138

Telephone: 504-558-9622   Fax: 504-523-7174
Address: 920 St. Charles Ave.; New Orleans, LA 70130

Restrictions:
Accommodations offered to (M/F/Families): M/F/Family. If M/F then must be over None yrs.
Pets: Not permitted; Alcohol: Not permitted; Smoking: Bedroom only
Reservation requirements: None
Reservations are accepted up to 14 days w/dep in advance. Seasonal closing: None

ACCOMMODATIONS:
Single room: Bedding included ?: Yes; Bath: Shared
Rate for 1 day: $30+$5 dep; Rate for 1 week: $180+$5 dep
Room fee includes membership in Y

Double room: Bedding included ?: Yes; Bath: Shared
Rate for 1 day: $35+$5/person dep; Rate for 1 week: $224+$5/pers dep

Main amenities: Laundry machine; Pool; Gym; Steam room; ;
Meals are offered in their own cafeteria.

MAINE

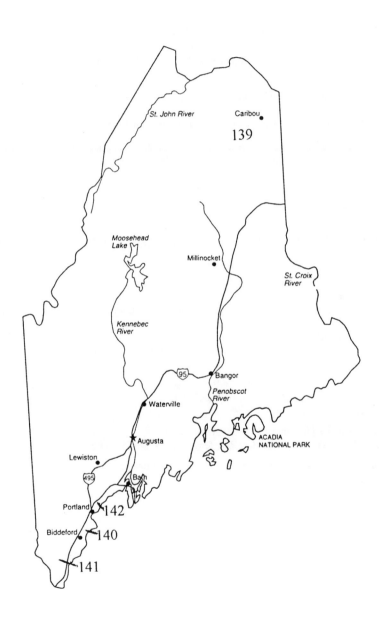

St. John River

Caribou

139

Moosehead
Lake

Millinocket

St. Croix
River

Kennebec
River

95

Bangor

Penobscot
River

Waterville

Augusta

ACADIA
NATIONAL PARK

Lewiston

495

Bath

Portland 142

Biddeford 140

141

NAME OF CENTER: Baptist Park   Listing ID #: 139

Telephone: 207-764-1832; Fax: ; E-mail:
Address: 60 Park Dr.; Mapleton; ME; 04757
Nearest Interstate: I-95, Last exit on I-95 is 50 miles; Nearest State/US Hwy: US 1; 5 miles.

Restrictions: Age: None; Pets: Not in bldgs (Cabins OK); Alcohol: Not permitted; Smoking: Designated outdoor area; Reservation Req'd: 7 days; Max. Adv. Reser.: Open; Seasonal closing: mid Sept - May 31

RV/Campers overnight hookups: Yes; Water: Yes; Electric: Yes; Septic: n/a
Basic Rate/Night: $3.00/ veh

ACCOM: Mon. night thru Thurs. night rates for winterized (check if this is critical) rooms w/o meals unless otherwise indicated.

Dorm; Max. Pers: ** 2; Bedding incl ?: Yes; Bath: Shared; A/C: No:
Rate for: Room; **
** FREE WILL DONATION Will put up to 2 mattresses on floor

Cabin; Max. Pers: 6; Bedding incl ?: No; Bath: Shared; A/C: No
Rate for: Entire cabin: **
** FREE WILL DONATION

Main amenities available: Indoor pool; Laundry machine; Children's playground; Incidentals store; VCR-TV; Tennis/ Bsk-ball
Meals are served in dining room for transients only when other groups are present. Approx. dinner price: $3.00; $2 under 13 yrs; free under 5.

NAME OF CENTER: Bayview Villa Convent   Listing ID #: 140

Telephone: 207-286-9762; Fax: 207-202-7376; E-mail:
Address: Rte 9; 187 Bay View Rd.; Saco; ME; 04072
Nearest Interstate: I-95, Exit 5; 4 miles.

Restrictions: Age: 5; Pets: Not permitted; Alcohol: Not permitted; Smoking: Outdoors only; Reservation Req'd: 7 days w/dep; Max. Adv. Reser.: 1 yr; Seasonal closing: None

RV/Campers overnight hookups: No

ACCOM: Mon. night thru Thurs. night rates for winterized (check if this is critical) rooms w/o meals unless otherwise indicated.

Motel; Max. Pers: 2; Bedding incl ?: Yes; Bath: Private; A/C: Yes:
Rate for: Person; ***
*** Bay View is located at the beach. Call ahead for all rates.

Main amenities available: Beach; Gift shop; Quiet areas; Children's swings; Screened in Veranda; Hiking
Meals are served in dining room for transients with advanced reservations.. Approx. dinner price: $6.00.

NAME OF CENTER: Notre Dame Spiritual Center   Listing ID #: 141

Telephone: 207-324-6612; Fax: 207-324-5044; E-mail:
Address: Shaker Hill Rd.; PO Box 159; Alfred; ME; 04002
Nearest Interstate: I-95, Exit 12 miles; Nearest State/US Hwy: Rte 202; 0 miles.

Restrictions: Age: None; Pets: Not permitted; Alcohol: Not permitted; Smoking: Outdoors only; Reservation Req'd: 14 days; Max. Adv. Reser.: 1 mo; Seasonal closing: None

RV/Campers overnight hookups: No

ACCOM: Mon. night thru Thurs. night rates for winterized (check if this is critical) rooms w/o meals unless otherwise indicated.

Dorm; Max. Pers: 3; Bedding incl ?: Yes; Bath: Shared; A/C: No:
Rate for: Room; $20; Child Rate: n/a

Motel; Max. Pers: 3; Bedding incl ?: Yes; Bath: Semi-private; A/C: No
Rate for: Room: $30; Child Rate: n/a

Main amenities available: 540 acres; V-ball; Bsk-ball; Laundry machine; Ping pong Pool table; Tennis; Hiking
Meals are served in dining room for transients only when other groups are present. Approx. dinner price: $7.00.

NAME OF CENTER: Sky-Hy Conference & Retreat Ctr.   Listing ID #: 142

Telephone: 207-725-7577; Fax: 207-725-7678; E-mail: servant@servant.net
Address: 32 Sky-Hy Dr.; Topsham; ME; 04086
Nearest Interstate: I-95, Exit 24; 7 miles.

Restrictions: Age: None; Pets: Permitted w/adv notice; Alcohol: Not permitted; Smoking: Designated outdoor area; Reservation Req'd: None; Max. Adv. Reser.: 14 days; Seasonal closing: None

RV/Campers overnight hookups: No

ACCOM: Mon. night thru Thurs. night rates for winterized (check if this is critical) rooms w/o meals unless otherwise indicated.

Bunkroom; Max. Pers: 4-8; Bedding incl ?: Yes; Bath: Shared; A/C: No:
Rate for: Person; $15; Rate for #2 pers: $15; Rate for #3 pers: $15; Child Rate: n/a

Dorm; Max. Pers: 2; Bedding incl ?: Yes; Bath: Shared; A/C: No
Rate for: Person: $15; Rate for #2 pers: $15; Rate for #3 pers: $15; Child Rate: n/a

Main amenities available: Laundry machine; Volleyball; Bookstore; VCR-TV; Horse shoes;
Meals are served in dining room for transients only when other groups are present. Approx. dinner price: $8.00.

NAME OF CENTER: YMCA - Portland Listing ID: 143

Telephone: 207-874-1111   Fax: 207-874-1114
Address: 75 Forest Ave.; Portland, ME 04101

Restrictions:
Accommodations offered to (M/F/Families): M. If M/F then must be over 18 yrs.
Pets: Not permitted; Alcohol: Not permitted; Smoking: Bedroom only
Reservation requirements: None
Reservations are accepted up to 5 hrs in advance. Seasonal closing: None

ACCOMMODATIONS:
Single room: Bedding included ?: Yes; Bath: Shared
Rate for 1 day: $36+$10 dep; Rate for 1 week: $90+$10 dep

Main amenities: Pool ; Gym; Laundry machine; Sauna; Racquetball; TV
Meals are not offered in their own cafeteria.

NAME OF CENTER: YWCA - Mount Desert Island Listing ID: 144

Telephone: 207-288-5008   Fax:
Address: 36 Mount St.; Bar Harbor, ME 04609

Restrictions:
Accommodations offered to (M/F/Families): F. If M/F then must be over 16 yrs.
Pets: Not permitted; Alcohol: Not permitted; Smoking: Outdoors only
Reservation requirements: None
Reservations are accepted up to 1 yr w/full dep in advance. Seasonal closing: None

ACCOMMODATIONS:
Single room: Bedding included ?: Yes; Bath: Shared
Rate for 1 day: $30; Rate for 1 week: $90

Double room: Bedding included ?: Yes; Bath: Shared
Rate for 1 day: $25; Rate for 1 week: $75

Main amenities: Laundry machine; TV; Kitchen privileges
Meals are offered in their own cafeteria.

MARYLAND

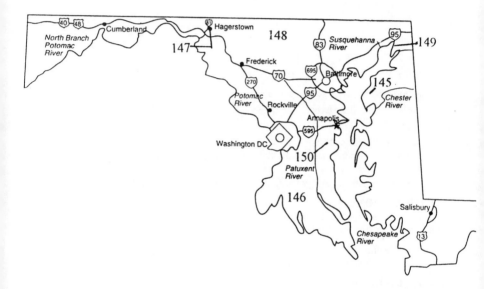

NAME OF CENTER: Drayton Retreat Center   Listing ID #: 145

Telephone: 410-778-2869; Fax: 410-778-9180; E-mail: drayton@juno.com
Address: 12651 Cooper Lane; Worton; MD; 21678
Nearest State/US Hwy: Rte 301; 15 miles.

Restrictions: Age: None; Pets: Not permitted; Alcohol: Not permitted; Smoking: Outdoors only; Reservation Req'd: None; Max. Adv. Reser.: Open; Seasonal closing: None

RV/Campers overnight hookups: No

ACCOM: Mon. night thru Thurs. night rates for winterized (check if this is critical) rooms w/o meals unless otherwise indicated.

Motel; Max. Pers: 5; Bedding incl ?: Yes; Bath: Private; A/C: Yes:
Rate for: Person; $32; Rate for #2 pers: $10; Rate for #3 pers: $11; Child Rate: n/a
Family max: $53

Main amenities available: Swimming; Volleyball; Bowling alley; Tennis; Library; Hiking
Meals are served in dining room for transients only when other groups are present. Approx. dinner price: $15.00.

NAME OF CENTER: Loyola Retreat House   Listing ID #: 146

Telephone: 301-870-3515; Fax: 301-392-0808; E-mail: sg_arrity@erois.com
Address: PO Box 9; Faulkner; MD; 20632
Nearest Interstate: I-495, Exit 20 miles; Nearest State/US Hwy: Rte 301; 1 miles.

Restrictions: Age: 18; Pets: Not permitted; Alcohol: Not permitted; Smoking: Outdoors only; Reservation Req'd: 14 days; Max. Adv. Reser.: Open; Seasonal closing: None

RV/Campers overnight hookups: No

ACCOM: Mon. night thru Thurs. night rates for winterized (check if this is critical) rooms w/o meals unless otherwise indicated.

Single room; Max. Pers: 1; Bedding incl ?: Yes; Bath: Private; A/C: Yes:
Rate for: Person; ** $60
** Includes 3 meals

Main amenities available: Book store; Meditation areas; On Potomac River; Chapel
Meals are served in dining room for transients . Approx. dinner price: Varies

REMEMBER TO CALL AHEAD

NAME OF CENTER: Mt. Aetna Camp & Retreat Center   Listing ID #: 147

Telephone: 301-824-6045; Fax: 301-824-6373; E-mail:
Address: 21905 Mt. Aetna Rd.; Hagerstown; MD; 21742
Nearest Interstate: I-70, Exit 35; 3 miles; Nearest State/US Hwy: Rte 66; 2 miles.

Restrictions: Age: None; Pets: Not permitted; Alcohol: Not permitted; Smoking: Nowhere; Reservation Req'd: 14 days; Max. Adv. Reser.: Open; Seasonal closing: None

RV/Campers overnight hookups: Yes; Water: No; Electric: Yes; Septic: No
Basic Rate/Night: $12.00/ veh

ACCOM: Mon. night thru Thurs. night rates for winterized (check if this is critical) rooms w/o meals unless otherwise indicated.

Motel; Max. Pers: 2; Bedding incl ?: Yes; Bath: Private; A/C: Yes:
Rate for: Person; $37; Rate for #2 pers: $32; Child Rate: n/a

Bunkroom; Max. Pers: 8; Bedding incl ?: No; Bath: Shared; A/C: No
Rate for: Person: $12; Rate for #2 pers: $12; Rate for #3 pers: $12; Child Rate: n/a

Main amenities available: Swimming; Volleyball; Basketball; Canoeing; Ping-pong; Hiking
Meals are served in dining room for transients only when other groups are present. Approx. dinner price: $7.50.

NAME OF CENTER: New Windsor Conference Center   Listing ID #: 148

Telephone: 800-766-1553; Fax: 410-635-8719; E-mail:
new_windsor_conferencectr@compuserve.com
Address: 500 Main St.; PO Box 188; New Windsor; MD; 21776
Nearest Interstate: I-70, Exit 15 miles; Nearest State/US Hwy: Rte 140; 7 miles.

Restrictions: Age: None; Pets: Not permitted; Alcohol: Not permitted; Smoking: Outdoors only; Reservation Req'd: None; Max. Adv. Reser.: Open; Seasonal closing: None

RV/Campers overnight hookups: No

ACCOM: Mon. night thru Thurs. night rates for winterized (check if this is critical) rooms w/o meals unless otherwise indicated.

Motel; Max. Pers: 4 or 6; Bedding incl ?: Yes; Bath: Private; A/C: Yes:
Rate for: Person; $30; Rate for #2 pers: $5; Rate for #3 pers: $5; Child Rate: n/a

Dorm; Max. Pers: 4; Bedding incl ?: Yes; Bath: Shared; A/C: Yes
Rate for: Person: $25; Rate for #2 pers: $5; Rate for #3 pers: $5; Child Rate: n/a

Bunkroom; Max. Pers: 16; Bedding incl ?: Yes; Bath: Shared; A/C: Yes:
Rate for: Person: $25; Rate for #2 pers: $5; Rate for #3 pers: $5; Child Rate: n/a

Main amenities available: Indoor V-ball & Bsk-ball; Ping-pong; Shuffleboard; Children's playground; Indoor tennis; Bookstore
Meals are served in dining room for transients only when other groups are present. Approx. dinner price: $7.75-7.95.

NAME OF CENTER: Sandy Cove Min. Hotel & Conf. Ctr.   Listing ID #: 149

Telephone: 800-234-2683; Fax: 410-287-3196; E-mail:
Address: PO Box B; North East; MD; 21901
Nearest Interstate: I-95, Exit 7 miles; Nearest State/US Hwy: Rte 272; 1 miles.

Restrictions: Age: None; Pets: Not permitted; Alcohol: Not permitted; Smoking: Nowhere;
Reservation Req'd: 11AM of day; Max. Adv. Reser.: 14 days; Seasonal closing: None

RV/Campers overnight hookups: Yes; Water: Yes; Electric: Yes; Septic: Yes
Basic Rate/Night: * $16.00/ veh

ACCOM: Mon. night thru Thurs. night rates for winterized (check if this is critical) rooms w/o
meals unless otherwise indicated.

Motel; Max. Pers: 4; Bedding incl ?: Yes; Bath: Private; A/C: Yes:
Rate for: Person; **$59; Rate for #2 pers: **$0; Rate for #3 pers: **$16; Child Rate: $8 under
17 yrs; free under 6
**These rates avail. all yr except July 3 - Aug 27. Incl. Bkfst; * RV avail. May, June, Sept

Motel; Max. Pers: 4; Bedding incl ?: Yes; Bath: Private; A/C: Yes
Rate for: Person: ***$136; Rate for #2 pers: ***$ 52; Rate for #3 pers: *** $52; Child Rate:
$40 under 17 yrs; $25 under 12; $15 under 3
*** From July 3 - Aug. 27. Includes 3 meals

Main amenities available: Swimming; V-ball; Bsk -ball; Library/Bookstore; Ping-pong; VCR-TV; Hiking
Meals are served in dining room for transients only when other groups are present. Approx. dinner price:
$10-14.00.

NAME OF CENTER: West River Retreat Center   Listing ID #: 150

Telephone: 410-867-0991; Fax: 410-867-3741; E-mail: westrivercenter@juno.com
Address: 5100 Chalk Point rd; West River; MD; 20778
Nearest Interstate: I-95, Exit 25 miles; Nearest State/US Hwy: MD 2; 5 miles.

Restrictions: Age: None; Pets: Permitted; Alcohol: Not permitted; Smoking: Outdoors only;
Reservation Req'd. None, Max. Adv. Reser.: 1 yr; Seasonal closing: Crowded JJA

RV/Campers overnight hookups: No

ACCOM: Mon. night thru Thurs. night rates for winterized (check if this is critical) rooms w/o
meals unless otherwise indicated.

Cabin; Max. Pers: 7; Bedding incl ?: No; Bath: Shared; A/C: No:
Rate for: Entire cabin; $45

Main amenities available: Outdoor pool; Volleyball; Basketball; Canoeing; On the Chesapeake; Shuffleboard
Meals are served in dining room for transients only when other groups are present. Approx. dinner price: $7.50.

NAME OF CENTER: YMCA - Hagerstown Listing ID: 151

Telephone: 301-739-3990   Fax: 301-739-3992
Address: 149 N. Potomac St.; Hagerstown, MD 21740

Restrictions:
Accommodations offered to (M/F/Families): M. If M/F then must be over 18 yrs.
Pets: Not permitted; Alcohol: Not permitted; Smoking: Bedroom only
Reservation requirements: None
Reservations are accepted up to 0 days in advance. Seasonal closing: None

ACCOMMODATIONS:
Single room: Bedding included ?: Yes; Bath: Shared
Rate for 1 day: $18+$ dep; Rate for 1 week: $60+$15 dep

Main amenities: TV lounge;
Meals are not offered in their own cafeteria.

MASSACHUSETTS

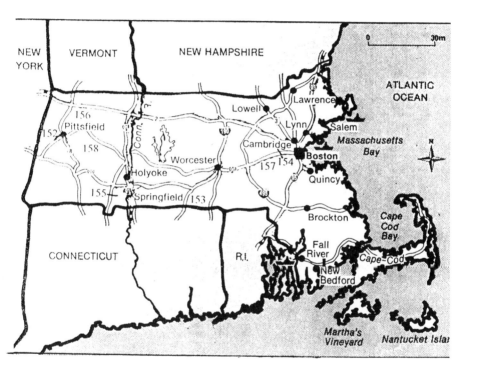

NAME OF CENTER: **Lakeside Christian Camp & Conf Ctr**   Listing ID #: 152

Telephone: 413-447-8930; Fax: 413-447-8934; E-mail: lakesidecc@aol.com
Address: 195 Cloverdale St.; Pittsfield; MA; 01701
Nearest Interstate: I-90, Exit 12 miles; Nearest State/US Hwy: Rte 20; 1 miles.

Restrictions: Age: None; Pets: Not permitted; Alcohol: Not permitted; Smoking: Outdoors only; Reservation Req'd: 1 day; Max. Adv. Reser.: Open; Seasonal closing: None

RV/Campers overnight hookups: No

ACCOM: Mon. night thru Thurs. night rates for winterized (check if this is critical) rooms w/o meals unless otherwise indicated.

Motel; Max. Pers: 4; Bedding incl ?: ** $5 surcharge; Bath: Private; A/C: No:
Rate for: Person; $25; Rate for #2 pers: $5; Rate for #3 pers: $5; Child Rate: n/a
** Adv notice required

Main amenities available: Swimming; Volleyball; Basketball; Ping pong; Tennis/Canoeing; Hiking
Meals are served in dining room for transients only when other groups are present. Approx. dinner price: $6-8.00.

NAME OF CENTER: **Bement Camp & Conference Ctr**   Listing ID #: 153

Telephone: 508-248-7811; Fax: ; E-mail:
Address: 73 Jones Rd.; Charlton Depot; MA; 01509
Nearest Interstate: I-90, Exit 7 miles.

Restrictions: Age: None; Pets: Permitted on leash; Alcohol: Not permitted; Smoking: Outdoors only; Reservation Req'd: 7 days; Max. Adv. Reser.: 1 mo; Seasonal closing: Not available June 15 - Sept 1; Not avail Fri/Sat nights

RV/Campers overnight hookups: No

ACCOM: Mon. night thru Thurs. night rates for winterized (check if this is critical) rooms w/o meals unless otherwise indicated.

Dorm/House; Max. Pers: 4; Bedding incl ?: No; Bath: Shared; A/C: No:
Rate for: Person; $40; Rate for #2 pers: $40; Rate for #3 pers: $40; Child Rate: $15 under 12 yrs
Hse w/three bedrooms w/four beds each

Main amenities available: Basketball; Volleyball; Hiking
Meals are not served in dining room for transients .

NAME OF CENTER: Espousal Ret Hse & Conf Ctr   Listing ID #: 154

Telephone: 781-647-0033; Fax: 781-893-0291; E-mail: espousal@aol.com
Address: 554 Lexington St.; Waltham; MA; 02452
Nearest Interstate: I-95, Exit 2 miles; Nearest State/US Hwy: Rte 128; 2 miles.

Restrictions: Age: None; Pets: Not permitted; Alcohol: Not permitted; Smoking: Outdoors only; Reservation Req'd: 2 days; Max. Adv. Reser.: 14 days; Seasonal closing: None

RV/Campers overnight hookups: No

ACCOM: Mon. night thru Thurs. night rates for winterized (check if this is critical) rooms w/o meals unless otherwise indicated.

Dorm; Max. Pers: 5; Bedding incl ?: Yes (w/notice); Bath: Shared; A/C: Yes:
Rate for: Person; $35; Rate for #2 pers: $35; Rate for #3 pers: $35; Child Rate: n/a

Main amenities available: Quiet areas
Meals are served in dining room for transients only when other groups are present. Approx. dinner price: $6-16.00.

NAME OF CENTER: Genesis Spiritual Life Center   Listing ID #: 155

Telephone: 413-562-3627; Fax: 413-572-1060; E-mail: genretc@exit3.com
Address: 53 Mill St.; Westfield; MA; 01085
Nearest Interstate: I-90, Exit 3; 3 miles; Nearest State/US Hwy: Rte 202; 1 miles.

Restrictions: Age: None; Pets: Not permitted; Alcohol: Not permitted; Smoking: Outdoors only; Reservation Req'd: 10 days; Max. Adv. Reser.: Open; Seasonal closing: June - Aug.

RV/Campers overnight hookups: No

ACCOM: Mon. night thru Thurs. night rates for winterized (check if this is critical) rooms w/o meals unless otherwise indicated.

Dorm; Max. Pers: 5; Bedding incl ?: Yes (w/notice); Bath: Shared; A/C: No:
Rate for: Person; $35; Rate for #2 pers: $35; Rate for #3 pers: $35; Child Rate: n/a

Main amenities available: Bookstore; Library; TV; Quiet areas
Meals are served in dining room for transients only when other groups are present. Approx. dinner price: $5-12.00.

NAME OF CENTER: Stump Sprout Lodge   Listing ID #: 156

Telephone: 413-339-4265; Fax: ; E-mail:
Address: West Hill Rd; West Hawley; MA; 01339
Nearest Interstate: I-91, Exit 25 miles; Nearest State/US Hwy: Rte 2; 6 miles.

Restrictions: Age: None; Pets: Not permitted; Alcohol: Permitted; Smoking: Outdoors only; Reservation Req'd: None; Max. Adv. Reser.: Open; Seasonal closing: None

RV/Campers overnight hookups: No

ACCOM: Mon. night thru Thurs. night rates for winterized (check if this is critical) rooms w/o meals unless otherwise indicated.

Dorm; Max. Pers: 5; Bedding incl ?: No; Bath: Shared; A/C: No:
Rate for: Person; **$22; Rate for #2 pers: **$22; Rate for #3 pers: **$22; Child Rate: 20% off under 17 yrs; 50% off under 11; 80% under 3
Winter rate $49; Lodge is frequented by Christian gps but is not specifically Christian.

Main amenities available: Recreation room; Volleyball; Pool table; Ping pong; X-Ctry skiing; Hiking
Meals are served in dining room for transients only when other groups are present. Approx. dinner price: $10.00.

NAME OF CENTER: UCC Conference Center   Listing ID #: 157

Telephone: 508-875-5233; Fax: 508-875-5481; E-mail:
Address: 1 Badger Rd. (PO Box 2246); Framingham; MA; 01703
Nearest Interstate: I-90, Exit 12; 1 miles.

Restrictions: Age: None; Pets: Not permitted; Alcohol: Permitted; Smoking: Outdoors only; Reservation Req'd: 3 PM of day; Max. Adv. Reser.: 3 mo; Seasonal closing: Closed all except July/Aug.

RV/Campers overnight hookups: No

ACCOM: Mon. night thru Thurs. night rates for winterized (check if this is critical) rooms w/o meals unless otherwise indicated.

Dorm; Max. Pers: 4; Bedding incl ?: $7 surcharge; Bath: Shared; A/C: No:
Rate for: Person; $10; Rate for #2 pers: $10; Rate for #3 pers: $10; Child Rate: Free under 12 yrs

Main amenities available: Child playground (after 6 PM); Volleyball; Basketball; VCR-TV; Hiking;
Meals are not served in dining room for transients .

NAME OF CENTER: YMCA Camp Hi-Rock   Listing ID #: 158

Telephone: 413-528-1227; Fax: 413-528-4234; E-mail: info@camphirock.com
Address: 162 East Street; Mt. Washington; MA; 01258
Nearest Interstate: I-91 , Exit 2; 35 miles; Nearest State/US Hwy: Rte 7; 15 miles.

Restrictions: Age: None; Pets: Not permitted; Alcohol: Not permitted; Smoking: Outdoors only;
Reservation Req'd: 14 days; Max. Adv. Reser.: 1 yr; Seasonal closing: Available May, Sept,
Oct (not heated)

RV/Campers overnight hookups: No

ACCOM: Mon. night thru Thurs. night rates for winterized (check if this is critical) rooms w/o
meals unless otherwise indicated.

Bunkroom; Max. Pers: 13; Bedding incl ?: No; Bath: Separate bldg; A/C: No:
Rate for: Person; $10; Rate for #2 pers: $10; Rate for #3 pers: $10; Child Rate: n/a

Main amenities available: Swimming; Tennis; Basketball; Boating; X-Ctry skiing; Hiking
Meals are served in dining room for transients only when other groups are present. Approx. dinner price: $6.00
with adv. notice.

NAME OF CENTER: YMCA - Pittsfield Listing ID: 159

Telephone: 413-499-7650   Fax: 413-443-6791
Address: 292 North St.; Pittsfield, MA 01201

Restrictions:
Accommodations offered to (M/F/Families): M&F. If M/F then must be over 18 yrs.
Pets: Not permitted; Alcohol: Not permitted; Smoking: Bedroom only
Reservation requirements: None
Reservations are accepted up to 2 days in advance. Seasonal closing: None

ACCOMMODATIONS:
Single room: Bedding included ?: Yes; Bath: Shared
Rate for 1 day: $27; Rate for 1 week: $73

Main amenities: Pool; Gym; TV; Laundromat adjacent; Hiking
Meals are not offered in their own cafeteria.

REMEMBER TO CALL AHEAD

NAME OF CENTER: YWCA - Cambridge Listing ID: 160

Telephone: 617-491-6050   Fax: 617-491-4108
Address: 7 Temple St.; Cambridge, MA 02139

Restrictions:
Accommodations offered to (M/F/Families): F. If M/F then must be over 18 yrs.
Pets: Not permitted; Alcohol: Not permitted; Smoking: Bedroom only
Reservation requirements: None
Reservations are accepted up to 3 mo w/dep in advance. Seasonal closing: None

ACCOMMODATIONS:
Single room: Bedding included ?: Yes; Bath: Shared
Rate for 1 day: $40; Rate for 1 week: $150

Main amenities: TV; Laundry machine
Meals are not offered in their own cafeteria.

MICHIGAN

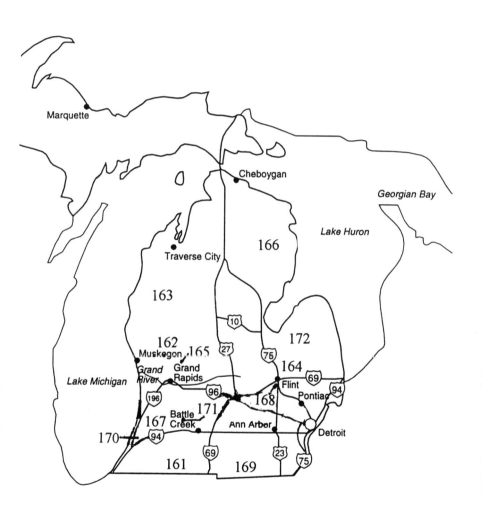

Marquette

Cheboygan

Georgian Bay

Lake Huron

166

Traverse City

163

10

162 .165 27
Muskegon

172

75

164 69

Grand Grand
River Rapids

Flint 94

Pontiac

196 96

168

167 Battle 171
Creek

Ann Arbor Detroit

170 94

161 69 169 23 75

Lake Michigan

NAME OF CENTER: Amigo Center   Listing ID #: 161

Telephone: 616-651-2811; Fax: 616-659-0084; E-mail: info@amigocentre.org
Address: 26455 Banker Rd.; Sturgis; MI; 49091
Nearest Interstate: I-80 Exit 8 miles; Nearest State/US Hwy: Rte 66; 2 miles.

Restrictions: Age: None; Pets: Not permitted; Alcohol: Not permitted; Smoking: Outdoors only;
Reservation Req'd: None; Max. Adv. Reser.: 1 wk; Seasonal closing: None

RV/Campers overnight hookups: Yes; Water: Yes; Electric: No; Septic: No
Basic Rate/Night: $12.00/ veh

ACCOM: Mon. night thru Thurs. night rates for winterized (check if this is critical) rooms w/o
meals unless otherwise indicated.

Motel; Max. Pers: 5; Bedding incl ?: Yes; Bath: Private; A/C: Yes:
Rate for: Couple; **$54; Child Rate: Free under 10 yrs
** $13 for each additional person

Main amenities available: V-ball; Bsk ball; Ball field; Laundry machine; Boat/canoeing; Hiking
Meals are served in dining room for transients only when other groups are present. Approx. dinner price: $7.60.

NAME OF CENTER: Camp Henry   Listing ID #: 162

Telephone: 616-459-2267; Fax: 616-456-1461; E-mail: info@camphenry.org
Address: 5575 Gordon Rd.; Newaygo; MI; 49337
Nearest Interstate: US 131, Exit 24 miles; Nearest State/US Hwy: M37; 4 miles.

Restrictions: Age: None; Pets: Not permitted; Alcohol: Not permitted; Smoking: Designated
outdoor area; Reservation Req'd: 7 days; Max. Adv. Reser.: Open; Seasonal closing: Mid June -
mid Aug

RV/Campers overnight hookups: No

ACCOM: Mon. night thru Thurs. night rates for winterized (check if this is critical) rooms w/o
meals unless otherwise indicated.

Cabin; Max. Pers: Over 5; Bedding incl ?: No; Bath: Shared; A/C: No:
Rate for: Person; $10; Rate for #2 pers: $10; Rate for #3 pers: $10; Child Rate: n/a
Includes: kitchenette.   Please tidy up area

Dorm; Max. Pers: 5; Bedding incl ?: No ; Bath: shared; A/C: No
Rate for: Person: $16; Rate for #2 pers: $16; Rate for #3 pers: $16; Child Rate: n/a
Please tidy up area

Motel; Max. Pers: 5; Bedding incl ?: No; Bath: Private; A/C: No:
Rate for: Person: $16; Rate for #2 pers: $16; Rate for #3 pers: $16; Child Rate: n/a
Please tidy up area

Main amenities available: Swimming; V-ball; Bsk ball; Boat/Canoeing; Laundry machine; VCR-TV; Tennis
Meals are served in dining room for transients only when other groups are present. Dinner price: $6.50.

NAME OF CENTER: Camp Living Waters   Listing ID #: 163

Telephone: 616-797-5107; Fax: 616-797-5552; E-mail:
Address: Rte 2; Box 73; Luther; MI; 49656
Nearest Interstate: I-131, Exit 18 miles; Nearest State/US Hwy: Rte 37; 5 miles.

Restrictions: Age: None; Pets: Not permitted; Alcohol: Not permitted; Smoking: Outdoors only;
Reservation Req'd: 1 wk; Max. Adv. Reser.: 1 mo; Seasonal closing: None

RV/Campers overnight hookups: Yes; Water: Yes; Electric: Yes; Septic: No
Basic Rate/Night: $15-20.00/ veh

ACCOM: Mon. night thru Thurs. night rates for winterized (check if this is critical) rooms w/o
meals unless otherwise indicated.

Bunk/cabin; Max. Pers: 8; Bedding incl ?: No; Bath: Shared; A/C: No:
Rate for: Person; $15; Rate for #2 pers: $15; Rate for #3 pers: $15; Child Rate: n/a

Main amenities available: Lake swimming; Volleyball; Basketball; Incidentals store; Canoeing; Hiking
Meals are served in dining room for transients only when other groups are present. Approx. dinner price: $6.00.

NAME OF CENTER: Covenant Hills   Listing ID #: 164

Telephone: 810-631-4531; Fax: 810-631-4533; E-mail: covenanthills@bigfoot.com
Address: Box 96; 10359 E. Farrand Rd.; Otisville; MI; 48463
Nearest Interstate: I-69/I-75, Exit 13 miles; Nearest State/US Hwy: M15; 1 miles.

Restrictions: Age: None; Pets: Not permitted; Alcohol: Not permitted; Smoking: Outdoors only;
Reservation Req'd: None; Max. Adv. Reser.: 14 days; Seasonal closing: None

RV/Campers overnight hookups: Yes; Water: YEs; Electric: Yes; Septic: Yes
Basic Rate/Night: $15.00/ veh

ACCOM: Mon. night thru Thurs. night rates for winterized (check if this is critical) rooms w/o
meals unless otherwise indicated.

Dorm; Max. Pers: 2; Bedding incl ?: No; Bath: Shared; A/C: Yes:
Rate for: Room; $25; Child Rate: n/a

Main amenities available: Lake swimming; V-ball; Bsk ball; Boating; Bookstore; Hiking; Ropes course
Meals are served in dining room for transients only when other groups are present. Approx. dinner price: $6.00.
Meals avail May, Sept, Oct

NAME OF CENTER: **Greenwood Presbyterian Camp**   Listing ID #: 165

Telephone: 616-754-7258; Fax: 616-754-0906; E-mail: camp.greenwood@ecunet.org
Address: 13564 MacClain Rd.; Gowen; MI; 49326
Nearest Interstate: I-96, Exit 20 miles; Nearest State/US Hwy: Rte 67; 2 miles.

Restrictions: Age: None; Pets: Not permitted; Alcohol: Not permitted; Smoking: Outdoors only; Reservation Req'd: None; Max. Adv. Reser.: Open; Seasonal closing: June - Aug 15

RV/Campers overnight hookups: Yes; Water: Yes; Electric: Yes; Septic: No
Basic Rate/Night: $15.00/ veh

ACCOM: Mon. night thru Thurs. night rates for winterized (check if this is critical) rooms w/o meals unless otherwise indicated.

Cabin; Max. Pers: 10; Bedding incl ?: No; Bath: Shared; A/C: No:
Rate for: Entire cabin; $80
Please sweep and take out trash

Main amenities available: Children's playground; V-ball; Bsk ball; VCR-TV; Laundry machine; Boat/canoeing; Hiking
Meals are served in dining room for transients only when other groups are present. Approx. dinner price: $6.00.

NAME OF CENTER: **Michi-Lu-Ca Conference Ctr & Camp**   Listing ID #: 166

Telephone: 517-848-2230; Fax: 517-848-2230; E-mail: lormm-mlc@juno.com
Address: 3506 Garling Rd.; Fairview; MI; 48621
Nearest Interstate: I-75, Exit 40 miles; Nearest State/US Hwy: Rte 72; 5 miles.

Restrictions: Age: None; Pets: Not permitted; Alcohol: Not permitted; Smoking: Designated outdoor area; Reservation Req'd: None; Max. Adv. Reser.: 1 yr; Seasonal closing: None

RV/Campers overnight hookups: No

ACCOM: Mon. night thru Thurs. night rates for winterized (check if this is critical) rooms w/o meals unless otherwise indicated.

Cottage; Max. Pers: Over 5; Bedding incl ?: No; Bath: Shared; A/C: No:
Rate for: Entire Cottage; $50
Includes: living rm; bedrooms; dining rm; kitchen; bath

Dorm; Max. Pers: 5; Bedding incl ?: No; Bath: Shared; A/C: No
Rate for: Person: $35; Rate for #2 pers: $35; Rate for #3 pers: $35; Child Rate: n/a

Main amenities available: Incidentals store (summer); Swimming; Basketball; VCR-TV; Laundry machine; Hiking/canoeing
Meals are served in dining room for transients only when other groups are present. Approx. dinner price: $6.00.

NAME OF CENTER: Miracle Camp   Listing ID #: 167

Telephone: 616-624-6161; Fax: 616-624-1566; E-mail: donpearce@aol.com
Address: 25281 80th Ave.; Lawton; MI; 49065
Nearest Interstate: I-94, Exit 8 miles; Nearest State/US Hwy: US 131; 8 miles.

Restrictions: Age: None; Pets: Not permitted; Alcohol: Not permitted; Smoking: Outdoors only;
Reservation Req'd: None; Max. Adv. Reser.: Open; Seasonal closing: None

RV/Campers overnight hookups: Yes; Water: Yes; Electric: Yes; Septic: No
Basic Rate/Night: $10.00/ veh

ACCOM: Mon. night thru Thurs. night rates for winterized (check if this is critical) rooms w/o
meals unless otherwise indicated.

Bunkroom; Max. Pers: 6-18; Bedding incl ?: $5 surcharge; Bath: Shared; A/C: **:
Rate for: Person; $15; Rate for #2 pers: $15; Rate for #3 pers: $15; Child Rate: n/a
** Some are Y; some N

Dorm; Max. Pers: 4; Bedding incl ?: $5 surcharge; Bath: Shared; A/C: No
Rate for: Couple: $30; $5 for third; $5 for fourth person; Child Rate: n/a

Main amenities available: Game room; Volleyball; Basketball; Gym; Hiking
Meals are served in dining room for transients only when other groups are present. Approx. dinner price: $6.50.

NAME OF CENTER: Myers Lake   Listing ID #: 168

Telephone: 800-994-5050; Fax: 810-266-6037; E-mail: myerslake@shianet.org
Address: 10575 Silver Lake Rd; Byron; MI; 48418
Nearest Interstate: I-75, Exit 29 Silver lake Rd; 18 miles; Nearest State/US Hwy: US
23; 10 miles.

Restrictions: Age: None; Pets: Permitted; Alcohol: Not permitted; Smoking: Outdoors only;
Reservation Req'd: None; Max. Adv. Reser.: 1 yr; Seasonal closing: Nov 1 - April 30

RV/Campers overnight hookups: Yes; Water: Yes; Electric: Yes; Septic: Yes
Basic Rate/Night: $17-25.00/ veh

ACCOM: Mon. night thru Thurs. night rates for winterized (check if this is critical) rooms w/o
meals unless otherwise indicated.

Main amenities available: Lake swimming; Incidentals store; Laundry machine; Boats-all kinds; Recreation
hall; V-ball; Bsk ball
Meals are not served in dining room for transients .

NAME OF CENTER: Somerset Beach Campground   Listing ID #: 169

Telephone: 517-688-3783; Fax: 517-688-3621; E-mail: somersetbeach@juno.com
Address: 9822 Brooklawn Ct.; PO Box 307; Somerset Ctr.; MI; 49282
Nearest Interstate: I-94, Exit 19 miles; Nearest State/US Hwy: US 12; 1 miles.

Restrictions: Age: None; Pets: Permitted outside; Alcohol: Not permitted; Smoking: Outdoors only; Reservation Req'd: Yes; Max. Adv. Reser.: 1 yr; Seasonal closing: June - Aug.; RV is OK all yr.

RV/Campers overnight hookups: Yes; Water: No; Electric: Yes; Septic: No
Basic Rate/Night: $16.00/ veh

ACCOM: Mon. night thru Thurs. night rates for winterized (check if this is critical) rooms w/o meals unless otherwise indicated.

Bunkroom; Max. Pers: Over 5; Bedding incl ?: No; Bath: Shared; A/C: No:
Rate for: Person; $30; Rate for #2 pers: $30; Rate for #3 pers: $30; Child Rate: n/a
Family max: $60

Dorm; Max. Pers: 5; Bedding incl ?: No; Bath: Shared; A/C: Yes
Rate for: Person: $30; Rate for #2 pers: $30; Rate for #3 pers: $30; Child Rate: n/a
Family max: $60.

Motel; Max. Pers: 5; Bedding incl ?: No; Bath: Private; A/C: Yes:
Rate for: Person: $30; Rate for #2 pers: $30; Rate for #3 pers: $30; Child Rate: n/a
Family max: $60

Main amenities available: Swimming; V-ball; Bsk ball; Laundry machine; Boats/canoeing; Tennis; Hiking
Meals are served in dining room for transients only when other groups are present. Approx. dinner price: $5-6.00.

NAME OF CENTER: Warner Memorial Camp   Listing ID #: 170

Telephone: 616-434-6844; Fax: 616-434-6451; E-mail: warnercp@bci.com
Address: 60 55th St.; Grand Junction; MI; 49056
Nearest Interstate: I-196, Exit 10 miles; Nearest State/US Hwy: Rte 31; 10 miles.

Restrictions: Age: None; Pets: Not permitted; Alcohol: Not permitted; Smoking: Outdoors only; Reservation Req'd: 5 days; Max. Adv. Reser.: 1 mo; Seasonal closing: Mid June - Aug 10

RV/Campers overnight hookups: Yes; Water: Yes; Electric: Yes; Septic: n/a
Basic Rate/Night: $9 w A/C $12/ veh

ACCOM: Mon. night thru Thurs. night rates for winterized (check if this is critical) rooms w/o meals unless otherwise indicated.

Bunkroom; Max. Pers: Over 5; Bedding incl ?: No; Bath: Shared; A/C: No:
Rate for: Person; $10; Rate for #2 pers: $10; Rate for #3 pers: $10; Child Rate: Free under 6 yrs
Family max: $24.50

Dorm; Max. Pers: 5; Bedding incl ?: No; Bath: Shared; A/C: No
Rate for: Person: $10; Rate for #2 pers: $10; Rate for #3 pers: $10; Child Rate: Free under 6 yrs
Family max: $24.50

Motel; Max. Pers: 5; Bedding incl ?: No; Bath: Private; A/C: Yes:
Rate for: Person: $10; Rate for #2 pers: $10; Rate for #3 pers: $10; Child Rate: Free under 6 yrs
Family max: $24.50

Main amenities available: Swimming; V-ball; Bsk ball; Laundry machine; Bookstore; Canoeing; Hiking
Meals are served in dining room for transients only when other groups are present. Approx. dinner price: $5.50-7.50.

NAME OF CENTER: Wesley Woods   Listing ID #: 171

Telephone: 616-721-8291; Fax: 616-721-8291; E-mail: wwumcamp@aol.com
Address: 1700 Clear Lake; Dowling; MI; 49050
Nearest Interstate: I-94, Exit 19 miles; Nearest State/US Hwy: M37; 1 miles.

Restrictions: Age: None; Pets: Not permitted; Alcohol: Not permitted; Smoking: Outdoors only;
Reservation Req'd: None; Max. Adv. Reser.: 14 days; Seasonal closing: None

RV/Campers overnight hookups: No

ACCOM: Mon. night thru Thurs. night rates for winterized (check if this is critical) rooms w/o
meals unless otherwise indicated.

Dorm; Max. Pers: 2; Bedding incl ?: Yes; Bath: Shared; A/C: No:
Rate for: Person; $25; Rate for #2 pers: $25; Rate for #3 pers: n/a; Child Rate: n/a

Main amenities available: Heated outdoor pool; Volleyball; Kayak/Canoeing; VCR-TV
Meals are served in dining room for transients only when other groups are present. Approx. dinner price: $7.00.

NAME OF CENTER: Wesleyan Woods   Listing ID #: 172

Telephone: 517-823-8840; Fax: ; E-mail:
Address: 4320 Caine Road; Vassar; MI; 48768
Nearest Interstate: I-75, Exit 20 miles; Nearest State/US Hwy: Rte 46; 2 miles.

Restrictions: Age: None; Pets: Permitted outside; Alcohol: Not permitted; Smoking: Outdoors
only; Reservation Req'd: 14 days; Max. Adv. Reser.: Open; Seasonal closing: None

RV/Campers overnight hookups: Yes; Water: Yes; Electric: Yes; Septic: No
Basic Rate/Night: $9 w A/C $11/ veh

ACCOM: Mon. night thru Thurs. night rates for winterized (check if this is critical) rooms w/o
meals unless otherwise indicated.

Bunkroom; Max. Pers: Over 5; Bedding incl ?: No; Bath: Shared; A/C: No:
Rate for: Person; $8; Rate for #2 pers: $8; Rate for #3 pers: $8; Child Rate: n/a
Family max. $25, Vacuum floor when leaving.

Dorm; Max. Pers: 5; Bedding incl ?: No; Bath: Shared; A/C:
Rate for: Person: $8; Rate for #2 pers: $8; Rate for #3 pers: $8; Child Rate: n/a
Family max: $25; Vacuum floor when leaving.

Motel; Max. Pers: 5; Bedding incl ?: No; Bath: Private; A/C: Yes:
Rate for: Room: $28; Child Rate: n/a
Vacuum room when leaving.

Main amenities available: Swimming; V-ball; Bsk ball; Tennis; Ball field; Canoeing; Hiking
Meals are not served in dining room for transients .

NAME OF CENTER: YMCA - Ann Arbor Listing ID: 173

Telephone: 734-663-0536   Fax: 734-663-8232
Address: 350 S. 5th Ave.; Ann Arbor, MI 48104

Restrictions:
Accommodations offered to (M/F/Families): M&F. If M/F then must be over 18 yrs.
Pets: Not permitted; Alcohol: Permitted in bedroom; Smoking: Outdoors only
Reservation requirements: Yes
Reservations are accepted up to 1 yr in advance. Seasonal closing: None

ACCOMMODATIONS:
Single room: Bedding included ?: Yes; Bath: Shared
Rate for 1 day: ; Rate for 1 week: $90+$100 sec dep
Room fee excludes membership in Y

Main amenities: Volleyball; Basketball
Meals are not offered in their own cafeteria.

NAME OF CENTER: YMCA - Detroit Western Br. Listing ID: 174

Telephone: 313-554-2136   Fax: 313-961-0329
Address: 1601 Clark St.; Detroit, MI 48209

Restrictions:
Accommodations offered to (M/F/Families): M. If M/F then must be over 18 yrs.
Pets: Not permitted; Alcohol: Not permitted; Smoking: Outdoors only
Reservation requirements: No - 'phone interview req'd
Reservations are accepted up to 3 days in advance. Seasonal closing: None

ACCOMMODATIONS:
Single room: Bedding included ?: Yes; Bath: Shared
Rate for 1 day: ; Rate for 1 week: $75+$75 sec dep
Room fee includes membership in Y

Main amenities: Pool; Gym; Sauna; Jacuzzi; Laundry machine
Meals are not offered in their own cafeteria.

NAME OF CENTER: YMCA - Flint Listing ID: 175

Telephone: 810-232-9622   Fax: 810-232-9329
Address: 411 East 3rd St.; Flint, Mi 48503

Restrictions:
Accommodations offered to (M/F/Families): M. If M/F then must be over 18 yrs.
Pets: Not permitted; Alcohol: Not permitted; Smoking: Outdoors only
Reservation requirements: None
Reservations are accepted up to 0 days in advance. Seasonal closing: None

ACCOMMODATIONS:
Single room: Bedding included ?: Yes; Bath: Shared
Rate for 1 day: ; Rate for 1 week: $56
Room fee includes membership in Y

Main amenities: Pool; Gym; TV Lounge
Meals are not offered in their own cafeteria.

NAME OF CENTER: YMCA - Grand Rapids Downtown Br. Listing ID: 176

Telephone: 616-222-9626   Fax:
Address: 33 Library St. NE; Grand Rapids, MI 49503

Restrictions:
Accommodations offered to (M/F/Families): M. If M/F then must be over 18 yrs.
Pets: Not permitted; Alcohol: Not permitted; Smoking: Bedroom only
Reservation requirements: None
Reservations are accepted up to 3 days in advance. Seasonal closing: None

ACCOMMODATIONS:
Single room: Bedding included ?: Yes; Bath: Shared
Rate for 1 day: ; Rate for 1 week: $92
Room fee excludes membership in Y

Main amenities: TV; Hiking
Meals are not offered in their own cafeteria.

NAME OF CENTER: YMCA - Saginaw Listing ID: 177

Telephone: 517-753-7721   Fax: 517-755-9329
Address: 1915 Fordney St.; Saginaw, MI 48601

Restrictions:
Accommodations offered to (M/F/Families): M. If M/F then must be over 18 yrs.
Pets: Not permitted; Alcohol: Not permitted; Smoking: On residence floors
Reservation requirements: None
Reservations are accepted up to 0 days in advance. Seasonal closing: None

ACCOMMODATIONS:
Single room: Bedding included ?: Yes; Bath: Shared
Rate for 1 day: $24+$5 dep; Rate for 1 week: $88+$5 dep
Room fee includes membership in Y

Main amenities: Pool; Gym; Jacuzzi; Racquetball; Handball; Weight room
Meals are not offered in their own cafeteria.

MINNESOTA

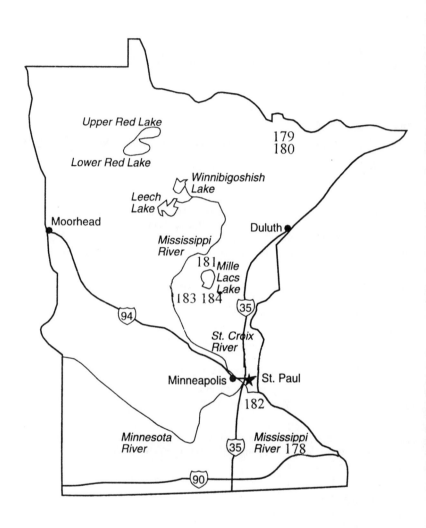

Upper Red Lake

Lower Red Lake

179
180

Winnibigoshish Lake

Leech Lake

Moorhead

Mississippi River

Duluth

181 Mille Lacs Lake

183 184

94

35

St. Croix River

Minneapolis

St. Paul

182

Minnesota River

35

Mississippi River 178

90

NAME OF CENTER: Assisi Community Center   Listing ID #: 178

Telephone: 507-280-2180; Fax: 507-282-7762; E-mail: acomc@aol.com
www.acomc.org
Address: 1001 14th St. NW; Suite 200; Rochester; MN; 55901
Nearest Interstate: I-90, Exit 10 miles; Nearest State/US Hwy: Rte 52; 2 miles.

Restrictions: Age: 18; Pets: Not permitted; Alcohol: Not permitted; Smoking: Nowhere;
Reservation Req'd: 10 days; Max. Adv. Reser.: Open; Seasonal closing: None

RV/Campers overnight hookups: No

ACCOM: Mon. night thru Thurs. night rates for winterized (check if this is critical) rooms w/o
meals unless otherwise indicated.

Dormitory; Max. Pers: 2; Bedding incl ?: Yes; Bath: Shared; A/C: No:
Rate for: Person; $23; Rate for #2 pers: $2; Rate for #3 pers: n/a; Child Rate: n/a
Reservation & referrals req'd from clergy or employer by TP or fax

Main amenities available: Labyrinth; Library; Outdoor pathway; Bookstore; Hiking
Meals are served in dining room for transients . Dinner price: $7.00.

NAME OF CENTER: Camp Hiawatha   Listing ID #: 179

Telephone: 218-666-5465; Fax: 218-666-5700; E-mail: vlm@vermilionnet.com
Address: PO Box 1076; Cook; MN; 55723
Nearest Interstate: I-94, Exit 220 miles; Nearest State/US Hwy: Rte 169; 15 miles.

Restrictions: Age: None; Pets: Permitted; Alcohol: Not permitted; Smoking: Outdoors only;
Reservation Req'd: 2 wks; Max. Adv. Reser.: Open; Seasonal closing: None

RV/Campers overnight hookups: Yes; Water: unk; Electric: unk; Septic: n/a
Basic Rate/Night: $11.00/ veh

ACCOM: Mon. night thru Thurs. night rates for winterized (check if this is critical) rooms w/o
meals unless otherwise indicated.

Bunkroom; Max. Pers: 10; Bedding incl ?: No; Bath: Shared; A/C: No:
Rate for: Person; $15; Rate for #2 pers: $15; Rate for #3 pers: $15; Child Rate: n/a

Main amenities available: Swimming; V-ball; Bsk-ball; VCR-TV; Sauna; Boat/canoe; Ping pong
Meals are served in dining room for transients only when other groups are present. Approx. dinner price:
$5-7.00.

REMEMBER TO CALL AHEAD

NAME OF CENTER: Camp Vermilion   Listing ID #: 180

Telephone: 218-666-5465; Fax: 218-666-5700; E-mail: vlm@vermilionnet.com
Address: PO Box 1076; Cook; MN; 55723
Nearest Interstate: I-94, Exit 220 miles; Nearest State/US Hwy: Rte 52; 8 miles.

Restrictions: Age: None; Pets: Not permitted; Alcohol: Not permitted; Smoking: Outdoors only;
Reservation Req'd: 2 wks; Max. Adv. Reser.: Open; Seasonal closing: None

RV/Campers overnight hookups: Yes; Water: unk; Electric: unk; Septic: n/a
Basic Rate/Night: $11.00/ veh

ACCOM: Mon. night thru Thurs. night rates for winterized (check if this is critical) rooms w/o
meals unless otherwise indicated.

Bunkroom; Max. Pers: 10; Bedding incl ?: No; Bath: Shared; A/C: No:
Rate for: Person; $15; Rate for #2 pers: $15; Rate for #3 pers: $15; Child Rate: n/a

Main amenities available: Swimming; V-ball; Bsk-ball; VCR-TV; Sauna; Boat/canoe; Ping pong
Meals are served in dining room for transients only when other groups are present. Approx. dinner price:
$5-7.00.

NAME OF CENTER: Clearwater Forest   Listing ID #: 181

Telephone: 218-678-2325; Fax: 218-678-3196; E-mail: clearwaterforest.org
Address: 3314 Crooked Lake Rd. NE; Deerwood; MN; 56444
Nearest Interstate: I-94, Exit 120 miles; Nearest State/US Hwy: Rte 6; 0 miles.

Restrictions: Age: None; Pets: Not permitted; Alcohol: Not permitted; Smoking: Designated
outdoor area; Reservation Req'd: None; Max. Adv. Reser.: 2 yrs; Seasonal closing: None

RV/Campers overnight hookups: Yes; Water: No; Electric: $14; Septic: No
Basic Rate/Night: $12.00/ veh

ACCOM: Mon. night thru Thurs. night rates for winterized (check if this is critical) rooms w/o
meals unless otherwise indicated.

Motel; Max. Pers: 5; Bedding incl ?: $5 surcharge; Bath: Semi-private; A/C: No:
Rate for: Room; $35; Child Rate: n/a
Located on 1100 acre lake

Main amenities available: Swimming; Volleyball; Horse shoes; Hiking
Meals are served in dining room for transients depending upon the retreat group present. Approx. dinner price:
$8.00.

NAME OF CENTER: Mt. Olivet Retreat Center   Listing ID #: 182

Telephone: 612-469-2175; Fax: 612-469-5564; E-mail:
Address: 7984 257th St. West; Farmington; MN; 55024
Nearest Interstate: I-35, Exit 2 miles.

Restrictions: Age: None; Pets: Not permitted; Alcohol: Not permitted; Smoking: Designated outdoor area; Reservation Req'd: 2 days; Max. Adv. Reser.: 14 days; Seasonal closing: Christmas, Easter, Thanksgiving

RV/Campers overnight hookups: No

ACCOM: Mon. night thru Thurs. night rates for winterized (check if this is critical) rooms w/o meals unless otherwise indicated.

Bunkroom; Max. Pers: 12; Bedding incl ?: No; Bath: Shared; A/C: No:
Rate for: Person; $10; Rate for #2 pers: $10; Rate for #3 pers: $10; Child Rate: n/a

Motel; Max. Pers: 5; Bedding incl ?: Yes; Bath: Private; A/C: No
Rate for: Person: $25; Rate for #2 pers: $25; Rate for #3 pers: $25; Child Rate: Free under 16 yrs
Open to small families & individuals on private retreats for min. 24 hr stay.

Main amenities available: Sauna; Volleyball; Tennis; Indoor swimming; Pool table ; Ping pong
Meals are served in dining room for transients only when other groups are present. Approx. dinner price: $9; $7.50 under 16 yrs; free under 2.

NAME OF CENTER: St. Francis Center   Listing ID #: 183

Telephone: 320-632-2981; Fax: 320-632-1714; E-mail:
Address: 116 8th Ave SE; Little Falls; MN; 56345
Nearest Interstate: I-94, Exit 40 miles; Nearest State/US Hwy: Rte 10; 2 miles.

Restrictions: Age: None; Pets: Not permitted; Alcohol: Hard liquor not permitted; Smoking: Outdoors only; Reservation Req'd: 15 days; Max. Adv. Reser.: Open; Seasonal closing: None

RV/Campers overnight hookups: No

ACCOM: Mon. night thru Thurs. night rates for winterized (check if this is critical) rooms w/o meals unless otherwise indicated.

Dormitory; Max. Pers: 4; Bedding incl ?: Yes (w/notice); Bath: Shared; A/C: Yes:
Rate for: Person; $21; Rate for #2 pers: $15; Rate for #3 pers: $15; Child Rate: Negotiated

Main amenities available: Swimming; Volleyball; Basketball; Tennis; Sauna; Hot tub
Meals are served in dining room for transients only when other groups are present. Approx. dinner price: $6.00.

113

MISSISSIPPI

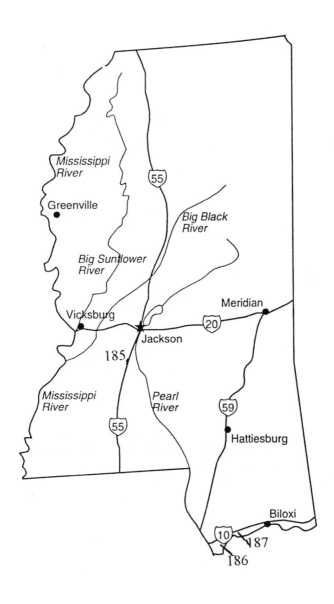

NAME OF CENTER: Timber Bay Camp & Retreat Center   Listing ID #: 184

Telephone: 320-532-3200; Fax: 320-532-3199; E-mail: markritchie@timberbay.org
Address: 18955 Woodland Rd; Onamia; MN; 56359
Nearest Interstate: I-94, Exit Rte 60 N; 18 miles; Nearest State/US Hwy: Rte 169; 7 miles.

Restrictions: Age: None; Pets: Not permitted; Alcohol: Not permitted; Smoking: Outdoors only; Reservation Req'd: 3 wks; Max. Adv. Reser.: Open; Seasonal closing: None

RV/Campers overnight hookups: Yes; Water: No; Electric: Yes; Septic: n/a
Basic Rate/Night: $25.00/ veh

ACCOM: Mon. night thru Thurs. night rates for winterized (check if this is critical) rooms w/o meals unless otherwise indicated.

Motel; Max. Pers: 4; Bedding incl ?: No; Bath: Private; A/C: No:
Rate for: Person; $20; Rate for #2 pers: $10; Rate for #3 pers: $10; Child Rate: Free under 3 yrs

Main amenities available: Swimming; Volleyball; Basketball; Ping pong; Boat/canoe; Hiking
Meals are served in dining room for transients only when other groups are present. Approx. dinner price: $4-7.00.

NAME OF CENTER: Camp Wesley Pines   Listing ID #: 185

Telephone: 601-892-2341; Fax: 601-892-2341; E-mail: wpines7944@aol.com
Address: Wesley Pines Rd (mail PO Box 307); Gallman; MS; 39077
Nearest Interstate: I-55, Exit 55; 1 miles.

Restrictions: Age: None; Pets: Not permitted; Alcohol: Not permitted; Smoking: Outdoors only; Reservation Req'd: None; Max. Adv. Reser.: 1 yr; Seasonal closing: None

RV/Campers overnight hookups: No

ACCOM: Mon. night thru Thurs. night rates for winterized (check if this is critical) rooms w/o meals unless otherwise indicated.

Motel; Max. Pers: 4; Bedding incl ?: $5 surcharge; Bath: Private; A/C: Yes:
Rate for: Person; ** $39; Rate for #2 pers: ** $33; Rate for #3 pers: ** $27; Child Rate: n/a
** Includes 3 meals.

Guest Hse; Max. Pers: 8; Bedding incl ?: $5 surcharge; Bath: Semi-private; A/C: Yes
Rate for: Person: $33; Rate for #2 pers: $0; Rate for #3 pers: $8; Child Rate: n/a
Each additional person $8.

Main amenities available: Swimming; Volleyball; Basketball; Canoeing; Horse shoes; Hiking
Meals are served in dining room for transients only when other groups are present. Approx. dinner price: Varies.

NAME OF CENTER: Gulfside Assembly   Listing ID #: 186

Telephone: 228-467-4909; Fax: 228-467-4909; E-mail:
Address: 950 S. Beach Blvd.; Waveland; MS; 39576
Nearest Interstate: I-10, Exit 13; 4 miles.

Restrictions: Age: One member of gp must be at least 55 yrs.; Pets: Not permitted; Alcohol: Not permitted; Smoking: Designated outdoor area; Reservation Req'd: 3 mos advised; Max. Adv. Reser.: 1 yr; Seasonal closing: None

RV/Campers overnight hookups: No; Water: n/a; Electric: n/a; Septic: n/a
Basic Rate/Night: n/a/ veh

ACCOM: Mon. night thru Thurs. night rates for winterized (check if this is critical) rooms w/o meals unless otherwise indicated.

Cabins; Max. Pers: 8; Bedding incl ?: Yes; Bath: Semi-private; A/C: Yes:
Rate for: Person; $40; Rate for #2 pers: $10; Rate for #3 pers: $10; Child Rate: n/a
Cabin includes: Kitchenette; 2 bedrooms w 2 double beds each; located on Gulf

Main amenities available: Swimming in Gulf; Volleyball; Basketball; Tennis; Hiking
Meals are served in dining room for transients only when other groups are present. Approx. dinner price: $7.00.

NAME OF CENTER: St. Augustine Retreat Center   Listing ID #: 187

Telephone: 228-467-9837; Fax: 228-466-4393; E-mail:
Address: 199 Seminary Dr.; Bay St. Louis; MS; 39520
Nearest Interstate: I-10, Exit 2W; 5 miles.

Restrictions: Age: 13; Pets: Not permitted; Alcohol: Not permitted; Smoking: Outdoors only; Reservation Req'd: 2 mo; Max. Adv. Reser.: 6 mo; Seasonal closing: None

RV/Campers overnight hookups: No

ACCOM: Mon. night thru Thurs. night rates for winterized (check if this is critical) rooms w/o meals unless otherwise indicated.

Motel; Max. Pers: 5; Bedding incl ?: Yes; Bath: Private; A/C: Yes:
Rate for: Person; $20; Rate for #2 pers: $20; Rate for #3 pers: $20; Child Rate: n/a

Main amenities available: Library; TV-VCR; Ball field; Quiet area; Chapel
Meals are served in dining room for transients only when other groups are present. Approx. dinner price: $5.00.

MISSOURI

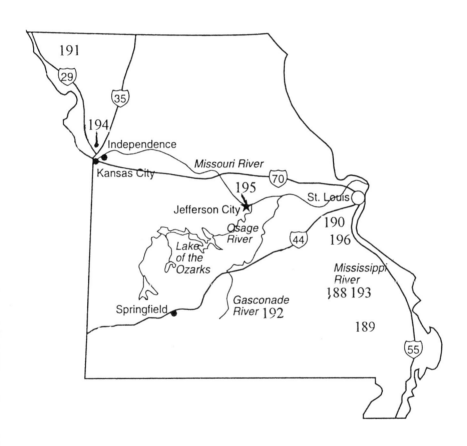

191

(29)

(35)

194

Independence

Kansas City

Missouri River

(70)

195

St. Louis

Jefferson City

Osage River

190

196

Lake of the Ozarks

(44)

Mississippi River

188 193

Springfield

Gasconade River 192

189

(55)

NAME OF CENTER: Blue Mountain   Listing ID #: 188

Telephone: 573-546-2923; Fax: 573-546-6574; E-mail: www.gbgm.umc.org/ep.blue
Address: Box 118; Arcadia; MO; 63621
Nearest Interstate: I-67, Exit 13 miles; Nearest State/US Hwy: MO 72; 1 miles.

Restrictions: Age: None; Pets: Permitted w/adv notice; Alcohol: Not permitted; Smoking: Nowhere; Reservation Req'd: 1 day; Max. Adv. Reser.: 1 yr; Seasonal closing: None

RV/Campers overnight hookups: Yes; Water: Yes; Electric: Yes; Septic: No
Basic Rate/Night: $10.00/ veh

ACCOM: Mon. night thru Thurs. night rates for winterized (check if this is critical) rooms w/o meals unless otherwise indicated.

Half cabin; Max. Pers: 8; Bedding incl ?: No; Bath: Shared; A/C: Y/N:
Rate for: Person; $10; Rate for #2 pers: $10; Rate for #3 pers: $10; Child Rate: n/a
Min: $30; Includes kitchenette

Main amenities available: Swimm in 500 acre lake; Volleyball; Basketball; VCR-TV ($5); Canoeing; Hiking
Meals are served in dining room for transients only when other groups are present. Approx. dinner price: $5.00.

NAME OF CENTER: Camp Allen   Listing ID #: 189

Telephone: 573-224-3826; Fax: ; E-mail:
Address: Rte #1; Box 45; Greenville; MO; 63944
Nearest Interstate: I-55, Exit 60 miles; Nearest State/US Hwy: Rte 67; 3 miles.

Restrictions: Age: None; Pets: Not permitted; Alcohol: Not permitted; Smoking: Outdoors only; Reservation Req'd: None; Max. Adv. Reser.: Open; Seasonal closing: RV camp open summers only.

RV/Campers overnight hookups: Yes; Water: Yes; Electric: Yes; Septic: No
Basic Rate/Night:$10/ veh

ACCOM: Mon. night thru Thurs. night rates for winterized (check if this is critical) rooms w/o meals unless otherwise indicated.

Motel; Max. Pers: 4; Bedding incl ?: Yes; Bath: Private; A/C: Yes
Rate for: Room: $25; Child Rate: n/a

Main amenities available: Waterslides; VCR-TV; Bookstore; Ball field
Meals are served in dining room for transients only when other groups are present. Approx. dinner price: Price varies.

118

NAME OF CENTER: Camp Mihaska   Listing ID #: 190

Telephone: 573-732-5239; Fax: 573-732-5027; E-mail: mihaska@fidnet.com
Address: SR N, Box 23; Bourbon; MO; 65441
Nearest Interstate: I-44, Exit 3 miles.

Restrictions: Age: None; Pets: Permitted in RV area; Alcohol: Not permitted; Smoking: Outdoors only; Reservation Req'd: None; Max. Adv. Reser.: Open; Seasonal closing: None

RV/Campers overnight hookups: Yes; Water: Yes; Electric: Yes; Septic: No
Basic Rate/Night: $10 w A/C $15/ veh

ACCOM: Mon. night thru Thurs. night rates for winterized (check if this is critical) rooms w/o meals unless otherwise indicated.

Bunkroom; Max. Pers: Over 5; Bedding incl ?: Yes; Bath: Shared; A/C: Yes:
Rate for: Person; $12; Rate for #2 pers: $12; Rate for #3 pers: $12; Child Rate: Youth $9; child $0

Main amenities available: Hiking
Meals are not served in dining room for transients .

NAME OF CENTER: Conception Abbey   Listing ID #: 191

Telephone: 660-944-2809; Fax: 660-944-2885; E-mail:
Address: Abbey Ctr for Prayer & Ministry; Concep. Abbey; Conception; MO; 64433
Nearest Interstate: I-35, Exit 60 miles; Nearest State/US Hwy: US 136; 0 miles.

Restrictions: Age: None; Pets: Not permitted; Alcohol: Not permitted; Smoking: Designated outdoor area; Reservation Req'd: 1 day; Max. Adv. Reser.: 6 mo; Seasonal closing: None

RV/Campers overnight hookups: No

ACCOM: Mon. night thru Thurs. night rates for winterized (check if this is critical) rooms w/o meals unless otherwise indicated.

Motel; Max. Pers: 2; Bedding incl ?: Yes; Bath: Semi-private; A/C: Yes:
Rate for: Person; $20; Rate for #2 pers: $14; Child Rate: Negotiable at time of reservation

Main amenities available: Quiet areas; Abbey chapel; Basketball
Meals are served in dining room for transients only when other groups are present. Approx. dinner price: $4.90
"All you can eat, home baked bread".

REMEMBER TO CALL AHEAD

NAME OF CENTER: Discovery Ministries   Listing ID #: 192

Telephone: 573-226-3213; Fax: ; E-mail:
Address: HCR 3; Box 32; Eminence; MO; 65466
Nearest Interstate: I-44, Exit US 63; 75 miles; Nearest State/US Hwy: Rte 106; 3 miles.

Restrictions: Age: None; Pets: Permitted on leash; Alcohol: Not permitted; Smoking: Outdoors only; Reservation Req'd: Rec. 10 days; Max. Adv. Reser.: Open; Seasonal closing: None

RV/Campers overnight hookups: Yes; Water: Yes; Electric: Yes; Septic: Yes
Basic Rate/Night: **$3/pers ($10 max)/ veh
** RV hookups w/water & elec add $4; plus A/C add $2; plus sewer add $6

ACCOM: Mon. night thru Thurs. night rates for winterized (check if this is critical) rooms w/o meals unless otherwise indicated.

Motel; Max. Pers: 7; Bedding incl ?: No; Bath: Shared; A/C: No:
Rate for: Person; $21; Rate for #2 pers: $3; Rate for #3 pers: $3; Child Rate: n/a

Cabin; Max. Pers: 10; Bedding incl ?: No; Bath: Shared; A/C: Yes
Rate for: Person: $31; Rate for #2 pers: $3; Rate for #3 pers: $3; Child Rate: n/a
Includes: Living area; microware; refrig.

Main amenities available: Swimming pool; V-ball; Bsk ball; Laundry machine; Horse shoes; Children's playground; VCR-TV
Meals are served in dining room for transients only when other groups are present, if OK w/them. Approx. dinner price: $5.00.

NAME OF CENTER: Epworth Among the Hills   Listing ID #: 193

Telephone: 573-546-2923; Fax: 573-546-6574; E-mail: www.gbgm.umc.org/ep.blue
Address: Box 118; Arcadia; MO; 63621
Nearest Interstate: I-67, Exit 20 miles; Nearest State/US Hwy: MO 72; 1 miles.

Restrictions: Age: None; Pets: Permitted w/adv notice; Alcohol: Not permitted; Smoking: Nowhere; Reservation Req'd: 1 day; Max. Adv. Reser.: 1 yr; Seasonal closing: None

RV/Campers overnight hookups: No

ACCOM: Mon. night thru Thurs. night rates for winterized (check if this is critical) rooms w/o meals unless otherwise indicated.

Half cabin; Max. Pers: 8; Bedding incl ?: No; Bath: Shared; A/C: No:
Rate for: Person; $10; Rate for #2 pers: $10; Rate for #3 pers: $10; Child Rate: n/a
Min: $30; Includes: kitchenette

Dorm "Rustic"; Max. Pers: 2; Bedding incl ?: No; Bath: Shared; A/C: No
Rate for: Person: $10; Rate for #2 pers: $10; Child Rate: n/a

Main amenities available: Pool; V-ball; Bsk ball; VCR-TV ($5); Ball field; Hiking
Meals are served in dining room for transients only when other groups are present. Approx. dinner price: $5.00.

NAME OF CENTER: New Hope Baptist Camp & Retreat Ctr Listing ID #: 194

Telephone: 816-320-3515; Fax: ; E-mail:
Address: 21209 NE 188 St.; Holt; MO; 64048
Nearest Interstate: I-35, Exit 33; 2 miles; Nearest State/US Hwy: Rte 33; 2 miles.

Restrictions: Age: None; Pets: Not permitted; Alcohol: Not permitted; Smoking: Outdoors only; Reservation Req'd: None; Max. Adv. Reser.: 3 wks; Seasonal closing: None

RV/Campers overnight hookups: Yes; Water: No; Electric: Yes; Septic: No
Basic Rate/Night: Unk at this time

ACCOM: Mon. night thru Thurs. night rates for winterized (check if this is critical) rooms w/o meals unless otherwise indicated.

Bunkroom; Max. Pers: 10; Bedding incl ?: No; Bath: Shared; A/C: Yes:
Rate for: Person; $12; Rate for #2 pers: $12; Rate for #3 pers: $12; Child Rate: n/a
Individual rates apply Sept - Apr; At other times $144 min. fee

Guest Hse; Max. Pers: 12; Bedding incl ?: No; Bath: Shared; A/C: No
Rate for: Person: $10; Rate for #2 pers: $10; Rate for #3 pers: $10; Child Rate: n/a

Main amenities available: Swimming; V-ball; Bsk ball; Basketball; Incidentals store; Bookstore; Hiking
Meals are served in dining room for transients only when other groups are present. Approx. dinner price: $5.00.

NAME OF CENTER: **The Rickman Center** Listing ID #: 195

Telephone: 563-635-0848; Fax: 573-635-0591; E-mail:
Address: 3519 Bennett Lane; Jefferson City; MO; 65110
Nearest Interstate: I-70, Exit 30 miles; Nearest State/US Hwy: MO 54; 0 miles.

Restrictions: Age: None; Pets: Not permitted; Alcohol: Not permitted; Smoking: Outdoors only; Reservation Req'd: 1 day; Max. Adv. Reser.: 1 mo; Seasonal closing: None

RV/Campers overnight hookups: Yes; Water: Yes; Electric: Yes; Septic: No
Basic Rate/Night: $10.00/ veh

ACCOM. Mon. night thru Thurs. night rates for winterized (check if this is critical) rooms w/o meals unless otherwise indicated.

Bunkroom; Max. Pers: 10; Bedding incl ?: $4 surcharge; Bath: Shared; A/C: Yes:
Rate for: Person; $11; Rate for #2 pers: $11; Rate for #3 pers: $11; Child Rate: n/a

Cottage; Max. Pers: 4; Bedding incl ?: Yes; Bath: Semi-private; A/C: Yes
Rate for: Person: ** 20; Rate for #2 pers: $20; Rate for #3 pers: $20; Child Rate: n/a
Min: $28; Two bedrooms; one bath

Motel; Max. Pers: 5; Bedding incl ?: Yes; Bath: Private; A/C: Yes:
Rate for: Person: ** $20; Rate for #2 pers: $20; Rate for #3 pers: $20; Child Rate: n/a
Min: $28 (Crib $5)

Main amenities available: Swimming; Volleyball; VCR-TV; Basketball; Children's playground; Hiking
Meals are served in dining room for transients only when other groups are present. Approx. dinner price: $9.25; 50% off under 12 yrs; free under 3.

NAME OF CENTER: YMCA of the Ozarks   Listing ID #: 196

Telephone: 573-438-2154; Fax: 573-438-5752; E-mail: www.ymcastlouis.org
Address: Rte 2; Box 240; Potosi; MO; 63664
Nearest Interstate: I-44, Exit 60 miles.

Restrictions: Age: None; Pets: Not permitted; Alcohol: Not permitted; Smoking: Nowhere; Reservation Req'd: Open w/dep; Max. Adv. Reser.: Over 1 yr; Seasonal closing: None

RV/Campers overnight hookups: No

ACCOM: Mon. night thru Thurs. night rates for winterized (check if this is critical) rooms w/o meals unless otherwise indicated.

Hotel; Max. Pers: Over 4; Bedding incl ?: Yes; Bath: Private; A/C: Yes:
Rate for: Person; **$88-116; Rate for #2 pers: $38-52; Rate for #3 pers: $33-42; Child Rate: $38 under 17 yrs; Free under 14 (excl. holidays)
** Rates include 3 meals. Rates vary w/season

Main amenities available: Virtually everything; 4800 acres; Basketball; Tennis; Sailing; Canoeing
Meals are served in dining room for transients . Approx. dinner price: Wide range.

MONTANA

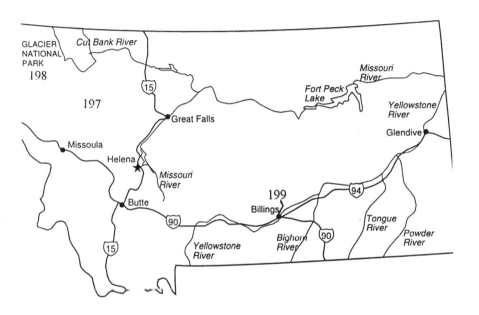

GLACIER
NATIONAL
PARK
198

Cut Bank River

197

15

Missoula

Helena

★

Butte

90

15

Great Falls

Missouri
River

Yellowstone
River

Missouri
River

Fort Peck
Lake

Yellowstone
River

Glendive

199

Billings

94

90

Tongue
River

Bighorn
River

Powder
River

NAME OF CENTER: Diamond Bar X Christian Guest Ranch   Listing ID #: 197

Telephone: 888-903-2279; Fax: 406-562-3503; E-mail: dbarx@dbarx.com
Address: PO Box 529; Augusta; MT; 59410
Nearest Interstate: I-15, Exit 34 miles; Nearest State/US Hwy: Rte 200; 14 miles.

Restrictions: Age: None; Pets: Permitted; Alcohol: Not permitted; Smoking: Not permitted in bedroom; Reservation Req'd: Open; Max. Adv. Reser.: Open; Seasonal closing: None

RV/Campers overnight hookups: Yes; Water: unk; Electric: unk; Septic: unk
Basic Rate/Night: $15.00/ veh

ACCOM: Mon. night thru Thurs. night rates for winterized (check if this is critical) rooms w/o meals unless otherwise indicated.

Bunkroom; Max. Pers: 22; Bedding incl ?: Yes (w/notice); Bath: Shared; A/C: No:
Rate for: Person; ** $25; Rate for #2 pers: $25; Rate for #3 pers: $25; Child Rate: $12.50 under 8 yrs; free under 4
** Room fee includes 3 meals

Dormitory; Max. Pers: 4; Bedding incl ?: Yes (w/notice); Bath: Shared; A/C: No
Rate for: Person: ** $30; Rate for #2 pers: $30; Rate for #3 pers: $30; Child Rate: $12.50 under 8 yrs; free under 4
** Room fee includes 3 meals

Motel; Max. Pers: 10; Bedding incl ?: Yes (w/notice); Bath: Private; A/C: No:
Rate for: Person: ** $40; Rate for #2 pers: $40; Rate for #3 pers: $40; Child Rate: $17.50 under 8 yrs; free under 4
** room fee includes 3 meals

Main amenities available: Library; Volleyball; Climbing wall; Ropes course; Horseback riding; Hiking
Meals are served in dining room for transients . Approx. dinner price: $5-7.00.

NAME OF CENTER: Flathead Lake UMC Camp   Listing ID #: 198

Telephone: 406-844-3483; Fax: ; E-mail: camp@digisys.net
Address: PO Box 88; Rollins; MT; 59931
Nearest State/US Hwy: Rte 93; 1 miles.

Restrictions: Age: None; Pets: Not permitted; Alcohol: Not permitted; Smoking: Designated outdoor area; Reservation Req'd: 1 mo; Max. Adv. Reser.: Open; Seasonal closing: None

RV/Campers overnight hookups: Yes; Water: Yes; Electric: Yes; Septic: unk
Basic Rate/Night: $12.00/ veh

ACCOM: Mon. night thru Thurs. night rates for winterized (check if this is critical) rooms w/o meals unless otherwise indicated.

Bunkroom; Max. Pers: Over 5; Bedding incl ?: No; Bath: Shared; A/C: No:
Rate for: Person; $13; Rate for #2 pers: $13; Rate for #3 pers: $13; Child Rate: n/a

Dormitory; Max. Pers: 5; Bedding incl ?: No; Bath: Shared; A/C: No
Rate for: Person: $13; Rate for #2 pers: $13; Rate for #3 pers: $13; Child Rate: n/a

Motel; Max. Pers: 5; Bedding incl ?: No; Bath: Private; A/C: No:
Rate for: Person: $15; Rate for #2 pers: $15; Rate for #3 pers: $15; Child Rate: n/a

Main amenities available: Lake swimming; V-ball; Bsk-ball; Fishing; Incidentals store; Ping pong; Chapel
Meals are served in dining room for transients only when other groups are present. Approx. dinner price: $5-7.00.

NAME OF CENTER: **Sacred Heart Renewal Center**   Listing ID #: 199

Telephone: 406-252-0322; Fax: ; E-mail:
Address: 26 Wyoming Ave.; Billings; MT; 59101
Nearest Interstate: I-90, Exit; 3 miles.

Restrictions: Age: None; Pets: Not permitted; Alcohol: Not permitted; Smoking: Outdoors only;
Reservation Req'd: 2 days; Max. Adv. Reser.: 2 mo; Seasonal closing: Christmas wk & Easter
wk

RV/Campers overnight hookups: No

ACCOM: Mon. night thru Thurs. night rates for winterized (check if this is critical) rooms w/o
meals unless otherwise indicated.

Dormitory; Max. Pers: 2; Bedding incl ?: Yes; Bath: Shared; A/C: No;
Rate for: Person; $15; Rate for #2 pers: $7;   Child Rate: n/a

Motel; Max. Pers: 2; Bedding incl ?: Yes; Bath: Private; A/C: No
Rate for: Person: $20; Rate for #2 pers: $7; Child Rate: n/a

Main amenities available: Library; Quiet area; Laundry machine; Kitchen available
Meals are not served in dining room for transients .

NEBRASKA

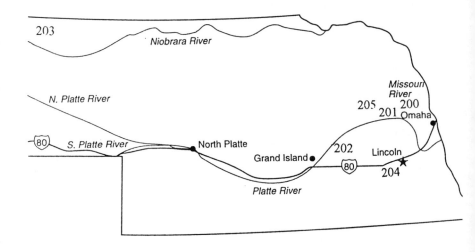

203

Niobrara River

N. Platte River

Missouri
River
205 201 200
Omaha

(80) S. Platte River

North Platte

Grand Island

202

(80)

Lincoln

204

Platte River

126

NAME OF CENTER: Calvin Crest Camp/Conf & Ret. Ctr.   Listing ID #: 200

Telephone: 402-628-6455; Fax: 402-628-8255; E-mail: calvin_crest@navix.net
Address: 2870 County Rd. 13; Fremont; NE; 68025
Nearest Interstate: I-80, Exit 45 miles; Nearest State/US Hwy: Rte 77; 3 miles.

Restrictions: Age: None; Pets: Not permitted; Alcohol: Not permitted; Smoking: Outdoors only; Reservation Req'd: 2 days; Max. Adv. Reser.: Open; Seasonal closing: None

RV/Campers overnight hookups: Yes; Water: Yes; Electric: unk; Septic: unk
Basic Rate/Night: $12.00/ veh

ACCOM: Mon. night thru Thurs. night rates for winterized (check if this is critical) rooms w/o meals unless otherwise indicated.

Bunkroom; Max. Pers: 16; Bedding incl ?: No; Bath: Shared; A/C: No:
Rate for: Person; $15; Rate for #2 pers: $15; Rate for #3 pers: $15; Child Rate: $26

Dormitory; Max. Pers: 4; Bedding incl ?: Yes; Bath: Shared; A/C: Yes
Rate for: Person: $22; Rate for #2 pers: $22; Rate for #3 pers: $22; Child Rate: $26

Motel; Max. Pers: 4; Bedding incl ?: Yes; Bath: Private; A/C: Yes:
Rate for: Person: $26; Rate for #2 pers: $26; Rate for #3 pers: $26; Child Rate: $26

Main amenities available: Swimming; Volleyball; Basketball
Meals are served in dining room for transients only when other groups are present. Approx. dinner price: $6.00.

NAME OF CENTER: Camp Moses Merrill   Listing ID #: 201

Telephone: 402-666-5639; Fax: 402-556-1910; E-mail:
Address: Rte #1; Box 170A; Linwood; NE; 68036
Nearest Interstate: I-80, Exit 50 miles; Nearest State/US Hwy: Rte 79; 6 miles.

Restrictions: Age: None; Pets: Not permitted; Alcohol: Not permitted; Smoking: Designated outdoor area; Reservation Req'd: 14 days (cabins & house); Max. Adv. Reser.: 1 yr; Seasonal closing: June 1 - July 31 (cabins & house)

RV/Campers overnight hookups: Yes; Water: Yes; Electric: Yes; Septic: Yes
Basic Rate/Night: $11.00/ veh

ACCOM: Mon. night thru Thurs. night rates for winterized (check if this is critical) rooms w/o meals unless otherwise indicated.

Cabin; Max. Pers: 10; Bedding incl ?: No; Bath: Shared; A/C: No:
Rate for: Person; $20; Rate for #2 pers: $20; Rate for #3 pers: $20; Child Rate: n/a

House; Max. Pers: 12; Bedding incl ?: No; Bath: Semi-private; A/C: No
Rate for: Entire House: $60
Includes kitchen, living room, dining roon, 2 baths

Main amenities available: Swimming pool; Basketball; Laundry machine; Ping-pong; Horseback riding; Hiking
Meals are served in dining room for transients only when other groups are present. Approx. dinner price: $5.00; 5 days advanced notice req'd.

NAME OF CENTER: **Covenant Cedars Camp & Conf. Ctr**   Listing ID #: 202

Telephone: 402-757-3241; Fax: 402-757-3250; E-mail: cedars@hamilton.net
Address: PO Box 68; Hordville; NE; 68846
Nearest Interstate: I-80, Exit 20 miles.

Restrictions: Age: None; Pets: Not permitted; Alcohol: Not permitted; Smoking: Outdoors only;
Reservation Req'd: 7 days; Max. Adv. Reser.: Open; Seasonal closing: None

RV/Campers overnight hookups: Yes; Water: Yes; Electric: Yes; Septic: n/a
Basic Rate/Night: $13.00/ veh

ACCOM: Mon. night thru Thurs. night rates for winterized (check if this is critical) rooms w/o
meals unless otherwise indicated.

Motel; Max. Pers: 4; Bedding incl ?: Yes; Bath: Private; A/C: Yes:
Rate for: Person; $45; Rate for #2 pers: $10; Rate for #3 pers: $10; Child Rate: n/a

Main amenities available: Swimming; V-ball; Bsk-ball; Boat/Canoe; Ping pong; Bookstore; Hiking
Meals are served in dining room for transients only when other groups are present. Approx. dinner price:
$4-6.00.

NAME OF CENTER: **Norwesca Camp & Retreat Ctr.**   Listing ID #: 203

Telephone: 308-478-3872; Fax: ; E-mail:
Address: 77 Camp Norwesca Rd.; Chadron; NE; 69337
Nearest Interstate: I-80, Exit 110 miles; Nearest State/US Hwy: US 20; 1 miles.

Restrictions: Age: None; Pets: Not permitted; Alcohol: Not permitted; Smoking: Designated
outdoor area; Reservation Req'd: 7 days; Max. Adv. Reser.: 1 yr; Seasonal closing: None

RV/Campers overnight hookups: Yes; Water: Yes; Electric: Yes; Septic: No
Basic Rate/Night: $8.50/ veh

ACCOM: Mon. night thru Thurs. night rates for winterized (check if this is critical) rooms w/o
meals unless otherwise indicated.

Cabin; Max. Pers: 13; Bedding incl ?: No; Bath: Separate bldg; A/C: No:
Rate for: Person; $9; Rate for #2 pers: $9; Rate for #3 pers: $9; Child Rate: n/a
Summer only

Motel; Max. Pers: 2; Bedding incl ?: Yes; Bath: Semi-private; A/C: No
Rate for: Person: $19; Rate for #2 pers: $19; Child Rate: n/a
Roll-away bed - $3.

Main amenities available: Swimming; Volleyball; Basketball; Fishing; Horseback riding
Meals are served in dining room for transients only when other groups are present. Dinner price: Varies.

NAME OF CENTER: Riverside Camp & Retreat Center   Listing ID #: 204

Telephone: 402-761-2406; Fax: 402-761-3784; E-mail:
Address: 717 238th Rd; Milford; NE; 68405
Nearest Interstate: I-80, Exit 2 miles.

Restrictions: Age: None; Pets: Permitted on leash; Alcohol: Not permitted; Smoking: Outdoors only; Reservation Req'd: 1 day; Max. Adv. Reser.: 14 days; Seasonal closing: None

RV/Campers overnight hookups: Yes; Water: Yes; Electric: Yes; Septic: No
Basic Rate/Night: $15.00/ veh

ACCOM: Mon. night thru Thurs. night rates for winterized (check if this is critical) rooms w/o meals unless otherwise indicated.

Guest Hse; Max. Pers: 2; Bedding incl ?: No; Bath: Shared; A/C: No:
Rate for: Room; $10; Rate for #2 pers: n/a; Child Rate: n/a
Available May - Oct.

Main amenities available: Swimming (1 mile); Volleyball; Basketball; VCR-TV; Hiking
Meals are served in dining room for transients only when other groups are present. Dinner price: $6-7.00 (call ahead).

NAME OF CENTER: St. Benedict Center   Listing ID #: 205

Telephone: 402-352-8819; Fax: 402-352-8884; E-mail: benedict.center@navix.net
Address: PO Box 528; Schuyler; NE; 68661
Nearest Interstate: I-80, Exit 15 miles.

Restrictions: Age: 12; Pets: Not permitted; Alcohol: Beer & wine w/permission; Smoking: Outdoors only; Reservation Req'd: None; Max. Adv. Reser.: Open; Seasonal closing: None

RV/Campers overnight hookups: No

ACCOM: Mon. night thru Thurs. night rates for winterized (check if this is critical) rooms w/o meals unless otherwise indicated.

Motel; Max. Pers: 2; Bedding incl ?: Yes; Bath: Private; A/C: Yes:
Rate for: Person; $21; Rate for #2 pers: $21; Child Rate: n/a
Requested to strip beds and fold blankets.

Main amenities available: Volleyball; Basketball; Hiking
Meals are served in dining room for transients only when other groups are present. Dinner price: Varies.

NAME OF CENTER: YMCA - Omaha Listing ID: 206

Telephone: 402-341-1600   Fax: 402-341-8214
Address: 430 S. 20th St.; Omaha, NE 68102

Restrictions:
Accommodations offered to (M/F/Families): M/F. If M/F then must be over 19 yrs.
Pets: Not permitted; Alcohol: Not permitted; Smoking: Outdoors only
Reservation requirements: None
Reservations are accepted up to 0 days in advance. Seasonal closing: None

ACCOMMODATIONS:
Single room: Bedding included ?: Yes; Bath: Shared
Rate for 1 day: $11+$10 dep; Rate for 1 week: $69+$10 dep
Membership in Y at $5/day

Single room: Bedding included ?: Yes; Bath: Private
Rate for 1 day: $12+$10 dep; Rate for 1 week: $78+$10 dep
Membership in Y at $5/day

Main amenities: Laundry across st.; Pool; Gym
Meals are not offered in their own cafeteria.

NEVADA

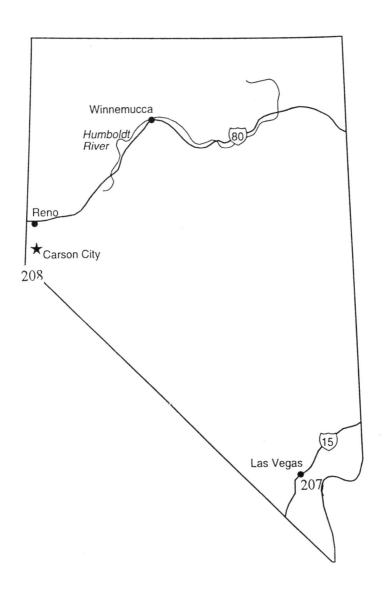

NAME OF CENTER: Wellspring Retreat House   Listing ID #: 207

Telephone: 702-293-4988; Fax: 702-293-7208; E-mail:
Address: 701 Park Pl.; PO Box 60818; Boulder City; NV; 89006
Nearest Interstate: I- 15, Exit 6 miles.

Restrictions: Age: 21; Pets: Not permitted; Alcohol: Not permitted; Smoking: Designated outdoor area; Reservation Req'd: 7 days; Max. Adv. Reser.: 1 mo; Seasonal closing: July-Aug.; Christmas wk & wk after

RV/Campers overnight hookups: No

ACCOM: Mon. night thru Thurs. night rates for winterized (check if this is critical) rooms w/o meals unless otherwise indicated.

Dormitory; Max. Pers: 4; Bedding incl ?: Yes; Bath: Shared; A/C: Yes:
Rate for: Room; ** $55; Rate for #2 pers: n/a; Rate for #3 pers: n/a; Child Rate: n/a
** Includes breakfast

Main amenities available: Library; Bookstore; Basketball; Hiking
Meals are not served in dining room for transients .
Restaurants within easy walk.

NAME OF CENTER: Zephyr Point Presbyterian Conf. Ctr.   Listing ID #: 208

Telephone: 702-588-6759; Fax: 702-588-1095; E-mail: zpoint@aol.com
Address: 660 Hwy 50; PO Box 289; Zephyr Cove; NV; 89448
Nearest Interstate: I- 80 , Exit 0 miles; Nearest State/US Hwy: Rte 50; 0 miles.

LOCATED ON LAKE TAHOE

Restrictions: Age: None; Pets: Not permitted; Alcohol: Not permitted in public places; Smoking: Designated outdoor area; Reservation Req'd: 1 day; Max. Adv. Reser.: Open; Seasonal closing: None

RV/Campers overnight hookups: No

ACCOM: Mon. night thru Thurs. night rates for winterized (check if this is critical) rooms w/o meals unless otherwise indicated.

Motel; Max. Pers: 3; Bedding incl ?: Yes; Bath: Private; A/C: Yes:
Rate for: Person; $56; Rate for #2 pers: $0; Rate for #3 pers: $6; Child Rate: n/a

Main amenities available: Swim in Lake Tahoe; Volleyball; Horse shoes; Hike Tahoe shores; Indoor games
Meals are served in dining room for transients only when other groups are present. Dinner price: $7.50.

REMEMBER TO CALL AHEAD

NEW HAMPSHIRE

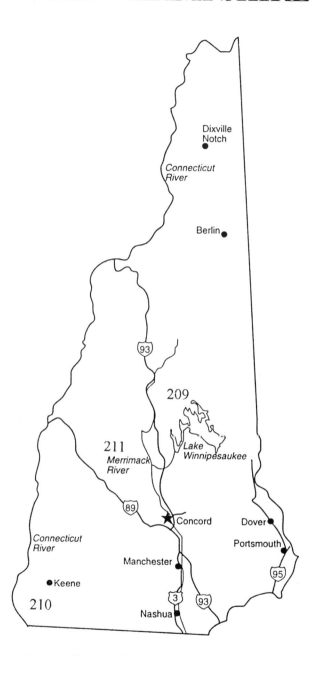

Dixville
Notch
●

*Connecticut
River*

Berlin ●

93

209

211
*Merrimack
River*

Lake
Winnipesaukee

89

★ Concord

Dover ●

Portsmouth ●

*Connecticut
River*

Manchester ●

95

● Keene

210

3   93

Nashua ●

NAME OF CENTER: Geneva Point Center   Listing ID #: 209

Telephone: 603-253-4366; Fax: 603-253-4883; E-mail: geneva@genevapoint.org
Address: HC 62; Box 469; Center Harbor; NH; 03226
Nearest Interstate: I-93, Exit 18 miles; Nearest State/US Hwy: Rte 25; 6 miles.

Restrictions: Age: None; Pets: Not permitted; Alcohol: Permitted in room; Smoking: Not permitted in bedroom; Reservation Req'd: 1 day; Max. Adv. Reser.: 5 mo; Seasonal closing: Oct 15 - May 15

RV/Campers overnight hookups: Yes; Water: unk; Electric: unk; Septic: unk
Basic Rate/Night: *** $14/ veh

ACCOM: Mon. night thru Thurs. night rates for winterized (check if this is critical) rooms w/o meals unless otherwise indicated.

Motel; Max. Pers: 5; Bedding incl ?: $5 surcharge; Bath: Private; A/C: No:
Rate for: Person; ** $90; Rate for #2 pers: ** $58; Rate for #3 pers: ** $59; Child Rate: $27-35 under 16 yrs; $21-27 under 9; free under 3
** Inclues 3 meals/day, only breakfast on day of departure*** Must take meals at GPC

Bunkroom; Max. Pers: Over 5; Bedding incl ?: $5 surcharge; Bath: Shared; A/C: No
Rate for: Person: ** $51; Rate for #2 pers: ** $37; Rate for #3 pers: ** $38; Child Rate: $27-35 under 16 yrs; $21-27 under 9; free under 3

Main amenities available: Volleyball; Basketball; Hiking
Meals are served in dining room for transients only when other groups are present. Dinner price: Varies.

NAME OF CENTER: Pilgrim Pines Conference Center   Listing ID #: 210

Telephone: 603-352-0443; Fax: 603-357-7660; E-mail: info@pilgrimpines.org
Address: PO Box 40; West Swanzey; NH; 03469
Nearest Interstate: I-91, Exit 30 miles; Nearest State/US Hwy: Rte 10/32; 4 miles.

Restrictions: Age: None; Pets: Not permitted; Alcohol: Not permitted; Smoking: Outdoors only; Reservation Req'd: None; Max. Adv. Reser.: Open; Seasonal closing: None

RV/Campers overnight hookups: Yes; Water: Yes; Electric: Yes; Septic: No
Basic Rate/Night: $25-30/ veh

ACCOM: Mon. night thru Thurs. night rates for winterized (check if this is critical) rooms w/o meals unless otherwise indicated.

Motel; Max. Pers: 4; Bedding incl ?: **$5 surcharge; Bath: Private; A/C: No:
Rate for: Person; $35; Rate for #2 pers: $5; Rate for #3 pers: $5; Child Rate: 50% off under 13 yrs; free under 4
** Adv. notice req'd

Dorm; Max. Pers: 4; Bedding incl ?: ** $5 surcharge; Bath: Shared/semi-private; A/C: No
Rate for: Person: ** $30; Rate for #2 pers: $5; Rate for #3 pers: $5; Child Rate: 50% off under 13 yrs; free under 4
** Adv. notice reqd

Main amenities available: Swimming; V-ball; Bsk ball; Tennis; Boat/canoeing; Ping-pong; Hiking
Meals are served in dining room for transients only when other groups are present. Dinner price: $10.00.

NAME OF CENTER: **Wilmot Center**   Listing ID #: 211

Telephone: 603-526-6392; Fax: 603-768-3409; E-mail:
Address: RD #1; Box 158; N. Wilmot Rd.; Danbury; NH; 03230
Nearest Interstate: I-89, Exit 20 miles.

Restrictions: Age: None; Pets: Permitted; Alcohol: Not permitted; Smoking: Designated
outdoor area; Reservation Req'd: 7 days; Max. Adv. Reser.: 1 mo; Seasonal closing: Cabins not
avail Oct 1 - May 31; During July-Aug avail. only Sat.

RV/Campers overnight hookups: Yes; Water: Yes; Electric: Yes; Septic: No
Basic Rate/Night: $10.00/ veh

ACCOM: Mon. night thru Thurs. night rates for winterized (check if this is critical) rooms w/o
meals unless otherwise indicated.

Cabin; Max. Pers: 10; Bedding incl ?: No; Bath: Shared; A/C: No:
Rate for: Person; $15; Rate for #2 pers: $15; Rate for #3 pers: $15; Child Rate: 50% off under
13 yrs; free under 4

Main amenities available: Swimming; V-ball; Bsk ball; Laundry machine; Canoeing; VCR-TV; Ping-pong
Meals are served in dining room for transients only when other groups are present. Dinner price: $6.00.

NEW JERSEY

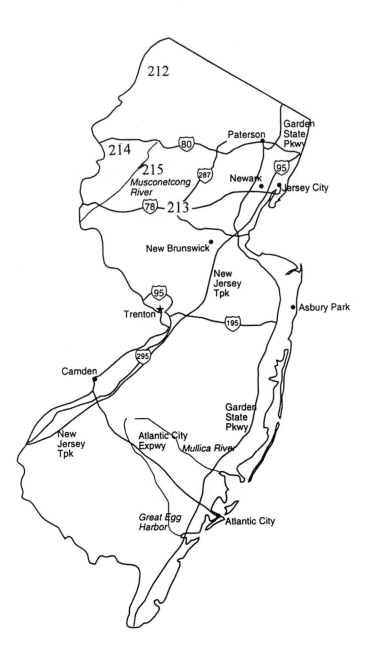

212

214

215
*Musconetcong
River*

80 Paterson

Garden
State
Pkwy

287 Newark

95

Jersey City

78 213

New Brunswick

New
Jersey
Tpk

95

Trenton

195

Asbury Park

295

Camden

New
Jersey
Tpk

Atlantic City
Expwy

Garden
State
Pkwy

Mullica River

Great Egg
Harbor

Atlantic City

NAME OF CENTER: Aldersgate   Listing ID #: 212

Telephone: 973-383-5978; Fax: 973-383-4428; E-mail:
Address: 1 Mary Jones Rd.; Swartswood; NJ; 07877
Nearest Interstate: I-80, Exit 30 miles; Nearest State/US Hwy: Rte 206; 7 miles.

Restrictions: Age: None; Pets: Not permitted; Alcohol: Not permitted; Smoking: Outdoors only;
Reservation Req'd: 7 days; Max. Adv. Reser.: 1 yr; Seasonal closing: None

RV/Campers overnight hookups: No

ACCOM: Mon. night thru Thurs. night rates for winterized (check if this is critical) rooms w/o
meals unless otherwise indicated.

Dorm; Max. Pers: 5; Bedding incl ?: No; Bath: Shared; A/C: No:
Rate for: Person; $20; Rate for #2 pers: $20; Rate for #3 pers: $20; Child Rate: $15 under 13
yrs; free under 5

Main amenities available: Swimming; Volleyball; Basketball; Laundry machine; Ball field; Hiking
Meals are served in dining room for transients only when other groups are present. Dinner price: $7-9.00.

NAME OF CENTER: Fellowship Conference Center   Listing ID #: 213

Telephone: 908-647-1777; Fax: 908-647-4117; E-mail:
Address: 3575 Valley Rd; PO Box 204; Liberty Corner; NJ; 07938
Nearest Interstate: I-287, Exit 2 miles; Nearest State/US Hwy: I-78; 1 miles.

Restrictions: Age: None; Pets: Not permitted; Alcohol: Not permitted; Smoking: Outdoors only;
Reservation Req'd: None; Max. Adv. Reser.: Open; Seasonal closing: None

RV/Campers overnight hookups: No

ACCOM: Mon. night thru Thurs. night rates for winterized (check if this is critical) rooms w/o
meals unless otherwise indicated.

Dorm; Max. Pers: 3; Bedding incl ?: Yes; Bath: Shared; A/C: Yes:
Rate for: Person; $34; Rate for #2 pers: $34; Rate for #3 pers: $34; Child Rate: 50% off under
12 yrs; 75% off under 6; free under 1

Motel; Max. Pers: 3; Bedding incl ?: Yes; Bath: Private; A/C: Yes
Rate for: Person: $46; Rate for #2 pers: $46; Rate for #3 pers: $46; Child Rate: see above

Main amenities available: Swimming; V-ball; Bsk ball; Laundry machine; VCR-TV; Tennis; Bookstore
Meals are served in dining room for transients only when other groups are present. Dinner price: $10.30-12.65
including tax and gratuity..

NAME OF CENTER: Hope Conference & Renewal Center   Listing ID #: 214

Telephone: 908-459-4435; Fax: 908-459-5571; E-mail: hcrc@juno.com
Address: PO Box 165; 35 Ridgeway Ave.; Hope; NJ; 07844
Nearest Interstate: I-80, Exit 12; 4 miles; Nearest State/US Hwy: Rte 519; 1 miles.

Restrictions: Age: None; Pets: Not permitted; Alcohol: Not permitted; Smoking: Outdoors only; Reservation Req'd: Yes w/dep; Max. Adv. Reser.: Open; Seasonal closing: None

RV/Campers overnight hookups: Yes; Water: No; Electric: Yes; Septic: No
Basic Rate/Night: $14 w elect. $19/ veh

ACCOM: Mon. night thru Thurs. night rates for winterized (check if this is critical) rooms w/o meals unless otherwise indicated.

Rustic cabin; Max. Pers: 10-12; Bedding incl ?: No; Bath: Separate bldg; A/C: No:
Rate for: Person; $25; Rate for #2 pers: $25; Rate for #3 pers: $25; Child Rate: 25% off under 11 yrs; 40% off under 6; free under 3
Some cabins are heated; others are not.

Main amenities available: Swimming; Volleyball; Basketball; Boat/canoeing; Ping-pong; Hiking
Meals are served in dining room for transients only when other groups are present. Dinner price: $9.25.

NAME OF CENTER: Liebenzell Guest House   Listing ID #: 215

Telephone: 908-852-6002; Fax: 908-852-4531; E-mail:
Address: 13 Heath Lane (PO Box 66); Schooley's Mountain; NJ; 07870
Nearest Interstate: I-80, Exit 26; 10 miles; Nearest State/US Hwy: Rte 24; 5 miles.

Restrictions: Age: None; Pets: Not permitted; Alcohol: Not permitted; Smoking: Outdoors only; Reservation Req'd: 1 mo; Max. Adv. Reser.: Open; Seasonal closing: Christmas Day

RV/Campers overnight hookups: No

ACCOM: Mon. night thru Thurs. night rates for winterized (check if this is critical) rooms w/o meals unless otherwise indicated.

Bunkroom; Max. Pers: Over 5; Bedding incl ?: Yes; Bath: Shared; A/C: No:
Rate for: Person; $21; Rate for #2 pers: $21; Rate for #3 pers: $21; Child Rate: n/a

Dorm; Max. Pers: 5; Bedding incl ?: Yes; Bath: Shared; A/C: Yes
Rate for: Person: $23; Rate for #2 pers: $23; Rate for #3 pers: $23; Child Rate: 50% under 12 yrs; free under 7

Motel; Max. Pers: 5; Bedding incl ?: Yes; Bath: Private; A/C: Yes:
Rate for: Person: $23; Rate for #2 pers: $23; Rate for #3 pers: $23; Child Rate: 50% under 12 yrs; free under 7

Main amenities available: Swimming; Volleyball; Basketball; Tennis; Incidentals store; Ball field
Meals are served in dining room for transients only when other groups are present. Dinner price: $5.50-7.50.

NAME OF CENTER: YMCA - Newark - Central Br. Listing ID: 216

Telephone: 973-624-8900   Fax: 973-624-3024
Address: 600 Broad St.; Newark, NJ 07102

Restrictions:
Accommodations offered to (M/F/Families): M&F&Couples. If M/F then must be over 18 yrs.
Pets: Not permitted; Alcohol: Not permitted; Smoking: Outdoors only
Reservation requirements: None
Reservations are accepted up to an indefinite time in advance. Seasonal closing: None

ACCOMMODATIONS:
Single room: Bedding included ?: Yes; Bath: Shared
Rate for 1 day: $40; Rate for 1 week: $280

Double room: Bedding included ?: Yes; Bath: Shared
Rate for 1 day: $50/1 pers; $60/2 pers; Rate for 1 week: $350

Main amenities: Pool; Gym; Laundry machine; Racquetball.
Meals are not offered in their own cafeteria.

NEW MEXICO

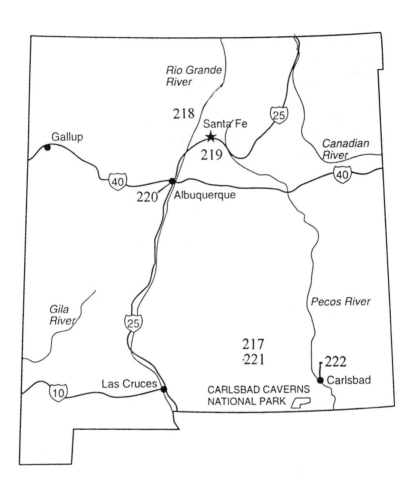

Rio Grande River

218

Santa Fe

25

Gallup

Canadian River

219

40

40

220

Albuquerque

Pecos River

Gila River

25

217

221

222

Las Cruces

CARLSBAD CAVERNS
NATIONAL PARK

Carlsbad

10

NAME OF CENTER: Camp Chimney Springs   Listing ID #: 217
Telephone: 505-687-3520; Fax: 505-687-3577
E-mail: chimneyspring@pvtnetworks.net
Address: 2679 Highway 82; Mayhill; NM; 88339
Nearest State/US Hwy: Rte 82 ; 0 miles.

Restrictions: Age: None; Pets: Permitted; Alcohol: Permitted in bedroom; Smoking: Outdoors only; Reservation Req'd: 7 days except JJA 90 days; Max. Adv. Reser.: 9 mo; Seasonal closing: None

RV/Campers overnight hookups: Yes; Water: Yes; Electric: Yes; Septic: unk
Basic Rate/Night: $15.00/ veh

ACCOM: Mon. night thru Thurs. night rates for winterized (check if this is critical) rooms w/o meals unless otherwise indicated.

Bunkroom; Max. Pers: 10; Bedding incl ?: No; Bath: Shared; A/C: No:
Rate for: Room; $50; Child Rate: n/a

Motel; Max. Pers: 4; Bedding incl ?: No; Bath: Private; A/C: No
Rate for: Room: $50; Child Rate: n/a
Incl. living rm & kitchenette

Main amenities available: Ball field; Volleyball; Basketball; Horse shoes; Frisbee golf; Hiking
Meals are served in dining room for transients only when other groups are present. Dinner price: $6.45; Child discount. Meals not available w/some gps.

NAME OF CENTER: Ghost Ranch Conference Center   Listing ID #: 218
Telephone: 505-685-4333; Fax: 505-685-4519; E-mail:
Address: HC 77, Box 11; Abiquiu; NM; 87510
Nearest Interstate: I-25, Exit 55 miles; Nearest State/US Hwy: Rte 84; 1 miles.

Restrictions: Age: None; Pets: Not permitted; Alcohol: Not permitted; Smoking: Not permitted in bedroom; Reservation Req'd: Noon of day; Max. Adv. Reser.: 6 mo; Seasonal closing: None

RV/Campers overnight hookups: Yes; Water: Yes; Electric: Yes; Septic: unk
Basic Rate/Night: $16.00/ veh

ACCOM: Mon. night thru Thurs. night rates for winterized (check if this is critical) rooms w/o meals unless otherwise indicated.

Bunkroom; Max. Pers: Over 5; Bedding incl ?: Yes; Bath: Shared; A/C: No:
Rate for: Couple; $32; Rate for #2 pers: n/a; Rate for #3 pers: n/a; Child Rate: 50% off under 14 yrs. Rate is double occupancy & includes 3 meals

Cabin; Max. Pers: n/a; Bedding incl ?: Yes; Bath: Shared; A/C: No
Rate for: Couple: $65; Rate for #2 pers: n/a; Rate for #3 pers: n/a; Child Rate: 50% off under 14 yrs. Rate is double occupancy and includes 3 meals

Motel; Max. Pers: 5; Bedding incl ?: Yes; Bath: Private; A/C: No:
Rate for: Couple: $65; Rate for #2 pers: n/a; Rate for #3 pers: n/a; Child Rate: 50% off under 14 Rate is double occupancy & incl. 3 meals

Main amenities avail: Swimming; Volleyball; Laundry machine; Library/Bookstore; Incidentals store; Hiking
Meals are served in dining room for transients only when other groups are present. Dinner price: $7.00.

NAME OF CENTER: Glorieta Conference Center   Listing ID #: 219

Telephone: 505-757-6161; Fax: 505-757-6149; E-mail:
Address: PO Box 8; Glorieta; NM; 87535
Nearest Interstate: I-25, Exit # 299; 0 miles.

Restrictions: Age: None; Pets: Not permitted; Alcohol: Not permitted; Smoking: Outdoors only;
Reservation Req'd: 7 weeks; Max. Adv. Reser.: Open; Seasonal closing: None

RV/Campers overnight hookups: Yes; Water: Yes; Electric: Yes; Septic: Yes
Basic Rate/Night: $30.00/ veh

ACCOM: Mon. night thru Thurs. night rates for winterized (check if this is critical) rooms w/o
meals unless otherwise indicated.

Kitchenette; Max. Pers: 2; Bedding incl ?: Yes; Bath: Private; A/C: Yes:
Rate for: Entire; $75

Sm Garden Apt I; Max. Pers: 4; Bedding incl ?: Yes; Bath: Private; A/C: No
Rate for: Apt: $86

Cabin; Max. Pers: 4; Bedding incl ?: No; Bath: Separate bldg; A/C: No:
Rate for: Entire cabin: $46
Kitchenette (excl utensils)

Main amenities available: Boating; Volleyball; Basketball; Horseback riding; Miniature golf; Hiking
Meals are served in dining room for transients only when other groups are present. Dinner price: Varies.

NAME OF CENTER: Madonna Retreat Center   Listing ID #: 220

Telephone: 505-831-8196; Fax: 505-831-8103; E-mail:
Address: 4040 St. Joseph Place; Albuquerque; NM; 87120
Nearest Interstate: I-40, Exit Coors N.; 1 miles.

Restrictions: Age: Adults; Pets: Not permitted; Alcohol: With permission; Smoking: Outdoors
only; Reservation Req'd: 2 days; Max. Adv. Reser.: 1 yr; Seasonal closing: End of Holy Wk &
Thanksgiving

RV/Campers overnight hookups: No

ACCOM: Mon. night thru Thurs. night rates for winterized (check if this is critical) rooms w/o
meals unless otherwise indicated.

Motel; Max. Pers: 2; Bedding incl ?: Yes; Bath: Private; A/C: unk:
Rate for: Person; $48; Rate for #2 pers: $7; Child Rate: n/a

Dorm; Max. Pers: 2; Bedding incl ?: Yes; Bath: Shared; A/C: unk
Rate for: Person: $23; Rate for #2 pers: $13; Child Rate: n/a

Dorm; Max. Pers: 2; Bedding incl ?: Yes; Bath: Semi-private; A/C: unk:
Rate for: Person: $35; Rate for #2 pers: $11; Child Rate: n/a
Bath shared between 2 rms

Main amenities available: Laundry machine; VCR-TV
Meals are served in dining room for transients with advanced notice.. Dinner price: $7.00.

NAME OF CENTER: Sacramento Methodist Assembly   Listing ID #: 221

Telephone: 800-667-3414; Fax: 505-687-3784; E-mail: sma@pvtnetworks.net
Address: Box 8; Sacramento, NM; 88347
Nearest State/US Hwy: Rte 24; 4 miles.

Restrictions: Age: None; Pets: Not permitted; Alcohol: Not permitted; Smoking: Designated outdoor area; Reservation Req'd: None; Max. Adv. Reser.: 1 yr; Seasonal closing: None

RV/Campers overnight hookups: Yes; Water: Yes; Electric: Yes; Septic: unk
Basic Rate/Night: $10.00/ veh

ACCOM: Mon. night thru Thurs. night rates for winterized (check if this is critical) rooms w/o meals unless otherwise indicated.

Dorm; Max. Pers: 5; Bedding incl ?: $5 surcharge; Bath: Shared; A/C: Yes:
Rate for: Person; $24; Rate for #2 pers: $24; Rate for #3 pers: $24; Child Rate: $2.50 under 17 yr. Husband/wife combined discount $3

Motel; Max. Pers: 5; Bedding incl ?: $5 surcharge; Bath: Private; A/C: Yes
Rate for: Person: $28; Rate for #2 pers: $28; Rate for #3 pers: $28; Child Rate: $2.50 under 17 yrs. Husband/wife combined discount $3

Bishop Apt; Max. Pers: 5; Bedding incl ?: Yes; Bath: Private; A/C: Yes:
Rate for: Person: $36; Rate for #2 pers: $36; Rate for #3 pers: $36; Child Rate: $2.50 under 17 yrs. Husband/wife combined discount $3; 2 bedrooms; lv rm; kitchenette

Main amenities available: Laundry machine; Volleyball; Basketball; Tennis; Incidentals store; Hiking
Meals are served in dining room for transients only when other groups are present. Dinner price: $5; Child discount.

NAME OF CENTER: Tres Rios Christian Growth Center   Listing ID #: 222

Telephone: 505-785-2361; Fax: 505-785-2344; E-mail: tresrios@carlsbadnm.com
Address: 1159 Black River Valley Rd; Carlsbad; NM; 88220
Nearest State/US Hwy: Rte 62/180; 4 miles.

Restrictions: Age: None; Pets: Not permitted; Alcohol: Not permitted; Smoking: Outdoors only; Reservation Req'd: 10 days; Max. Adv. Reser.: 1 yr; Seasonal closing: June

RV/Campers overnight hookups: Yes; Water: Yes; Electric: Yes; Septic: unk
Basic Rate/Night: $12.00/ veh

ACCOM: Mon. night thru Thurs. night rates for winterized (check if this is critical) rooms w/o meals unless otherwise indicated.

Motel; Max. Pers: 5; Bedding incl ?: $4.50 surcharge; Bath: Private; A/C: Yes:
Rate for: Person; $20; Rate for #2 pers: $10; Rate for #3 pers: $8; Child Rate: Free under 5 yr

Main amenities available: Swimming; Volleyball; Basketball; VCR-TV; Hot tub; Boating
Meals are served in dining room for transients only when other groups are present. Dinner price: $5.00-7.00.
Meals not available w/some gps.

NEW YORK

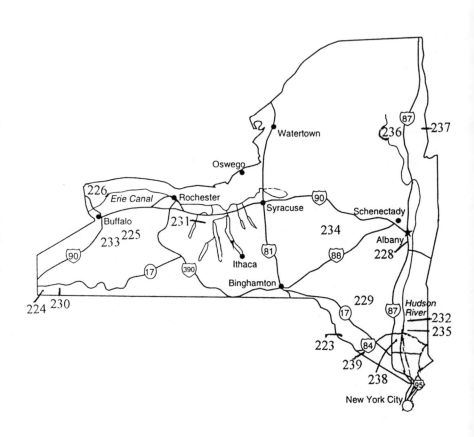

NAME OF CENTER: Camp Deerpark   Listing ID #: 223

Telephone: 914-754-8669; Fax: 914-754-8217; E-mail: campdeerpark@juno.com
Address: PO Box 394; Westbrookville; NY; 12785
Nearest Interstate: I-87, Exit 16; 20 miles; Nearest State/US Hwy: Rte 17; 7 miles.

Restrictions: Age: None; Pets: Not permitted; Alcohol: Not permitted; Smoking: Outdoors only;
Reservation Req'd: Noon of day; Max. Adv. Reser.: Open; Seasonal closing: None

RV/Campers overnight hookups: No

ACCOM: Mon. night thru Thurs. night rates for winterized (check if this is critical) rooms w/o
meals unless otherwise indicated.

Motel; Max. Pers: Over 2; Bedding incl ?: No; Bath: Private; A/C: No:
Rate for: Room; ** $35; Rate for #2 pers: n/a; Rate for #3 pers: n/a; Child Rate: n/a
** $40 for room w/kitchenette

Dorm; Max. Pers: 4; Bedding incl ?: No; Bath: Shared; A/C: No
Rate for: Person: $15; Rate for #2 pers: $15; Rate for #3 pers: $15; Child Rate: $10.00

Main amenities available: Swimming; V-ball; Bsk ball; Laundry machine; Ball field; Hiking
Meals are served in dining room for transients only when other groups are present. Dinner price: $7; $4 under
12 yrs; free under 5. One-time registration fee per pers; $5; $3 under 12 yrs

NAME OF CENTER: Camp Findley   Listing ID #: 224

Telephone: 716-769-7146; Fax: 716-769-7398; E-mail: dbfindley@juno.com
Address: 2334 Sunnyside Rd.; Clymer; NY; 14724
Nearest Interstate: I-90, Exit 15 miles; Nearest State/US Hwy: Rte 17; 2 miles.

Restrictions: Age: None; Pets: Not permitted; Alcohol: Not permitted; Smoking: Outdoors only;
Reservation Req'd: Noon of day; Max. Adv. Reser.: Open; Seasonal closing: None

RV/Campers overnight hookups: Yes; Water: Yes; Electric: Yes; Septic: Yes
Basic Rate/Night: $16; $18 w/septic/ veh

ACCOM: Mon. night thru Thurs. night rates for winterized (check if this is critical) rooms w/o
meals unless otherwise indicated.

House; Max. Pers: 8; Bedding incl ?: No; Bath: Shared; A/C: No:
Rate for: Entire Hse; ** $60
**$10/pers for over 5 persons

Main amenities available: Swimming; V-ball; Bsk ball; Bookstore; VCR-TV; Canoeing; Ball field
Meals are served in dining room for transients only when other groups are present. Dinner price: $9.00 ; $5
under 12 yrs; free under 3.

REMEMBER TO CALL AHEAD

NAME OF CENTER: Camp Vick   Listing ID #: 225

Telephone: 716-492-4494; Fax: ; E-mail:
Address: Sandbank Rd (PO Box 109); Sandusky; NY; 14133
Nearest Interstate: I-90, Exit 35 miles; Nearest State/US Hwy: Rte 98; 0 miles.

Restrictions: Age: None; Pets: Permitted on leash; Alcohol: Not permitted; Smoking: Nowhere;
Reservation Req'd: 7 days; Max. Adv. Reser.: Open; Seasonal closing: None

RV/Campers overnight hookups: Yes; Water: Yes; Electric: Yes; Septic: Yes
Basic Rate/Night: $10; $18 w/electric/ veh

ACCOM: Mon. night thru Thurs. night rates for winterized (check if this is critical) rooms w/o
meals unless otherwise indicated.

Cabin; Max. Pers: 8; Bedding incl ?: No; Bath: Separate bldg; A/C: No:
Rate for: Entire cabin; $20
Not heated

Main amenities available: Swimming; Sailboat; Canoeing; Vollyball; Hiking
Meals are not served in dining room for transients . Dinner price: Varies.

NAME OF CENTER: Center of Renewal, Inc.   Listing ID #: 226

Telephone: 716-754-7376; Fax: 716-754-1223; E-mail:
Address: 4421 Lower River Rd; Stella Niagra; NY; 14144
Nearest Interstate: I-190, Exit 5 miles; Nearest State/US Hwy: Rte 104; 1 miles.

Restrictions: Age: None; Pets: Not permitted; Alcohol: Not permitted; Smoking: Outdoors only;
Reservation Req'd: 7 days; Max. Adv. Reser.: Open; Seasonal closing: None

RV/Campers overnight hookups: No

ACCOM: Mon. night thru Thurs. night rates for winterized (check if this is critical) rooms w/o
meals unless otherwise indicated.

Dorm; Max. Pers: 2; Bedding incl ?: Yes; Bath: Shared; A/C: No:
Rate for: Person; ** $38; Rate for #2 pers: ** $38; Rate for #3 pers: n/a; Child Rate: Ask when
making reservations
** Includes 3 meals. Strip beds when leaving

Main amenities available: Swimming (charge); Bookstore; Library; VCR-TV; Laundry machine; Hiking
Meals are served in dining room for transients . Dinner price: Varies.

NAME OF CENTER: Duffield   Listing ID #: 227

Telephone: 716-835-8056; Fax: 716-835-8072; E-mail:
Address: Worden Rd.; Delevan; NY; 14042
Nearest Interstate: I-90, Exit 25 miles; Nearest State/US Hwy: Rte 39; 2 miles.

Restrictions: Age: None; Pets: Permitted; Alcohol: Not permitted; Smoking: Nowhere; Reservation Req'd: 3 days; Max. Adv. Reser.: Open; Seasonal closing: None

RV/Campers overnight hookups: No

ACCOM: Mon. night thru Thurs. night rates for winterized (check if this is critical) rooms w/o meals unless otherwise indicated.

Cabin; Max. Pers: 12; Bedding incl ?: No; Bath: Shared; A/C: No:
Rate for: Person; $12; Rate for #2 pers: $12; Rate for #3 pers: $12; Child Rate: n/a
Includes kitchenette

Main amenities available: Swimming; Volleyball; Ball field; Fishing; Hiking
Meals are served in dining room for transients only when other groups are present. Dinner price: $5-7.00 (Not in winter).

NAME OF CENTER: Emmanuel Christian Church Center   Listing ID #: 228

Telephone: 518-463-1296; Fax: ; E-mail:
Address: 31 Retreat Hse Rd.; Glenmont; NY; 12077
Nearest Interstate: I-87 (NY Thruway), Exit 23; 2 miles.

Restrictions: Age: None; Pets: Not permitted; Alcohol: Not permitted; Smoking: Nowhere; Reservation Req'd: 2 days; Max. Adv. Reser.: 14 days; Seasonal closing: None

RV/Campers overnight hookups: No

ACCOM: Mon. night thru Thurs. night rates for winterized (check if this is critical) rooms w/o meals unless otherwise indicated.

Dorm; Max. Pers: 4; Bedding incl ?: Yes; Bath: Semi-private; A/C: No:
Rate for: Person; $23; Rate for #2 pers: $23; Rate for #3 pers: $23; Child Rate: n/a
$3 for kitchen use

Motel; Max. Pers: 2; Bedding incl ?: Yes; Bath: Private; A/C: No
Rate for: Person: $23; Rate for #2 pers: $23; Rate for #3 pers: $23; Child Rate:
$3 for kitchen use

Main amenities available: Volleyball
Meals are not served in dining room for transients . Dinner price: Varies.

NAME OF CENTER: Frost Valley - YMCA   Listing ID #: 229

Telephone: 914-985-2291; Fax: 914-985-0056; E-mail: www.frostvalley.org
Address: 2000 Frost Valley Rd.; Claryville; NY; 12725
Nearest Interstate: I-87(NY Thruway), Exit 17; 40 miles.

Restrictions: Age: None; Pets: Not permitted; Alcohol: Not permitted; Smoking: Outdoors only; Reservation Req'd: Yes w/dep; Max. Adv. Reser.: Open; Seasonal closing: None

RV/Campers overnight hookups: No

ACCOM: Mon. night thru Thurs. night rates for winterized (check if this is critical) rooms w/o meals unless otherwise indicated.

Dorm; Max. Pers: 2; Bedding incl ?: $5 surcharge; Bath: Shared/Private ($Lo/$Hi); A/C: No: Rate for: Person; ** $129-154; Rate for #2 pers: ** $129-154; Child Rate: $99-110 under 15 yrs; $88-99 under 10; $55-61 under 6; free under 3
** Includes 2 nights lodging & 5 meals

Dorm; Max. Pers: 3-6; Bedding incl ?: $5 surcharge; Bath: Shared/Private($Lo/$Hi); A/C: No Rate for: Person: ** $108-131; Rate for #2 pers: ** $108-131; Rate for #3 pers: ** $108-131; Child Rate: $93-99 under 15 yrs; $77-88 under 10; $50-55 under 6; free under 3
** Includes 2 nights lodging & 5 meals

Main amenities available: 4900 acre major resort center
Meals are served in dining room for transients . Dinner price: Varies.

NAME OF CENTER: **Lake Chautauqua Lutheran Center**   Listing ID #: 230

Telephone: 716-386-4125; Fax: 716-386-5714; E-mail:
Address: 5013 Rte 430; Bemus Point; NY; 14712
Nearest Interstate: I-90, Exit 15 miles; Nearest State/US Hwy: Rte 17; 4 miles.

Restrictions: Age: None; Pets: Not permitted; Alcohol: Permitted; Smoking: Designated outdoor area; Reservation Req'd: None; Max. Adv. Reser.: Open; Seasonal closing: None

RV/Campers overnight hookups: No

ACCOM: Mon. night thru Thurs. night rates for winterized (check if this is critical) rooms w/o meals unless otherwise indicated.

Dorm; Max. Pers: 3; Bedding incl ?: Yes; Bath: Shared; A/C: No:
Rate for: Room; $45; Child Rate: n/a

Main amenities available: Lake swimming; Volleyball; VCR-TV; Hiking
Meals are served in dining room for transients only when other groups are present. Dinner price: $10.00.

NAME OF CENTER: LeTourneau Christian Conf. Ctr   Listing ID #: 231

Telephone: 716-554-3400; Fax: 716-554-3419; E-mail: lccc495@aol.com
Address: 4950 CR 11; Rushville; NY; 14544
Nearest Interstate: I-90, Exit 20 miles; Nearest State/US Hwy: Rte 5 & 20; 8 miles.

Restrictions: Age: None; Pets: Not permitted; Alcohol: Not permitted; Smoking: Not permitted in bedroom; Reservation Req'd: None; Max. Adv. Reser.: Open; Seasonal closing: None

RV/Campers overnight hookups: No

ACCOM: Mon. night thru Thurs. night rates for winterized (check if this is critical) rooms w/o meals unless otherwise indicated.

Dorm; Max. Pers: 5; Bedding incl ?: Yes; Bath: Shared; A/C: No:
Rate for: Person; $34; Rate for #2 pers: $12; Rate for #3 pers: $12; Child Rate: Free under 4 yrs

Main amenities available: Swimming; V-ball; Bsk ball; Boating; Canoeing; Bookstore; Hiking
Meals are served in dining room for transients only when other groups are present. Dinner price: $8.00.

NAME OF CENTER: Mt. Alvernia Retreat House   Listing ID #: 232

Telephone: 914-297-5707; Fax: 914-298-0309; E-mail:
Address: DeLavergne Ave.; Wappingers Falls; NY; 12590
Nearest Interstate: I-84, Exit Rte 9 Poughkeepsie; 15 miles; Nearest State/US Hwy: Rte 9D; 0 miles.

Restrictions: Age: None; Pets: Not permitted; Alcohol: Not permitted; Smoking: Outdoors only; Reservation Req'd: 7 days; Max. Adv. Reser.: 1 mo; Seasonal closing: None

RV/Campers overnight hookups: No

ACCOM: Mon. night thru Thurs. night rates for winterized (check if this is critical) rooms w/o meals unless otherwise indicated.

Dorm; Max. Pers: 2; Bedding incl ?: Yes; Bath: Shared; A/C: No:
Rate for: Person; $25; Rate for #2 pers: $25; Child Rate: n/a

Main amenities available: Meditative atm set on 1000 acres; Hiking
Meals are served in dining room for transients only when other groups are present. Dinner price: Varies

NAME OF CENTER: Odosagih Bible Conference   Listing ID #: 233

Telephone: 716-353-8555; Fax: 716-353-4219; E-mail: odosagih@juno.com
Address: 3204 Hazelmere; PO Box 107; Machias; NY; 14101
Nearest Interstate: I-90, Exit; 60 miles; Nearest State/US Hwy: Rte 16; 1 miles.

Restrictions: Age: None; Pets: Not permitted; Alcohol: Not permitted; Smoking: Outdoors only;
Reservation Req'd: None; Max. Adv. Reser.: Open; Seasonal closing: None

RV/Campers overnight hookups: Yes; Water: Yes; Electric: Yes; Septic: Yes
Basic Rate/Night: $22.00/ veh

ACCOM: Mon. night thru Thurs. night rates for winterized (check if this is critical) rooms w/o
meals unless otherwise indicated.

Motel; Max. Pers: 5; Bedding incl ?: Yes w/notice; Bath: Private; A/C: No:
Rate for: Person; $35; Rate for #2 pers: $5; Rate for #3 pers: $5; Child Rate: Free under 17 yrs

Cabin; Max. Pers: Over 5; Bedding incl ?: Yes w/notice; Bath: Shared; A/C: No
Rate for: Entire cabin: $55
Includes kitchenette

Main amenities available: Swimming; V-ball; Bsk ball; Bookstore; Tennis; Boat/canoeing; Hiking
Meals are served in dining room for transients only when other groups are present. Dinner price: $7-8.50
(Summer only).

NAME OF CENTER: Pathfinder Lodge   Listing ID #: 234

Telephone: 607-547-2300; Fax: ; E-mail:
Address: PO Box 350; Cooperstown; NY; 13326
Nearest Interstate: I-90, Exit 20 miles; Nearest State/US Hwy: Rte 20; 4 miles.

Restrictions: Age: None; Pets: Permitted on leash; Alcohol: Not permitted; Smoking: Nowhere;
Reservation Req'd: 7 days; Max. Adv. Reser.: Seasonal closing: None

RV/Campers overnight hookups: Yes; Water: Yes; Electric: Yes; Septic: Yes
Basic Rate/Night: $10; $18 w/electric/ veh

ACCOM: Mon. night thru Thurs. night rates for winterized (check if this is critical) rooms w/o
meals unless otherwise indicated.

Cabin; Max. Pers: 8; Bedding incl ?: No; Bath: Shared; A/C: No:
Rate for: Entire cabin; $25
Not heated; Kitchenette avail by reservation for $5

Main amenities available: Swimming; sailboat; Canoeing; Vollyball; Hiking
Meals are not served in dining room for transients

REMEMBER TO CALL AHEAD

NAME OF CENTER: Presbyterian Center at Holmes   Listing ID #: 235

Telephone: 914-878-6383; Fax: 914-878-7824; E-mail: holmespca@aol.com
Address: 183 Denton Lake Rd.; Holmes; NY; 12531
Nearest Interstate: I-84, Exit 2 miles.

Restrictions: Age: None; Pets: Not permitted; Alcohol: Not permitted; Smoking: Outdoors only; Reservation Req'd: 11AM of day; Max. Adv. Reser.: 3 days; Seasonal closing: June - Aug.

RV/Campers overnight hookups: Yes; Water: Yes; Electric: Yes; Septic: n/a
Basic Rate/Night: $20.00/ veh

ACCOM: Mon. night thru Thurs. night rates for winterized (check if this is critical) rooms w/o meals unless otherwise indicated.

Bunkroom; Max. Pers: Over 5; Bedding incl ?: **$9 surcharge; Bath: Shared; A/C: No:
Rate for: Person; $19; Rate for #2 pers: $19; Rate for #3 pers: $19; Child Rate: n/a
** Adv. notice req'd; Kitchenette included.

Motel; Max. Pers: 5; Bedding incl ?: ** $9 surcharge; Bath: Private; A/C: No
Rate for: Person: $22; Rate for #2 pers: $22; Rate for #3 pers: $22; Child Rate: n/a
** Adv. notice req'd

Cabin; Max. Pers: 5; Bedding incl ?: **$9 surcharge; Bath: Shared; A/C: No:
Rate for: Person: $14; Rate for #2 pers: $14; Rate for #3 pers: $14; Child Rate: n/a
** Adv. notice req'd

Main amenities available: Swimming; V-ball; Bsk ball; Boat/canoeing; VCR-TV; Ball field; Hiking
Meals are served in dining room for transients only when other groups are present. Dinner price varies.

NAME OF CENTER: Priory of St. Benedict   Listing ID #: 236

Telephone: 518-494-3733; Fax: 518-494-3733; E-mail:
Address: 135 Priory Rd.; Chestertown; NY; 12817
Nearest Interstate: I-87 (NY Northway), Exit 25; 5 miles.

Restrictions: Age: None; Pets: Not permitted; Alcohol: Not permitted; Smoking: Outdoors only; Reservation Req'd: 4 PM of day; Max. Adv. Reser.: Open; Seasonal closing: Christmas Day; Easter Day and week following both

RV/Campers overnight hookups: No

ACCOM: Mon. night thru Thurs. night rates for winterized (check if this is critical) rooms w/o meals unless otherwise indicated.

Dorm; Max. Pers: 3; Bedding incl ?: Yes; Bath: Shared; A/C: No:
Rate for: Person; $21; Rate for #2 pers: $21; Rate for #3 pers: $21; Child Rate: n/a

Main amenities available: X-Ctry skiing (6 mi trails); Library; Bookstore; Laundry machine; Quiet area; Hiking
Meals are served in dining room for transients only when other groups are present. Dinner price: $12.00.

NAME OF CENTER: Silver Bay Association YMCA   Listing ID #: 237

Telephone: 518-543-8833; Fax: 518-543-6733; E-mail: sbaconf@aol.com
Address: 87 Silver Bay Rd; Silver Bay; NY; 12874
Nearest Interstate: I-87 (NY Northway), Exit 24; 18 miles; Nearest State/US Hwy:
Rte 9N; 1 miles.

Restrictions: Age: None; Pets: Not permitted; Alcohol: Not permitted; Smoking: Designated
outdoor area; Reservation Req'd: 1 day; Max. Adv. Reser.: 1 yr; Seasonal closing: None

RV/Campers overnight hookups: No

ACCOM: Mon. night thru Thurs. night rates for winterized (check if this is critical) rooms w/o
meals unless otherwise indicated.

Cabin; Max. Pers: 4 and up; Bedding incl ?: Yes; Bath: Shared; A/C: No:
Rate for: Entire cabin; **$110 & up
** $3 per person for req'd daily membership in Silver Bay Association.

Dorm; Max. Pers: 5; Bedding incl ?: Yes; Bath: Shared; A/C: No
Rate for: Room: ** $49 & up

Motel; Max. Pers: 5; Bedding incl ?: Yes; Bath: Private; A/C: No:
Rate for: Room: ** $59 & up; Child Rate: n/a

Main amenities available: Swimming; V-ball; Bsk ball; Library; Laundry machine; Canoeing/Tennis; Hiking
Meals are not served in dining room for transients . Dinner price varies.

NAME OF CENTER: Stony Point Center   Listing ID #: 238

Telephone: 914-786-5674; Fax: 914-786-5919; E-mail:
Address: 17 Crickettown Rd.; Stony Point; NY; 10980
Nearest Interstate: I-287, Exit 10 miles; Nearest State/US Hwy: Palisades Pkwy; 2
miles.

Restrictions: Age: None; Pets: Not permitted; Alcohol: Not permitted; Smoking: Outdoors only;
Reservation Req'd: 24 hrs; Max. Adv. Reser.: Open; Seasonal closing: None

RV/Campers overnight hookups: No

ACCOM: Mon. night thru Thurs. night rates for winterized (check if this is critical) rooms w/o
meals unless otherwise indicated.

Dorm; Max. Pers: 2; Bedding incl ?: Yes; Bath: Shared; A/C: No:
Rate for: Person; ** $25; Rate for #2 pers: ** $15; Child Rate: 50% off
** Includes continental breakfast

Guest Hse; Max. Pers: 5; Bedding incl ?: Yes; Bath: Private; A/C: Yes
Rate for: Person: ** $52-72; Rate for #2 pers: ** $15; Rate for #3 pers: ** $15; Child Rate:
50% off
** Includes continental breakfast

Main amenities available: Incidentals store (1/4 mi); Volleyball; VCR-TV; Bookstore; 2 mi Harriman State Pk;
Hiking
Meals are served in dining room for transients only when other groups are present. Dinner price varies.

NAME OF CENTER: The Warwick Center   Listing ID #: 239

Telephone: 914-986-1164; Fax: 914-986-8874; E-mail:
Address: PO Box 349; Hoyt Rd.; Warwick; NY; 10990
Nearest Interstate: I-84, Exit 20 miles; Nearest State/US Hwy: Rte 94; 1 miles.

Restrictions: Age: None; Pets: Not permitted; Alcohol: Not permitted; Smoking: Outdoors only; Reservation Req'd: 7 days; Max. Adv. Reser.: Open; Seasonal closing: None

RV/Campers overnight hookups: Yes; Water: Yes; Electric: Yes; Septic: Yes
Basic Rate/Night: $20.00/ veh

ACCOM: Mon. night thru Thurs. night rates for winterized (check if this is critical) rooms w/o meals unless otherwise indicated.

Motel; Max. Pers: 2; Bedding incl ?: Yes; Bath: Private; A/C: Yes:
Rate for: Person; ** $89; Rate for #2 pers: **$69; Rate for #3 pers: n/a; Child Rate: n/a
** Includes 3 meals

Dorm; Max. Pers: 2; Bedding incl ?: Yes; Bath: Semi-private; A/C: No
Rate for: Person: ** $74; Rate for #2 pers: ** $44; Rate for #3 pers: n/a; Child Rate: n/a
** Includes 3 meals

Bunkroom; Max. Pers: Over 5; Bedding incl ?: $7 surcharge; Bath: Shared; A/C: No:
Rate for: Person: ** $51; Rate for #2 pers: ** $51; Rate for #3 pers: ** $51; Child Rate: n/a
** Includes 3 meals

Main amenities available: Swimming; Volleyball; Basketball; Ball field; Ping-pong; Hike on 465 acres
Meals are served in dining room for transients only when other groups are present. Dinner price: $10; Children $7.

NAME OF CENTER: YMCA - Binghamton Listing ID: 240

Telephone: 607-772-0560   Fax: 607-772-0563
Address: 61 Susquehanna St.; Binghamton, NY 13901

Restrictions:
Accommodations offered to (M/F/Families): M. If M/F then must be over 16 yrs.
Pets: Not permitted; Alcohol: Not permitted; Smoking: Bedroom only
Reservation requirements: None
Reservations are accepted up to 0 days in advance. Seasonal closing: None

ACCOMMODATIONS:
Single room: Bedding included ?: Yes; Bath: Shared
Rate for 1 day: $12+$15 dep; Rate for 1 week: $70+$15 dep
Room fee includes membership in Y

Main amenities: Pool; Gym; TV lounge; Sauna; Steam room; Laundry machine
Meals are offered in their own cafeteria.

NAME OF CENTER: YMCA - **Buffalo** Listing ID: 241

Telephone: 716-883-9622   Fax: 716-881-2989
Address: 347 E. Ferry St.; Buffalo, NY 14208

Restrictions:
Accommodations offered to (M/F/Families): M. If M/F then must be over 18 yrs.
Pets: Not permitted; Alcohol: Not permitted; Smoking: Bedroom only
Reservation requirements: None
Reservations are accepted up to 0 days in advance. Seasonal closing: None

ACCOMMODATIONS:
Single room: Bedding included ?: Yes; Bath: Shared
Rate for 1 day: $20+$15 dep; Rate for 1 week: $57+$15 dep
$6 daily guest fee for use of Y

Main amenities: Pool; Gym; Steam room
Meals are not offered in their own cafeteria.

NAME OF CENTER: YMCA - **Niagra Falls** Listing ID: 242

Telephone: 716-285-8491   Fax: 716-285-1030
Address: 1317 Portage Rd.; Niagra Falls, NY 14301

Restrictions:
Accommodations offered to (M/F/Families): M. If M/F then must be over 18 yrs.
Pets: Not permitted; Alcohol: Not permitted; Smoking: Outdoors only
Reservation requirements: Yes w/ID
Reservations are accepted up to 0 days in advance. Seasonal closing: None

ACCOMMODATIONS:
Single room: Bedding included ?: Yes; Bath: Shared
Rate for 1 day: $25+$10 dep; Rate for 1 week: $95+$10 dep
Room fee includes membership in Y

Main amenities: Pool; Gym; TV lounge
Meals are not offered in their own cafeteria.

NAME OF CENTER: YMCA - **NYC - Flushing Br.** Listing ID: 243

Telephone: 718-961-6880   Fax: 718-461-4691
Address: 138-46 Northern Blvd; Flushing, NY 11354

Restrictions:
Accommodations offered to (M/F/Families): M&F. If M/F then must be over 18 yrs.
Pets: Not permitted; Alcohol: Not permitted; Smoking: Bedroom only
Reservation requirements: Yes w/credit card
Reservations are accepted up to 1 mo in advance. Seasonal closing: None

ACCOMMODATIONS:
Single room: Bedding included ?: Yes; Bath: Shared
Rate for 1 day: $28-46 + $10 dep; Rate for 1 week: not offered
Room fee includes membership in Y

Double room: Bedding included ?: Yes; Bath: Shared
Rate for 1 day: $65+$10 dep; Rate for 1 week: not offered
Double room for married couples only.

Main amenities: Pool; Gym; Sauna; Steam room; Laundry machine;
Meals are not offered in their own cafeteria.

NAME OF CENTER: YMCA - NYC - McBurney Br. Listing ID: 244

Telephone: 212-741-9226   Fax: 212-741-0012
Address: 215 W. 23rd St.; New York, NY 10011

Restrictions:
Accommodations offered to (M/F/Families): M&F.   If M/F then must be over 18 yrs.
Pets: Not permitted; Alcohol: Not permitted; Smoking: Bedroom only
Reservation requirements: None
Reservations are accepted up to 1 mo in advance.   Seasonal closing: None

ACCOMMODATIONS:
Single room: Bedding included ?: Yes; Bath: Shared
Rate for 1 day: $55+$5 dep; Rate for 1 week: not offered
Room fee includes membership in Y

Double room: Bedding included ?: Yes; Bath: Shared
Rate for 1 day: $67+$5 dep; Rate for 1 week: $469+$10 dep

Main amenities: Pool; Gym
Meals are offered in their own cafeteria.

NAME OF CENTER: YMCA - Queens Central Br. Listing ID: 245

Telephone: 718-739-6600   Fax: 718-658-7233
Address: 8925 Parsons Bld.; Jamica, NY 11432

Restrictions:
Accommodations offered to (M/F/Families): M.   If M/F then must be over 18 yrs.
Pets: Not permitted; Alcohol: Not permitted; Smoking: Bedroom only
Reservation requirements: None
Reservations are accepted up to 14 days in advance.   Seasonal closing: None

ACCOMMODATIONS:
Single room: Bedding included ?: Yes; Bath: Shared
Rate for 1 day: $43+$10 dep; Rate for 1 week: not offered
Room fee includes membeship in Y

Main amenities: Pool; Gym
Meals are not offered in their own cafeteria.

NAME OF CENTER: YMCA - NYC - **Vanderbilt Br.** Listing ID: 246

Telephone: 212-756-9600   Fax: 212-755-7579
Address: 224 E. 47th St.; New York, NY 10017

Restrictions:
Accommodations offered to (M/F/Families): M&F&Families. If M/F then must be over 18 yrs.
Pets: Not permitted; Alcohol: Not permitted; Smoking: Outdoors only
Reservation requirements: None
Reservations are accepted up to 1 mo w/credit card in advance. Seasonal closing: None

ACCOMMODATIONS:
Single room: Bedding included ?: Yes; Bath: Shared
Rate for 1 day: $65; Rate for 1 week: not offered

Double room: Bedding included ?: Yes; Bath: Shared
Rate for 1 day: $78; Rate for 1 week:

Main amenities: Pool; Gym; Laundry machine
Meals are not offered in their own cafeteria.

NAME OF CENTER: YMCA - NYC - **West Side Br.** Listing ID: 247

Telephone: 212-875-4100   Fax: 212-580-0441
Address: 5 W. 63rd st.; New York, NY 10023

Restrictions:
Accommodations offered to (M/F/Families): M&F. If M/F then must be over 18 yrs.
Pets: Not permitted; Alcohol: Not permitted; Smoking: Outdoors only
Reservation requirements: 1 night's dep req'd
Reservations are accepted up to 14 days in advance. Seasonal closing: None

ACCOMMODATIONS:
Single room: Bedding included ?: Yes; Bath: Shared
Rate for 1 day: $65+$10 dep (W/TV); Rate for 1 week: not offered

Double room: Bedding included ?: Yes; Bath: Shared
Rate for 1 day: $75+$20 dep (w/TV); Rate for 1 week:

Main amenities: Pool ; Gym; Laundry machine
Meals are offered in their own cafeteria.

NAME OF CENTER: YMCA - Port Chester/Rye Brook Listing ID: 248

Telephone: 914-939-7800   Fax: 914-939-5407
Address: 400 Westchester Ave.; Port Chester, NY 10573

Restrictions:
Accommodations offered to (M/F/Families): M. If M/F then must be over 21 yrs.
Pets: Not permitted; Alcohol: Not permitted; Smoking: Bedroom only
Reservation requirements: None
Reservations are accepted up to 0 days in advance. Seasonal closing: None

ACCOMMODATIONS:
Single room: Bedding included ?: Yes; Bath: Shared
Rate for 1 day: not offered; Rate for 1 week: $90+$25 dep
Room fee includes membership in Y

Main amenities: Pool ; Gym; Fitness center; Sauna
Meals are not offered in their own cafeteria.

NAME OF CENTER: YMCA - Schenectady Listing ID: 249

Telephone: 518-374-9136   Fax: 518-370-5526
Address: 13 State St.; Schenectady, NY 12305

Restrictions:
Accommodations offered to (M/F/Families): M. If M/F then must be over 18 yrs.
Pets: Not permitted; Alcohol: Not permitted; Smoking: Bedroom only
Reservation requirements: None
Reservations are accepted up to 0 days in advance. Seasonal closing: None

ACCOMMODATIONS:
Single: Bedding included ?: Yes; Bath: Shared
Rate for 1 day: $22-24 + $10 dep; Rate for 1 week: $60-64 + $10 dep
Room fee includes membership in Y

Main amenities: Pool; Gym; TV lounge; Laundry machine
Meals are not offered in their own cafeteria.

NAME OF CENTER: YMCA - Syracuse - Downtown Br. Listing ID: 250

Telephone: 315-474-6851   Fax: 315-474-6857
Address: 340 Montgomery St.; Syracuse, NY 13202

Restrictions:
Accommodations offered to (M/F/Families): M. If M/F then must be over 18 yrs.
Pets: Not permitted; Alcohol: Not permitted; Smoking: Bedroom only
Reservation requirements: None
Reservations are accepted up to 0 days in advance. Seasonal closing: None

ACCOMMODATIONS:
Single: Bedding included ?: Yes; Bath: Shared
Rate for 1 day: $30+$3 dep; Rate for 1 week: $82+$3 dep
Room fee includes membership in Y

Main amenities: Pool; Gym; Laundry machine
Meals are not offered in their own cafeteria.

NAME OF CENTER: YMCA - Yonkers Listing ID: 251

Telephone: 914-963-0183   Fax: 914-963-0315
Address: 17 Riverdale Ave.; Yonkers, NY 10701

Restrictions:
Accommodations offered to (M/F/Families): M. If M/F then must be over 18 yrs.
Pets: Not permitted; Alcohol: Not permitted; Smoking: Bedroom only
Reservation requirements: None
Reservations are accepted up to 0 days in advance. Seasonal closing: None

ACCOMMODATIONS:
Single room: Bedding included ?: Yes; Bath: Shared
Rate for 1 day: not offered; Rate for 1 week: $90
$10 daily guest fee for use of Y

Main amenities: Laundry machine; Volleyball; Basketball; Hiking
Meals are not offered in their own cafeteria.

NAME OF CENTER: YWCA - Brooklyn Listing ID: 252

Telephone: 718-875-1190   Fax: 718-858-5731
Address: 30 Third Ave.; Brooklyn, NY 11217

Restrictions:
Accommodations offered to (M/F/Families): F. If M/F then must be over 18 yrs.
Pets: Not permitted; Alcohol: Not permitted; Smoking: Outdoors only
Reservation requirements: None
Reservations are accepted up to 0 days in advance. Seasonal closing: None

ACCOMMODATIONS:
Single room: Bedding included ?: Yes; Bath: Shared
Rate for 1 day: $30+$80 dep; Rate for 1 week: $210+$80 dep

Main amenities: TV lounge; Laundry machine
Meals are not offered in their own cafeteria.

NORTH CAROLINA

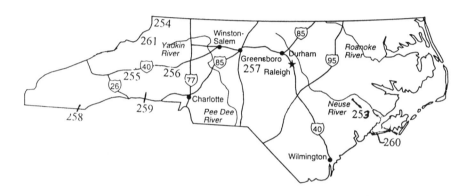

NAME OF CENTER: Camp Carolwood, Inc.　Listing ID #: 253

Telephone: 828-758-1468; Fax: ; E-mail:
Address: 1181 Camp Carolwood Rd.; Lenoir; NC; 28645
Nearest Interstate: US-321, Exit 13 miles; Nearest State/US Hwy: Rte 268; 1 miles.

Restrictions: Age: 1; Pets: Not permitted; Alcohol: Not permitted; Smoking: Outdoors only; Reservation Req'd: 5 days; Max. Adv. Reser.: Open; Seasonal closing: None

RV/Campers overnight hookups: No

ACCOM: Mon. night thru Thurs. night rates for winterized (check if this is critical) rooms w/o meals unless otherwise indicated.

Cabins-2 rooms; Max. Pers: 8 per rm; Bedding incl ?: No; Bath: Shared; A/C: :
Rate for: Person; $14; Rate for #2 pers: $14; Rate for #3 pers: $14; Child Rate: n/a
Sweep and mop area daily

Motel; Max. Pers: 2; Bedding incl ?: No; Bath: Private; A/C:
Rate for: Person: $14; Rate for #2 pers: $14; Child Rate:
Sweep and mop area daily

Main amenities available: Swimming; Volleyball; Basketball; Ball field; Hiking;
Meals are served in dining room for transients only when other groups are present. Dinner price: $5.00.

NAME OF CENTER: Camp Elk Shoals　Listing ID #: 254

Telephone: 336-877-4607; Fax: ; E-mail:
Address: 349 Methodist Camp Rd.; West Jefferson; NC; 28694
Nearest Interstate: I-81, Exit 35 miles; Nearest State/US Hwy: Rte 163; 2 miles.

Restrictions: Age: None; Pets: Not permitted; Alcohol: Not permitted; Smoking: Outdoors only; Reservation Req'd: None; Max. Adv. Reser.: 1 mo; Seasonal closing: None

RV/Campers overnight hookups: Yes; Water: Yes; Electric: Yes; Septic: Yes
Basic Rate/Night: $16.00/ veh

ACCOM: Mon. night thru Thurs. night rates for winterized (check if this is critical) rooms w/o meals unless otherwise indicated.

** Cottage; Max. Pers: 3 per rm; Bedding incl ?: No; Bath: Private; A/C: Yes:
Rate for: Room; $30
**Cottage has 4 bedrooms; Use of kitchen if all 4 rms rented.

Main amenities available: 354 acres on New River; Volleyball; Playground; Athletic field; Mountain biking
Meals are served in dining room for transients only when other groups are present. Dinner price: $5.00.

NAME OF CENTER: Camp Grier Listing ID #: 255

Telephone: 828-668-7793; Fax: 828-668-9096; E-mail:
Address: PO Box 490; Old Fort; NC; 28762
Nearest Interstate: I-40, Exit 73; 5 miles; Nearest State/US Hwy: Rte 70; 2 miles.

Restrictions: Age: None; Pets: Not permitted; Alcohol: Not permitted; Smoking: Outdoors only;
Reservation Req'd: None; Max. Adv. Reser.: 1 yr; Seasonal closing: None

RV/Campers overnight hookups: No

ACCOM: Mon. night thru Thurs. night rates for winterized (check if this is critical) rooms w/o
meals unless otherwise indicated.

Cabin; Max. Pers: 12-16; Bedding incl ?: No; Bath: Shared; A/C: No:
Rate for: Person; $11; Rate for #2 pers: $11; Rate for #3 pers: $11; Child Rate: Free under 4
yrs

Dorm; Max. Pers: 5; Bedding incl ?: No; Bath: Shared; A/C: No
Rate for: Person; $11; Rate for #2 pers: $11; Rate for #3 pers: $11; Child Rate: Free under 4
yrs.

Main amenities available: Swim in pool/lake; Volleyball; Boat/Canoeing; Horse shoes; Ball field; Hiking
Meals are served in dining room for transients only when other groups are present. Dinner price: $6.25; $5.25
under 10 yrs.

NAME OF CENTER: Catholic Conference Center Listing ID #: 256

Telephone: 888-536-7441; Fax: 828-327-0872; E-mail: www.catholicconference.org
Address: 1551 Trinity Lane; Hickory; NC; 28602
Nearest Interstate: I-40, Exit 12 miles; Nearest State/US Hwy: NC 10; 3 miles.

Restrictions: Age: None; Pets: Not permitted; Alcohol: Not permitted; Smoking: 5 smoking
rooms & outside; Reservation Req'd: 2 days; Max. Adv. Reser.: 1 yr (dep w far adv res.);
Seasonal closing: None

RV/Campers overnight hookups: No

ACCOM: Mon. night thru Thurs. night rates for winterized (check if this is critical) rooms w/o
meals unless otherwise indicated.

Motel; Max. Pers: 4; Bedding incl ?: Yes; Bath: Private; A/C: Yes:
Rate for: Person; $54; Rate for #2 pers: $16; Rate for #3 pers: $26; Child Rate: n/a

Main amenities available: Laundry machine; Game room; Ping-pong; V-ball; Bsk ball; Horse shoes; Hiking
Meals are served in dining room for transients only when other groups are present. Dinner price: $9.00.

REMEMBER TO CALL AHEAD

NAME OF CENTER: Mount Sheperd Retreat Center   Listing ID #: 257

Telephone: 336-629-4085; Fax: 336-629-4880; E-mail: mtsheph@asheboro.com
Address: 1045 Mount Shepherd Road Extension; Asheboro; NC; 27203
Nearest Interstate: I-85, Exit 15 miles; Nearest State/US Hwy: Rte 64; 2 miles.

Restrictions: Age: None; Pets: Not permitted; Alcohol: Not permitted; Smoking: Outdoors only;
Reservation Req'd: 3 days; Max. Adv. Reser.: 2 mo; Seasonal closing: None

RV/Campers overnight hookups: Yes; Water: Yes; Electric: Yes; Septic: No
Basic Rate/Night: $20.00/ veh

ACCOM: Mon. night thru Thurs. night rates for winterized (check if this is critical) rooms w/o
meals unless otherwise indicated.

**Cottage; Max. Pers: Over 8; Bedding incl ?: Yes w/notice; Bath: Private; A/C: Yes:
Rate for: Entire Cottage; $250
** Includes: living rm; dining rm; lge fireplace; multiple bedrooms; patio; kitchen

Main amenities available: Horseback riding; Canoeing; Basketball; Golf; Ropes course; Hiking
Meals are served in dining room for transients only when other groups are present. Dinner price: $4.65-6.10.

NAME OF CENTER: Mountain Retreat & Learning Center   Listing ID #: 258

Telephone: 828-526-5838; Fax: 828-526-2511; E-mail:
Address: 3872 Dillard Rd (PO Box 1299); Highlands; NC; 28741
Nearest Interstate: I-40, Exit 60 miles; Nearest State/US Hwy: US 441; 1 miles.

Restrictions: Age: None; Pets: Not permitted; Alcohol: Hard liquor not permitted; Smoking:
Designated outdoor area; Reservation Req'd: None; Max. Adv. Reser.: 6 mo; Seasonal closing:
None

RV/Campers overnight hookups: No

ACCOM: Mon. night thru Thurs. night rates for winterized (check if this is critical) rooms w/o
meals unless otherwise indicated.

Motel; Max. Pers: 2; Bedding incl ?: Yes; Bath: Private; A/C: No:
Rate for: Person; $43; Rate for #2 pers: $43; Child Rate: n/a

Cabin; Max. Pers: 2-4; Bedding incl ?: Yes; Bath: Private; A/C: No
Rate for: Person: $38; Rate for #2 pers: $38; Rate for #3 pers: $38; Child Rate: Free under 17
yrs

Main amenities available: Lake; Volleyball; Foosball; Boating; Ropes/Climbing wall; Hiking
Meals are served in dining room for transients only when other groups are present. Dinner price: $9.00.

NAME OF CENTER: South Mountain Christian Camp   Listing ID #: 259

Telephone: 828-245-3322; Fax: 828-245-1659; E-mail: smcc@blueridge.net
Address: 1129 South Mountain Rd.; Bostic; NC; 28018
Nearest Interstate: I-40, Exit 25 miles; Nearest State/US Hwy: Rte 74; 10 miles.

Restrictions: Age: None; Pets: Not permitted; Alcohol: Not permitted; Smoking: Outdoors only;
Reservation Req'd: 15 days; Max. Adv. Reser.: Open; Seasonal closing: Bunkroom not
available May 15 - Aug 31

RV/Campers overnight hookups: No

ACCOM: Mon. night thru Thurs. night rates for winterized (check if this is critical) rooms w/o
meals unless otherwise indicated.

Bunkroom; Max. Pers: 24; Bedding incl ?: No; Bath: Shared; A/C: Yes:
Rate for: Person; $10; Rate for #2 pers: $10; Rate for #3 pers: $10; Child Rate: n/a
Min: $120

Cabin; Max. Pers: 5; Bedding incl ?: Yes; Bath: Private; A/C: Yes
Rate for: Person: $35; Rate for #2 pers: $5; Rate for #3 pers: $5; Child Rate: n/a

Main amenities available: Fishing; Volleyball; Basketball; Ball field; Ropes course; Hiking
Meals are served in dining room for transients only when other groups are present. Dinner price: $4.00.

NAME OF CENTER: Trinity Center   Listing ID #: 260

Telephone: 252-247-5000; Fax: 252-247-3290; E-mail: trinity@mail.clis.com
Address: PO Box 380; Salter Path; NC; 28575
Nearest Interstate: I-40, Exit 2 hrs hours; Nearest State/US Hwy: US 70; 5 miles.

Restrictions: Age: None; Pets: Not permitted; Alcohol: Permitted w/discretion; Smoking:
Outdoors only; Reservation Req'd: None; Max. Adv. Reser.: 14 days; Seasonal closing:
Christmas Eve & Day; Thanksgiving (Thurs & Fri)

RV/Campers overnight hookups: No

ACCOM: Mon. night thru Thurs. night rates for winterized (check if this is critical) rooms w/o
meals unless otherwise indicated.

Motel; Max. Pers: 5; Bedding incl ?: Yes; Bath: Private; A/C: Yes:
Rate for: Person; $30; Rate for #2 pers: $5; Rate for #3 pers: $3; Child Rate: n/a

Main amenities available: Living room for ea cluster of 12 bedrooms; Ocean front; Basketball; Swimming;
VCR-TV; Pool
Meals are served in dining room for transients only when other groups are present. Dinner price: $8.00.

NAME OF CENTER: TVR Christian Camp   Listing ID #: 261

Telephone: 704-765-7860; Fax: 704-765-0690; E-mail:
Address: PO Box 10; 216 Teen Valley Ranch Rd.; Plumtree; NC; 28664
Nearest Interstate: I-40, Exit 50 miles; Nearest State/US Hwy: Rte 19E; 1 miles.

Restrictions: Age: None; Pets: Not permitted; Alcohol: Not permitted; Smoking: Outdoors only;
Reservation Req'd: None; Max. Adv. Reser.: Open; Seasonal closing: None

RV/Campers overnight hookups: No

ACCOM: Mon. night thru Thurs. night rates for winterized (check if this is critical) rooms w/o
meals unless otherwise indicated.

Dorm; Max. Pers: 6-10; Bedding incl ?: No; Bath: Shared; A/C: No:
Rate for: Person; $35-40; Rate for #2 pers: $35-40; Rate for #3 pers: $35-40;   Child Rate:
Inquire for discount schedule

Motel; Max. Pers: 6; Bedding incl ?: No; Bath: Private; A/C: No
Rate for: Person: $35-40; Rate for #2 pers: $35-40; Rate for #3 pers: $35-40; Child Rate:
Inquire for discount schedule.

Main amenities available: Gym; Game room; Bookstore; Horseback riding; Swimming; Hiking
Meals are served in dining room for transients only when other groups are present. Dinner price: $5.00.

NAME OF CENTER: YMCA - Raleigh Capital Area Listing ID: 262

Telephone: 919-832-6602   Fax: 919-834-3506
Address: 1601 Hillsborough St; PO Box 10976; Raleigh, NC 27605

Restrictions:
Accommodations offered to (M/F/Families): M. If M/F then must be over 18 yrs.
Pets: Not permitted; Alcohol: Not permitted; Smoking: Bedroom only
Reservation requirements: None
Reservations are accepted up to 0 days in advance. Seasonal closing: None

ACCOMMODATIONS:
Single room: Bedding included ?: Yes; Bath: Shared
Rate for 1 day: $19+$2 dep; Rate for 1 week: n/a

Main amenities: TV lounge; Pool; Gym
Meals are offered in their own cafeteria.

NAME OF CENTER: YMCA - Rocky-Mount Listing ID: 263

Telephone: 252-972-9622   Fax: 252-972-3580
Address: PO Box 4063; Rocky Mount, NC 27803

Restrictions:
Accommodations offered to (M/F/Families): M. If M/F then must be over 18 yrs.
Pets: Not permitted; Alcohol: Not permitted; Smoking: Bedroom only
Reservation requirements: None
Reservations are accepted up to 7 days in advance. Seasonal closing: None

ACCOMMODATIONS:
Single room: Bedding included ?: Yes; Bath: Shared
Rate for 1 day: not offered; Rate for 1 week: not offered
Room fee includes membership in Y

Main amenities: Pool; Gym; TV lounge; Laundry machine
Meals are not offered in their own cafeteria.

NORTH DAKOTA

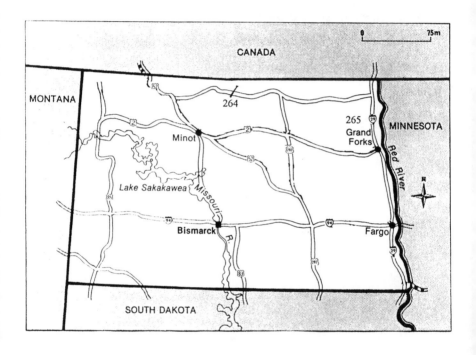

NAME OF CENTER: Metigoshe Lutheran Bible Camp   Listing ID #: 264

Telephone: 701-263-4788; Fax: 701-263-4250; E-mail: kaleberti@metigoshe.ndak.net
Address: 10605 Lake Loop Road East; Bottineau; ND; 58318
Nearest Interstate: I-94, Exit 150 miles; Nearest State/US Hwy: Rte 5; 16 miles.

Restrictions: Age: None; Pets: Not permitted; Alcohol: Not permitted; Smoking: Outdoors only;
Reservation Req'd: 2 days; Max. Adv. Reser.: 7 days; Seasonal closing: None

RV/Campers overnight hookups: Yes; Water: No; Electric: Yes; Septic: No
Basic Rate/Night: $5.00/ veh

ACCOM: Mon. night thru Thurs. night rates for winterized (check if this is critical) rooms w/o
meals unless otherwise indicated.

Dormitory; Max. Pers: 2; Bedding incl ?: No; Bath: Shared; A/C: Yes:
Rate for: Person; $6; Rate for #2 pers: $6; Child Rate: n/a

Motel; Max. Pers: 4; Bedding incl ?: Yes; Bath: Private; A/C: Yes
Rate for: Room: $35; Child Rate: n/a

Main amenities available: Lake; Volleyball; Basketball; Canoeing/Kyaking; Child swings; VCR-TV
Meals are served in dining room for transients only when other groups are present. Dinner price: $6; 50% off
under 12 yrs.

NAME OF CENTER: Park River Lutheran Bible Camp   Listing ID #: 265

Telephone: 701-284-6795; Fax: 701-284-6796; E-mail: quanbeck@polarcomm.com
Address: 106 Solid Rock Circle; Park River; ND; 58270
Nearest Interstate: I-29, Exit 35 miles; Nearest State/US Hwy: Rte 17; 1 miles.

Restrictions: Age: None; Pets: Permitted on leash; Alcohol: Not permitted; Smoking:
Designated outdoor area; Reservation Req'd: 2 days; Max. Adv. Reser.: 2 wks w/dep; Seasonal
closing: 2 weeks at Christmas

RV/Campers overnight hookups: Yes; Water: Yes; Electric: Yes; Septic: No
Basic Rate/Night: $6.00/ veh

ACCOM: Mon. night thru Thurs. night rates for winterized (check if this is critical) rooms w/o
meals unless otherwise indicated.

Cabin; Max. Pers: 12; Bedding incl ?: No; Bath: Separate bldg; A/C: No:
Rate for: Person; $13; Rate for #2 pers: $13; Rate for #3 pers: $13; Child Rate: Free under 5 yrs

Dorm; Max. Pers: 10; Bedding incl ?: No; Bath: Shared; A/C: No
Rate for: Person: $13; Rate for #2 pers: $13; Rate for #3 pers: $13; Child Rate: Free under 5 yrs

Motel; Max. Pers: 2; Bedding incl ?: Yes; Bath: Private; A/C: No:
Rate for: Person: $13; Rate for #2 pers: $13; Child Rate: n/a

Main amenities available: Child swings/slide; Volleyball; Basketball; VCR-TV; Hiking
Meals are not served in dining room for transients .

OHIO

NAME OF CENTER: Assemblies of God Camp   Listing ID #: 266

Telephone: 330-496-2381; Fax: 330-496-4105; E-mail:
Address: 13529 County Rd 100; Big Prairie; OH; 44611
Nearest Interstate: I-71, Exit 30 miles; Nearest State/US Hwy: Rte 226; 1 miles.

Restrictions: Age: None; Pets: Not permitted; Alcohol: Not permitted; Smoking: Outdoors only; Reservation Req'd: 1 day; Max. Adv. Reser.: Open; Seasonal closing: June - Aug

RV/Campers overnight hookups: Yes; Water: Yes; Electric: Yes; Septic: No
Basic Rate/Night: $12 + $1/pers >4/ veh

ACCOM: Mon. night thru Thurs. night rates for winterized (check if this is critical) rooms w/o meals unless otherwise indicated.

Cabin; Max. Pers: Over 4; Bedding incl ?: Yes; Bath: Shared; A/C: Yes:
Rate for: Entire cabin; $39
$6/person over 4 persons; includes kitchenette

Main amenities available: Putt-Putt 18 holes; V-ball; Bsk ball; Laundry machine; Bookstore; Canoeing; Hiking
Meals are served in dining room for transients only when other groups are present. Dinner price: $5-6.00.

NAME OF CENTER: Camp Gideon   Listing ID #: 267

Telephone: 330-738-6871; Fax: 330-493-1660; E-mail: efcer@aol.com
Address: 7261 salineville Rd; Mechanicstown; OH; 44651
Nearest Interstate: I-77, Exit 22 miles; Nearest State/US Hwy: Rte 39; 0 miles.

Restrictions: Age: None; Pets: Not permitted; Alcohol: Not permitted; Smoking: Outdoors only; Reservation Req'd: 5 days; Max. Adv. Reser.: Open; Seasonal closing: Limited to RV use June - Aug 15

RV/Campers overnight hookups: Yes; Water: n/a; Electric: n/a; Septic: n/a
Basic Rate/Night: $10.00/ veh

ACCOM: Mon. night thru Thurs. night rates for winterized (check if this is critical) rooms w/o meals unless otherwise indicated.

Motel; Max. Pers: 5; Bedding incl ?: No; Bath: Private; A/C: Yes:
Rate for: Person; $15; Rate for #2 pers: $15; Rate for #3 pers: $15; Child Rate: $5

Dorm; Max. Pers: 5; Bedding incl ?: No; Bath: Shared; A/C: Yes
Rate for: Person: $12; Rate for #2 pers: $12; Rate for #3 pers: $12; Child Rate: $5.00

Bunkroom; Max. Pers: Over 5; Bedding incl ?: No; Bath: shared; A/C: Yes:
Rate for: Person: $10; Rate for #2 pers: $10; Rate for #3 pers: $10; Child Rate: $5

Main amenities available: Waterfront activities; V-ball; Bsk ball; Canoeing; VCR-TV; Ball field; Hiking
Meals are served in dining room for transients only when other groups are present. Dinner price: $4-6.00.

NAME OF CENTER: Camp Mowana   Listing ID #: 268

Telephone: 419-589-7406; Fax: 419-589-3096; E-mail: mowana@aol.com
Address: 2276 Fleming Falls Rd.; Mansfield; OH; 44903
Nearest Interstate: I-71, Exit 5 miles; Nearest State/US Hwy: Rte 30; 3 miles.

Restrictions: Age: None; Pets: Not permitted; Alcohol: Not permitted; Smoking: Outdoors only;
Reservation Req'd: 1 day; Max. Adv. Reser.: Open; Seasonal closing: None

RV/Campers overnight hookups: No

ACCOM: Mon. night thru Thurs. night rates for winterized (check if this is critical) rooms w/o
meals unless otherwise indicated.

Dorm; Max. Pers: 4; Bedding incl ?: No; Bath: Shared; A/C: No:
Rate for: Person; $46; Rate for #2 pers: $46; Rate for #3 pers: $46; Child Rate: 50% off under
12 yrs; free under 4 1/2 yrs

Main amenities available: Swimming; V-ball; Bsk ball; Library/ VCR-TV; Laundry machine; Incidentals store;
Hiking
Meals are served in dining room for transients only when other groups are present. Dinner price varies.

NAME OF CENTER: Camp Otyokwah   Listing ID #: 269

Telephone: 419-883-3854; Fax: 419-883-3854; E-mail:
Address: 3380 Tugend Rd; Butler; OH; 44822
Nearest Interstate: I-71, Exit 10 miles.

Restrictions: Age: None; Pets: Not permitted; Alcohol: Not permitted; Smoking: Outdoors only;
Reservation Req'd: 2 days; Max. Adv. Reser.: Open; Seasonal closing: None

RV/Campers overnight hookups: Yes; Water: Yes; Electric: Yes; Septic: n/a
Basic Rate/Night: $12.00/ veh

ACCOM: Mon. night thru Thurs. night rates for winterized (check if this is critical) rooms w/o
meals unless otherwise indicated.

Dorm; Max. Pers: 4; Bedding incl ?: No; Bath: Semi-private; A/C: No:
Rate for: Room; $95; Child Rate: n/a

Bunkroom; Max. Pers: 20-40; Bedding incl ?: No; Bath: Shared; A/C: No
Rate for: Person: $12; Rate for #2 pers: $12; Rate for #3 pers: $12; Child Rate: Free under 4 yrs

Main amenities available: Swimming in pond; V-ball; Bsk ball; Ball field; Canoeing; Ping-pong; Hiking
Meals are served in dining room for transients only when other groups are present. Dinner price: $6.00.

REMEMBER TO CALL AHEAD

NAME OF CENTER: Epworth Center   Listing ID #: 270

Telephone: 740-484-4705; Fax: 740-484-0252; E-mail:
Address: 301 N. Main St.; PO box 538; Bethesda; OH; 43719
Nearest Interstate: I-70, Exit 4 miles.

Restrictions: Age: None; Pets: Permoitted on leash; Alcohol: Not permitted; Smoking:
Outdoors only; Reservation Req'd: 1 day; Max. Adv. Reser.: 1 yr; Seasonal closing: None

RV/Campers overnight hookups: Yes; Water: No; Electric: Yes; Septic: No
Basic Rate/Night: $7.00/ veh

ACCOM: Mon. night thru Thurs. night rates for winterized (check if this is critical) rooms w/o
meals unless otherwise indicated.

Cabin; Max. Pers: Over 8; Bedding incl ?: No; Bath: Shared; A/C: No:
Rate for: Person; $4; Rate for #2 pers: $4; Rate for #3 pers: $4; Child Rate: n/a
4 rms with 2-4 beds each

Cottage Hse; Max. Pers: 5; Bedding incl ?: No; Bath: Shared; A/C: No
Rate for: Entire Hse: $25
Avail April thru Nov; includes kitchen w/utensils

Main amenities available: Laundry machine; Volleyball; Basketball; Pool table/ping-pong; VCR-TV; Hiking
Meals are not served in dining room for transients .

NAME OF CENTER: **Faith Ranch**   Listing ID #: 271

Telephone: 740-946-2255; Fax: 740-946-7661; E-mail:
Address: Box 384; State Rte 9; Jewett; OH; 43986
Nearest Interstate: I-77, Exit 30 miles; Nearest State/US Hwy: US 22; 6 miles.

Restrictions: Age: None; Pets: Permitted; Alcohol: Not permitted; Smoking: Outdoors only;
Reservation Req'd: None; Max. Adv. Reser.: Open; Seasonal closing: None

RV/Campers overnight hookups: Yes; Water: Yes; Electric: Yes; Septic: No
Basic Rate/Night: $6/pers; max $18/ veh

ACCOM: Mon. night thru Thurs. night rates for winterized (check if this is critical) rooms w/o
meals unless otherwise indicated.

Cabin; Max. Pers: 8; Bedding incl ?: $3.50 surcharge; Bath: Shared; A/C: No:
Rate for: Person; $8; Rate for #2 pers: $8; Rate for #3 pers: $8; Child Rate: 50% off for
preschool children; free for babies

Motel; Max. Pers: 10; Bedding incl ?: $3.50 surcharge; Bath: Private; A/C: No
Rate for: Person: $12; Rate for #2 pers: $12; Rate for #3 pers: $12; Child Rate: 50% off for
preschool children; free for babies

Main amenities available: Petting" animals; Swimming; Boats; Canoeing; Horseback riding; Hiking
Meals are served in dining room for transients . Dinner price: $6.00.

NAME OF CENTER: **Franciscan Renewal Center**   Listing ID #: 272

Telephone: 419-396-7970; Fax: 419-396-3355; E-mail:
Address: 321 Clay St.; Carey; OH; 43316
Nearest State/US Hwy: Rte 15; Exit 2 miles

Restrictions: Age: 18; Pets: Not permitted; Alcohol: Not permitted; Smoking: Outdoors only; Reservation Req'd: 7 days; Max. Adv. Reser.: 7 days; Seasonal closing: Christmas wk; Holy wk; Thanksgiving wk

RV/Campers overnight hookups: No

ACCOM: Mon. night thru Thurs. night rates for winterized (check if this is critical) rooms w/o meals unless otherwise indicated.

Motel; Max. Pers: 2; Bedding incl ?: Yes; Bath: Private; A/C: Yes:
Rate for: Person; $35; Rate for #2 pers: $10; Child Rate: n/a

Dorm; Max. Pers: 2; Bedding incl ?: Yes; Bath: Shared; A/C: No
Rate for: Person: $20; Rate for #2 pers: $15; Child Rate: n/a

Main amenities available: Quiet areas; Chapel; Cable TV in lobby; Gift shop
Meals are served in dining room for transients only when other groups are present. Dinner price: $7.00.

NAME OF CENTER: **Geneva Hills Center**   Listing ID #: 273

Telephone: 740-746-8439; Fax: 740-746-7958; E-mail:
Address: 1380 Blue Valley Rd.; Lancaster; OH; 43130
Nearest Interstate: I-70, Exit 40 miles; Nearest State/US Hwy: OH 33; 2 miles.

Restrictions: Age: None; Pets: Not permitted; Alcohol: Not permitted; Smoking: Outdoors only; Reservation Req'd: 7 days; Max. Adv. Reser.: Open; Seasonal closing: None

RV/Campers overnight hookups: Yes; Water: No; Electric: No; Septic: No
Basic Rate/Night: $5/pers; max $17/ veh

ACCOM: Mon. night thru Thurs. night rates for winterized (check if this is critical) rooms w/o meals unless otherwise indicated.

Bunkroom; Max. Pers: Over 5; Bedding incl ?: Yes; Bath: Shared; A/C: No:
Rate for: Person; $22; Rate for #2 pers: $22; Rate for #3 pers: $22; Child Rate: 50% off under 13 yrs; free under 4

Dorm; Max. Pers: 5; Bedding incl ?: Yes; Bath: Shared; A/C: Yes
Rate for: Person: $22; Rate for #2 pers: $22; Rate for #3 pers: $22; Child Rate: 50% off under 13 yrs; free under 4

Main amenities available: Swimming; V-ball; Bsk ball; Laundry machine; VCR-TV; Canoeing; Hiking
Meals are served in dining room for transients only when other groups are present. Dinner price: $7.50.

NAME OF CENTER: Highlands Camp & Conference Center   Listing ID #: 274

Telephone: 216-241-3966; Fax: 216-241-3969; E-mail: highlands@unidial.com
Address: 4246 Sweetwest Rd. N.W.; Middlefield; OH; 44062
Nearest Interstate: I-80, Exit 30 miles; Nearest State/US Hwy: Rte 322; 2 miles.

Restrictions: Age: None; Pets: Not permitted; Alcohol: Not permitted; Smoking: Outdoors only; Reservation Req'd: Noon of day; Max. Adv. Reser.: Open; Seasonal closing: None

RV/Campers overnight hookups: No

ACCOM: Mon. night thru Thurs. night rates for winterized (check if this is critical) rooms w/o meals unless otherwise indicated.

Cabin; Max. Pers: Over 8; Bedding incl ?: No; Bath: Shared; A/C: No:
Rate for: Entire cabin; $120-300

Main amenities available: Swimming; Volleyball; Ball field; Canoeing
Meals are not served in dining room for transients .

NAME OF CENTER: Wildwood Christian Education Center   Listing ID #: 275

Telephone: 513-831-3241; Fax: 513-831-8248; E-mail:
Address: 941 Barg Salt Run; Milford; OH; 45150
Nearest Interstate: I-275, Exit 5 miles; Nearest State/US Hwy: Rte 50; 1 miles.

Restrictions: Age: None; Pets: Not permitted; Alcohol: Not permitted; Smoking: Designated outdoor area; Reservation Req'd: None; Max. Adv. Reser.: Open; Seasonal closing: June 16 - Aug 8

RV/Campers overnight hookups: No

ACCOM: Mon. night thru Thurs. night rates for winterized (check if this is critical) rooms w/o meals unless otherwise indicated.

Bunkroom; Max. Pers: Over 10; Bedding incl ?: No; Bath: shared; A/C: No:
Rate for: Person; $15; Rate for #2 pers: $15; Rate for #3 pers: $15; Child Rate: n/a
$15/pers under 10 persons; $12 otherwise

Main amenities available: Swimming pool; V-ball; Bsk ball; Ball field; VCR-TV; Laundry machine; Hiking
Meals are served in dining room for transients only when other groups are present. Dinner price: $7.00.

NAME OF CENTER: Woodland Alters   Listing ID #: 276

Telephone: 800-213-1161; Fax: 937-588-4431; E-mail: alters@bright.net
Address: 33200 State Rte 41; Peebles; OH; 45660
Nearest State/US Hwy: Rte 32; 7 miles.

Restrictions: Age: None; Pets: Permitted; Alcohol: Not permitted; Smoking: Outdoors only;
Reservation Req'd: None; Max. Adv. Reser.: Open; Seasonal closing: None

RV/Campers overnight hookups: Yes; Water: Yes; Electric: Yes; Septic: No
Basic Rate/Night: $14.00/ veh

ACCOM: Mon. night thru Thurs. night rates for winterized (check if this is critical) rooms w/o
meals unless otherwise indicated.

Chalet; Max. Pers: 6; Bedding incl ?: $5 surcharge; Bath: Semi-private; A/C: No:
Rate for: Entire Chalet; $70
Chalet includes: 3 bedrooms; kitchen; living room

Lodge; Max. Pers: 24; Bedding incl ?: $5 surcharge; Bath: Shared; A/C: Yes
Rate for: Person: $18; Rate for #2 pers: $18; Rate for #3 pers: $18; Child Rate: Min: $108

Main amenities available: Swimming; V-ball; Bsk ball; Laundry machine; Ping-pong; VCR-TV; Hiking
Meals are served in dining room for transients only when other groups are present. Dinner price: $5; 50% off
under 12 yrs; free under 3.

NAME OF CENTER: YMCA - Canton Listing ID: 277

Telephone: 330-456-7141   Fax: 330-456-0513
Address: 405 2nd St. N.W.; Canton, OH 44702

Restrictions:
Accommodations offered to (M/F/Families): M. If M/F then must be over 18 yrs.
Pets: Not permitted; Alcohol: Not permitted; Smoking: Bedroom only
Reservation requirements: None
Reservations are accepted up to 0 days in advance. Seasonal closing: None

ACCOMMODATIONS:
Single room: Bedding included ?: Yes; Bath: Shared
Rate for 1 day: $15 + $5 dep; Rate for 1 week: $43+$5 dep

Main amenities: Swimming pool; Gym; TV lounge; Laundry machine
Meals are not offered in their own cafeteria.

NAME OF CENTER: YMCA - Cleveland (Bklyn Br.) Listing ID: 278

Telephone: 216-749-2355   Fax: 216-749-0041
Address: ** Pearl Rd 3831; Brooklyn, OH 44109

Restrictions:
Accommodations offered to (M/F/Families): M. If M/F then must be over 21 yrs.
Pets: Permitted; Alcohol: Not permitted; Smoking: Outdoors only
Reservation requirements: None
Reservations are accepted up to 0 days in advance. Seasonal closing: None

ACCOMMODATIONS:
Single room: Bedding included ?: Yes; Bath: Shared
Rate for 1 day: $27+$10 dep; Rate for 1 week: $86+$10 dep
Y membership $6/day; $7.70/wk ** Extension of 25th St.

Main amenities: Laundry machine; TV lounge
Meals are not offered in their own cafeteria.

NAME OF CENTER: YMCA - Mansfield Listing ID: 279

Telephone: 419-522-3517   Fax: 419-525-3009
Address: 455 Park Ave. W.; Mansfield, OH 44906

Restrictions:
Accommodations offered to (M/F/Families): M. If M/F then must be over 18 yrs.
Pets: Not permitted; Alcohol: Not permitted; Smoking: Bedroom only
Reservation requirements: None
Reservations are accepted up to 1 mo in advance. Seasonal closing: None

ACCOMMODATIONS:
Single room: Bedding included ?: Yes; Bath: Shared
Rate for 1 day: $21+$5 dep; Rate for 1 week: $51+$5 dep

Main amenities: Swimming pool; Gym; TV lounge
Meals are not offered in their own cafeteria.

OKLAHOMA

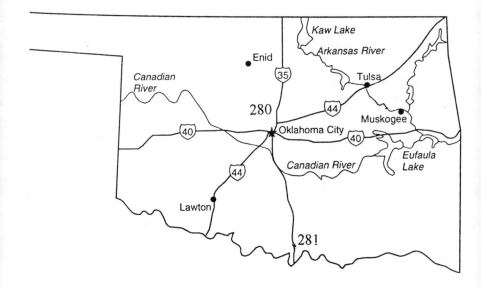

NAME OF CENTER: Central Christian Camp & Conf. Ctr.   Listing ID #: 280

Telephone: 405-282-2811; Fax: 405-282-1367; E-mail:
Address: One Twin Cedar Lane; Guthrie; OK; 73044
Nearest Interstate: I-35, Exit 2 miles; Nearest State/US Hwy: I-44; 15 miles.

Restrictions: Age: None; Pets: Permitted on leash; in cabin; Alcohol: Not permitted; Smoking: Designated outdoor area; Reservation Req'd: 10 AM of day; Max. Adv. Reser.: 14 days; Seasonal closing: None

RV/Campers overnight hookups: Yes; Water: Yes; Electric: Yes; Septic: No
Basic Rate/Night: $5.90+ $2.55/pers/ veh

ACCOM: Mon. night thru Thurs. night rates for winterized (check if this is critical) rooms w/o meals unless otherwise indicated.

Cabin; Max. Pers: 10; Bedding incl ?: No; Bath: Separate bldg; A/C: Yes:
Rate for: Person; ** $9; Rate for #2 pers: $9; Rate for #3 pers: $9; Child Rate: n/a
**Max for cabin: $47 plus $2.55 per person

Main amenities available: Swimming; V-ball; Bsk-ball; Canoe/boat; Laundry machine; Fishing; Hiking
Meals are served in dining room for transients only when other groups are present. Dinner price: $7.35; 25% off under 12 yrs; 50% off under 5; free under 2.

NAME OF CENTER: Cross Point Camp   Listing ID #: 281

Telephone: 580-564-2505; Fax: 580-564-2339; E-mail:
Address: HC 70; Box 1515; Kingston; OK; 73439
Nearest Interstate: I-35, Exit 39 miles; Nearest State/US Hwy: Rte 70; 5 miles.

Restrictions: Age: None; Pets: Not permitted; Alcohol: Not permitted; Smoking: Outdoors only; Reservation Req'd: 1 day; Max. Adv. Reser.: 1 yr; Seasonal closing: June - Aug.

RV/Campers overnight hookups: Yes; Water: Yes; Electric: Yes; Septic: Yes
Basic Rate/Night: $8.50+ $1/pers/ veh

ACCOM: Mon. night thru Thurs. night rates for winterized (check if this is critical) rooms w/o meals unless otherwise indicated.

Bunkroom; Max. Pers: 9; Bedding incl ?: No; Bath: Shared; A/C: No:
Rate for: Person; $15; Rate for #2 pers: $15; Rate for #3 pers: $15; Child Rate: $7.50 under 7 yrs; free under 1
Kitchen privileges

Cabins; Max. Pers: 4; Bedding incl ?: No; Bath: Private; A/C: No
Rate for: Person: $26; Rate for #2 pers: $9; Rate for #3 pers: $9; Child Rate: n/a
Max: $48; includes kitchenette

Main amenities available: Beach on lake; V-ball; Bsk-ball; Canoe/boat; Fishing; Horse shoes; Tetherball
Meals are served in dining room for transients only when other groups are present. Dinner price: $5.50; 50% off under 7 yrs; free under 1.

NAME OF CENTER: YMCA - Greater Tulsa Listing ID: 282

Telephone: 918-583-6201   Fax: 918-584-9622
Address: 515 S. Denver Ave.; Tulse, OK 74103

Restrictions:
Accommodations offered to (M/F/Families): M/F. If M/F then must be over 18 yrs.
Pets: Not permitted; Alcohol: Not permitted; Smoking: Bedroom only
Reservation requirements: None
Reservations are accepted up to 0 days in advance. Seasonal closing: None

ACCOMMODATIONS:
Single room: Bedding included ?: Yes; Bath: Shared
Rate for 1 day: $18+$10 dep; Rate for 1 week: $62+$10 dep

Main amenities: Laundry machine; Pool; Gym; Hot tub/sauna; Steam room; TV lounge
Meals are not offered in their own cafeteria.

OREGON

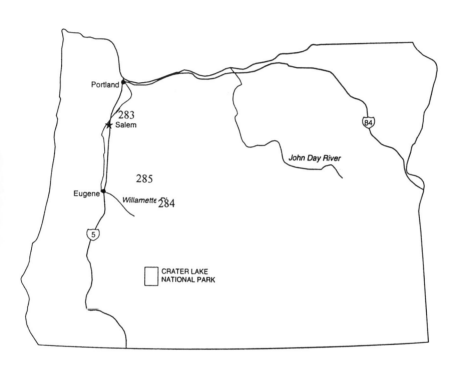

NAME OF CENTER: Christian Renewal Center   Listing ID #: 283

Telephone: 503-873-6743; Fax: 503-873-8300; E-mail:
Address: 22444 N. Fork Rd., SE; Silverton; OR; 97381
Nearest Interstate: I-5, Exit 28 miles; Nearest State/US Hwy: Rte 214; 1 miles.

Restrictions: Age: None; Pets: Not permitted; Alcohol: Not permitted; Smoking: Outdoors only;
Reservation Req'd: Noon of day; Max. Adv. Reser.: 14 days; Seasonal closing: None

RV/Campers overnight hookups: Yes; Water: Yes; Electric: Yes; Septic: n/a
Basic Rate/Night: $15.00/ veh

ACCOM: Mon. night thru Thurs. night rates for winterized (check if this is critical) rooms w/o
meals unless otherwise indicated.

Cabin; Max. Pers: 4; Bedding incl ?: $5 surcharge; Bath: Separate bldg; A/C: unk:
Rate for: Person; $16; Rate for #2 pers: $16; Rate for #3 pers: $16; Child Rate: n/a

Cabin; Max. Pers: 4; Bedding incl ?: $5 surcharge; Bath: In bldg, shared; A/C: unk
Rate for: Person: $25; Rate for #2 pers: $25; Rate for #3 pers: $25; Child Rate: n/a

Dorm; Max. Pers: 6; Bedding incl ?: $5 surcharge; Bath: Shared; A/C: unk:
Rate for: Person: $25; Rate for #2 pers: $25; Rate for #3 pers: $25; Child Rate: n/a

Main amenities available: Children playground; Volleyball; Basketball; Adj. to State Park; Hiking;
Meals are served in dining room for transients only when other groups are present. Dinner price varies.

NAME OF CENTER: Mountain Lakes Bible Camp   Listing ID #: 284

Telephone: 541-885-8161; Fax: 541-884-8725; E-mail:
Address: 21200 Varney Creek Rd.; Rocky Point; OR; 97601
Nearest Interstate: I-5, Exit 45 miles; Nearest State/US Hwy: Rte 140; 2 miles.

Restrictions: Age: 5; Pets: Not permitted; Alcohol: Not permitted; Smoking: Designated
outdoor area; Reservation Req'd: None; Max. Adv. Reser.: 3 mo; Seasonal closing: December

RV/Campers overnight hookups: Yes; Water: Yes; Electric: Yes; Septic: Yes
Basic Rate/Night: $13.00/ veh

ACCOM: Mon. night thru Thurs. night rates for winterized (check if this is critical) rooms w/o
meals unless otherwise indicated.

Cabin; Max. Pers: 12; Bedding incl ?: No; Bath: Separate bldg; A/C: No:
Rate for: Person; $12; Rate for #2 pers: $12; Rate for #3 pers: $12; Child Rate: n/a

Motel; Max. Pers: 5; Bedding incl ?: Yes; Bath: Private; A/C: No
Rate for: Person: $12; Rate for #2 pers: $12; Rate for #3 pers: $12; Child Rate: n/a

Dorm; Max. Pers: 10; Bedding incl ?: Yes; Bath: Shared; A/C: No:
Rate for: Person: $12; Rate for #2 pers: $12; Rate for #3 pers: $12; Child Rate: n/a
Lodge sleeps 10 in 4 bedrooms w/2 baths.

Main amenities available: VCR-TV; Volleyball; Basketball; Swimming; Incidentals store; Hiking
Meals are served in dining room for transients only when other groups are present. Dinner price: $5.00.

NAME OF CENTER: White Branch Youth Camp   Listing ID #: 285
Telephone: 541-822-3511; Fax: 541-822-8304; E-mail:
Address: 61500 Old McKenzie Highway; McKenzie Bridge; OR; 97413
Nearest Interstate: I-5, Exit 62 miles; Nearest State/US Hwy: Rte 126; 7 miles.

Restrictions: Age: None; Pets: Not permitted; Alcohol: Not permitted; Smoking: Outdoors only; Reservation Req'd: None; Max. Adv. Reser.: 7 days; Seasonal closing: June - August

RV/Campers overnight hookups: Yes; Water: Yes; Electric: Yes; Septic: unk
Basic Rate/Night: $13.00/ veh

ACCOM: Mon. night thru Thurs. night rates for winterized (check if this is critical) rooms w/o meals unless otherwise indicated.

Bunkroom; Max. Pers: 12; Bedding incl ?: No; Bath: Shared; A/C: No:
Rate for: Person; $12; Rate for #2 pers: $12; Rate for #3 pers: $12; Child Rate: n/a

Cabin; Max. Pers: 12; Bedding incl ?: No; Bath: Shared; A/C: No
Rate for: Person: $13; Rate for #2 pers: $13; Rate for #3 pers: $13; Child Rate: 50% off under 10 yrs, free under 6
Kitchenette

Main amenities available: Pool table; Volleyball; Basketball; Ping pong; Ball field; Hiking
Meals are served in dining room for transients only when other groups are present. Dinner price: $5.00.

REMEMBER TO CALL AHEAD

PENNSYLVANIA

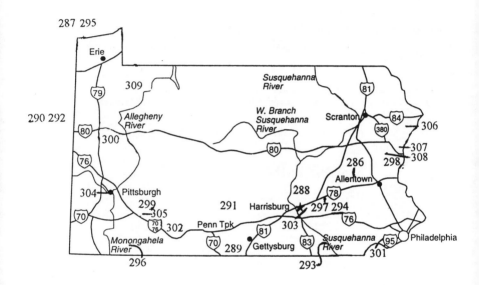

287 295

Erie

309

79

Susquehanna River

81

290 292

Allegheny River

W. Branch Susquehanna River

Scranton

84

306

80

380

307
308

300

298

76

80

286

78

Allentown

304

Pittsburgh

288

299

305

291

Harrisburg

297 294

70
76

302

Penn Tpk

81

303

76

70

70

289

Gettysburg

83

Susquehanna River

95

Philadelphia

Monongahela River

301

296

293

NAME OF CENTER: Blue Mountain Christian Retreat   Listing ID #: 286

Telephone: 570-386-2154; Fax: 570-386-1145; E-mail:
Address: Rd #2; Box 118A; New Ringgold; PA; 17960
Nearest Interstate: I-81, Exit 20 miles; Nearest State/US Hwy: Rte 895; 2 miles.

Restrictions: Age: None; Pets: Not permitted; Alcohol: Not permitted; Smoking: Outdoors only;
Reservation Req'd: None; Max. Adv. Reser.: Open; Seasonal closing: None

RV/Campers overnight hookups: Yes; Water: Yes; Electric: Yes; Septic: Yes
Basic Rate/Night: n/a

ACCOM: Mon. night thru Thurs. night rates for winterized (check if this is critical) rooms w/o
meals unless otherwise indicated.

Motel; Max. Pers: 4; Bedding incl ?: $1.25 surcharge; Bath: Private; A/C: Yes:
Rate for: Person; $30; Rate for #2 pers: $19; Rate for #3 pers: $19; Child Rate: n/a

Main amenities available: Swimming; V-ball; Bsk ball; Ping-pong; Bookstore; Tennis; Hiking
Meals are served in dining room for transients only when other groups are present. Dinner price: $4-$6.95.

NAME OF CENTER: Camp Fitch   Listing ID #: 287

Telephone: 814-922-3219; Fax: 814-922-7000; E-mail: campfitch@hotmail.com
Address: Camp Fitch; N. Springfield; PA; 16430
Nearest Interstate: I-90, Exit 5 miles; Nearest State/US Hwy: PA 215; 0 miles.

Restrictions: Age: None; Pets: Not permitted; Alcohol: Not permitted; Smoking: Outdoors only;
Reservation Req'd: 2 days; Max. Adv. Reser.: 1 mo; Seasonal closing: mid-June - 1 Sept.

RV/Campers overnight hookups: No

ACCOM: Mon. night thru Thurs. night rates for winterized (check if this is critical) rooms w/o
meals unless otherwise indicated.

**Bunkroom; Max. Pers: 15; Bedding incl ?: $5 surcharge; Bath: Shared; A/C: No:
Rate for: Person; $10; Rate for #2 pers: $10; Rate for #3 pers: $10; Child Rate: n/a
** Standard package. 2 nights in Bunkroom or Dorm plus 4 meals $45/pers.

**Dorm; Max. Pers: 5; Bedding incl ?: $5 surcharge; Bath: Shared; A/C: No
Rate for: Person: $10; Rate for #2 pers: $10; Rate for #3 pers: $10; Child Rate: n/a

Main amenities available: 1 mi frontage w/450 acre on L. Erie; V-ball; Bsk ball; Swimming; Incidentals store;
Laundry machine; Boat/canoeing
Meals are served in dining room for transients only when other groups are present. Dinner price: $6.50.

NAME OF CENTER: Camp Hebron   Listing ID #: 288

Telephone: 800-864-7747; Fax: 717-896-3391; E-mail: hebron@camphebron.org
Address: 957 Camp Hebron Rd.; Halifax; PA; 17032
Nearest Interstate: I-81, Exit 15 miles; Nearest State/US Hwy: Rte 225; 3 miles.

Restrictions: Age: None; Pets: Not permitted; Alcohol: Not permitted; Smoking: Designated outdoor area; Reservation Req'd: 14 days w/dep; Max. Adv. Reser.: 3+ mo; Seasonal closing: None

RV/Campers overnight hookups: Yes; Water: Yes; Electric: Yes; Septic: n/a
Basic Rate/Night: Vary; Res req'd w/dep/ veh

ACCOM: Mon. night thru Thurs. night rates for winterized (check if this is critical) rooms w/o meals unless otherwise indicated.

Motel; Max. Pers: 4; Bedding incl ?: Yes; Bath: Private; A/C: Yes:
Rate for: Person; **114; Rate for #2 pers: ** $74; Rate for #3 pers: ** $64; Child Rate: ** $58 under 19 yrs; $41 under 13; free under 5
** Weekend package rate includes 2 nights, 5 meals, 2 evening snacks

Bunkroom; Max. Pers: 10; Bedding incl ?: Surcharge; Bath: Shared; A/C: No
Rate for: Person: ** $16; Rate for #2 pers: ** $16; Rate for #3 pers: ** $16; Child Rate: n/a
Weekend package rates availale **Minimum charge $60

Main amenities available: Volleyball; Basketball; Hiking
Meals are served in dining room for transients only when other groups are present. Dinner price varies.

NAME OF CENTER: Camp Joy-El   Listing ID #: 289

Telephone: 717-369-4539; Fax: 717-369-2927; E-mail: joy_el@cvn.net
Address: 3741 Joy-El Drive; Greencastle; PA; 17225
Nearest Interstate: I-81, Exit 10 miles; Nearest State/US Hwy: I-70; 15 miles.

Restrictions: Age: None; Pets: Not permitted; Alcohol: Not permitted; Smoking: Outdoors only; Reservation Req'd: 7 days; Max. Adv. Reser.: Open; Seasonal closing: None

RV/Campers overnight hookups: No

ACCOM: Mon. night thru Thurs. night rates for winterized (check if this is critical) rooms w/o meals unless otherwise indicated.

Motel; Max. Pers: 2; Bedding incl ?: Yes; Bath: Private; A/C: No:
Rate for: Person; $28; Rate for #2 pers: $28; Child Rate: n/a

Main amenities available: Ball field; Volleyball; Basketball; Ping-pong; Hiking
Meals are not served in dining room for transients only when other groups are present. Dinner price varies.

NAME OF CENTER: **Camp Lamber**   Listing ID #: 290

Telephone: 814-922-7370; Fax: 724-662-1080; E-mail: capnwp@aol.com
Address: 114 W. Venango St.; Mercer; PA; 16137
Nearest Interstate: I-90, Exit 5 miles; Nearest State/US Hwy: PA 215; 1 miles.

Restrictions: Age: None; Pets: Not permitted; Alcohol: Not permitted; Smoking: Outdoors only; Reservation Req'd: 3 days; Max. Adv. Reser.: Open; Seasonal closing: June - Sept

RV/Campers overnight hookups: Yes; Water: No; Electric: Yes; Septic: No
Basic Rate/Night: $4/pers + $1/ veh

ACCOM: Mon. night thru Thurs. night rates for winterized (check if this is critical) rooms w/o meals unless otherwise indicated.

Cabin; Max. Pers: 8; Bedding incl ?: No; Bath: Shared; A/C: No:
Rate for: Person; $12; Rate for #2 pers: $12; Rate for #3 pers: $12; Child Rate: n/a
Some cabins heated

Main amenities available: On Lake Erie; Volleyball; Swimming; Tennis; Hiking
Meals are not served in dining room for transients . Dinner price varies.

NAME OF CENTER: **Camp Mantowagan**   Listing ID #: 291

Telephone: 814-658-3815; Fax: 814-658-3815; E-mail:
Address: PO Box 95; Little Valley Rd.; Saxton; PA; 16678
Nearest Interstate: I-76, Exit 30 miles; Nearest State/US Hwy: Rte 913; 3 miles.

Restrictions: Age: None; Pets: Not permitted; Alcohol: Not permitted; Smoking: Outdoors only; Reservation Req'd: 7 days; Max. Adv. Reser.: Open; Seasonal closing: None

RV/Campers overnight hookups: Yes; Water: Yes; Electric: Yes; Septic: No
Basic Rate/Night: $14.00/ veh

ACCOM: Mon. night thru Thurs. night rates for winterized (check if this is critical) rooms w/o meals unless otherwise indicated.

Motel, Max. Pers. 2; Bedding incl ?: No; Bath: Private; A/C: No:
Rate for: Person; $13; Rate for #2 pers: $13; Child Rate: 50% off under 17 yrs; free under 4

Dorm; Max. Pers: 3; Bedding incl ?: No; Bath: Shared; A/C: No
Rate for: Person: $13; Rate for #2 pers: $13; Rate for #3 pers: $13; Child Rate: 50% off under 17 yrs; free under 4

Bunkroom; Max. Pers: 8; Bedding incl ?: No; Bath: Shared; A/C: No:
Rate for: Person: $13; Rate for #2 pers: $13; Rate for #3 pers: $13; Child Rate: 50% off under 17 yrs; free under 4

Main amenities available: V-ball; Bsk ball; VCR-TV; Tennis; Ball field; Ping-pong; Hiking
Meals are not served in dining room for transients .

NAME OF CENTER: Camp Nazareth   Listing ID #: 292

Telephone: 724-662-4840; Fax: 724-662-4840; E-mail:
Address: 339 Pew Rd.; Mercer; PA; 16137
Nearest Interstate: I-80, Exit 7 miles; Nearest State/US Hwy: I-79; 2 miles.

Restrictions: Age: None; Pets: Not permitted; Alcohol: Not permitted; Smoking: Outdoors only; Reservation Req'd: 5 days; Max. Adv. Reser.: Open; Seasonal closing: June - Aug.

RV/Campers overnight hookups: No

ACCOM: Mon. night thru Thurs. night rates for winterized (check if this is critical) rooms w/o meals unless otherwise indicated.

Duplex cabin; Max. Pers: 7; Bedding incl ?: No; Bath: Semi-private; A/C: No:
Rate for: Entire cabin; $25
4 bedrooms and 2 baths

Main amenities available: Swimming; V-ball; Bsk ball; Laundry machine; VCR-TV; Tennis/mini golf; Horse shoes
Meals are served in dining room for transients only when other groups are present. Dinner price: $6.00.

NAME OF CENTER: Donegal Camp & Conference Ctr   Listing ID #: 293

Telephone: 717-862-3722; Fax: ; E-mail:
Address: 303 East Telegraph Rd.; Airville; PA; 17302
Nearest Interstate: I-83, Exit 25 miles; Nearest State/US Hwy: Rte 30; 25 miles.

Restrictions: Age: None; Pets: Not permitted; Alcohol: Not permitted; Smoking: Outdoors only; Reservation Req'd: None; Max. Adv. Reser.: Open; Seasonal closing: June - Aug

RV/Campers overnight hookups: No; Water: n/a; Electric: n/a; Septic: n/a
Basic Rate/Night: n/a/ veh

ACCOM: Mon. night thru Thurs. night rates for winterized (check if this is critical) rooms w/o meals unless otherwise indicated.

Cabin - 2 rooms; Max. Pers: 8; Bedding incl ?: No; Bath: Shared; A/C: No:
Rate for: Person; **; Rate for #2 pers: **; Rate for #3 pers: **; Child Rate: **
** $3 on weeknights; $5 Fri or Sat night; $8 Fri/Sat night together

Main amenities available: Hiking
Meals are served in dining room for transients only when other groups are present. Dinner price: $7.00.

NAME OF CENTER: **Grace Brethren Retreat Center**   Listing ID #: 294

Telephone: 717-336-2541; Fax: 717-336-2541; E-mail:
Address: 480 Forest Rd.; Denver; PA; 17517
Nearest Interstate: I-76 (PA Tpke), Exit 21; 11 miles; Nearest State/US Hwy: PA 897;
1 miles.

Restrictions: Age: None; Pets: Permitted; Alcohol: Not permitted; Smoking: Outdoors only;
Reservation Req'd: 1 day; Max. Adv. Reser.: Open; Seasonal closing: None

RV/Campers overnight hookups: No

ACCOM: Mon. night thru Thurs. night rates for winterized (check if this is critical) rooms w/o
meals unless otherwise indicated.

Bunkroom; Max. Pers: Over 5; Bedding incl ?: No; Bath: Separate bldg; A/C: No:
Rate for: Person; $15; Rate for #2 pers: $15; Rate for #3 pers: $15; Child Rate: $7.25 under 3
yrs

Cabin; Max. Pers: Over 5; Bedding incl ?: No; Bath: Private; A/C: No
Rate for: Person: $15; Rate for #2 pers: $15; Rate for #3 pers: $15; Child Rate: $7.25 under 3
yrs

Main amenities available: Swimming; Volleyball; Basketball; Boats; Ball field; Hiking
Meals are not served in dining room for transients.

NAME OF CENTER: **Judson Baptist Camp & Retreat Ctr**   Listing ID #: 295

Telephone: 814-922-3834; Fax: ; E-mail:
Address: 398 Holiday Rd; N. Springfield; PA; 16430
Nearest Interstate: I-90, Exit 4 miles; Nearest State/US Hwy: PA 215; 1 miles.

Restrictions: Age: None; Pets: Not permitted; Alcohol: Not permitted; Smoking: Outdoors only;
Reservation Req'd: None; Max. Adv. Reser.: Open; Seasonal closing: None

RV/Campers overnight hookups: Yes; Water: Yes; Electric: Yes; Septic: No
Basic Rate/Night: $17.00/ veh

ACCOM: Mon. night thru Thurs. night rates for winterized (check if this is critical) rooms w/o
meals unless otherwise indicated.

Dorm; Max. Pers: 4-5; Bedding incl ?: Yes; Bath: Shared; A/C: No:
Rate for: Person; $20; Rate for #2 pers: $20; Rate for #3 pers: $20; Child Rate: 50% off under
12 yrs; free under 4

Motel; Max. Pers: 2; Bedding incl ?: Yes; Bath: Private; A/C: No
Rate for: Person: $20; Rate for #2 pers: $20; Child Rate: 50% off under 12 yrs; free under 4

Main amenities available: On Lake Erie; Incidentals store; Basketball; Swimming
Meals are served in dining room for transients only when other groups are present. Dinner price: $7.15.

NAME OF CENTER: Jumenville   Listing ID #: 296

Telephone: 800-463-7688; Fax: 724-439-1415; E-mail: lrbeatty@aol.com
Address: 886 Jumonville Rd.; Hopwood; PA; 15445
Nearest Interstate: I-76/70 (PA Tpke), Exit 30 miles; Nearest State/US Hwy: Rte 40; 3 miles.

Restrictions: Age: None; Pets: Not permitted; Alcohol: Not permitted; Smoking: Outdoors only; Reservation Req'd: 1 day; Max. Adv. Reser.: Open; Seasonal closing: None

RV/Campers overnight hookups: No

ACCOM: Mon. night thru Thurs. night rates for winterized (check if this is critical) rooms w/o meals unless otherwise indicated.

Bunkroom; Max. Pers: Over 5; Bedding incl ?: **$3.50 surcharge; Bath: Shared; A/C: No: Rate for: Person; $29; Rate for #2 pers: $29; Rate for #3 pers: $29; Child Rate: 50% off under 13 yrs; free under 3 ** Adv. notice req'd

Motel; Max. Pers: Over 2; Bedding incl ?: **$3.50 surcharge; Bath: Private; A/C: Yes Rate for: Person: $65; Rate for #2 pers: $21; Child Rate: Call for children's rates ** Adv. notice req'd

Main amenities available: Swimming; V-ball; Bsk ball; Tennis; Bookstore; Ball field; Hiking
Meals are served in dining room for transients only when other groups are present. Dinner price: $6.50-7.00.

NAME OF CENTER: Kenbrook Bible Camp   Listing ID #: 297

Telephone: 717-865-4547; Fax: 717-865-0995; E-mail: kenbrook@redrose.net
Address: 190 Pine Meadow; Lebanon; PA; 17046
Nearest Interstate: I-78, Exit ; 5 miles; Nearest State/US Hwy: Rte 22; 3 miles.

Restrictions: Age: None; Pets: Not permitted; Alcohol: Not permitted; Smoking: Outdoors only; Reservation Req'd: 3 days; Max. Adv. Reser.: 1 yr for weekdays; 3 mo for wkend; Seasonal closing: None

RV/Campers overnight hookups: Yes; Water: Yes; Electric: Yes; Septic: No
Basic Rate/Night: $16 +$4 electric/ veh

ACCOM: Mon. night thru Thurs. night rates for winterized (check if this is critical) rooms w/o meals unless otherwise indicated.

Duplex Bkrm; Max. Pers: 10; Bedding incl ?: No; Bath: Shared; A/C: No: Rate for: Person; $16; Rate for #2 pers: $16; Rate for #3 pers: $16; Child Rate: Free under 20 yrs.
Kitchen privileges

Motel; Max. Pers: 4; Bedding incl ?: Yes; Bath: Private; A/C: No Rate for: Person: $48; Rate for #2 pers: $28; Rate for #3 pers: $28; Child Rate: Free under 20 yrs.

Main amenities available: Swimming; Volleyball; Boat/Canoeing; Ping-pong; Climbing wall/rope course; Hiking
Meals are served in dining room for transients only when other groups are present. Dinner price: $9.25.

NAME OF CENTER: Kirkridge   Listing ID #: 298

Telephone: 610-588-1793; Fax: 610-588-8510; E-mail:
Address: 2495 Fox Gap Rd.; Bangor; PA; 18013
Nearest Interstate: I-80, Exit 5 miles; Nearest State/US Hwy: Rte 191; 0 miles.

Restrictions: Age: None; Pets: Not permitted; Alcohol: Hard liquor not permitted; Smoking:
Outdoors only; Reservation Req'd: 5 days; Max. Adv. Reser.: Open; Seasonal closing: None

RV/Campers overnight hookups: No

ACCOM: Mon. night thru Thurs. night rates for winterized (check if this is critical) rooms w/o
meals unless otherwise indicated.

Dorm; Max. Pers: 2; Bedding incl ?: $5 surcharge; Bath: Shared; A/C: No:
Rate for: Person; $55; Rate for #2 pers: $20; Child Rate: 50% off under 10 yrs; free under 6

Main amenities available: Swimming; Volleyball; Bookstore/Library; Ping-pong; Ball field; Hiking
Meals are served in dining room for transients only when other groups are present. Dinner price: $12.00.

NAME OF CENTER: Ligonier Camp & Conference Center   Listing ID #: 299

Telephone: 724-238-6428; Fax: 724-238-6971; E-mail: lccc@westol.com
Address: RD #1; Box 16; Ligonier; PA; 15658
Nearest Interstate: I-76/70 (PA Tpke), Exit 14 miles; Nearest State/US Hwy: Rte 30;
2 miles.

Restrictions: Age: None; Pets: Not permitted; Alcohol: Not permitted; Smoking: Outdoors only;
Reservation Req'd: 11AM of day; Max. Adv. Reser.: Open; Seasonal closing: Limited in June -
Aug

RV/Campers overnight hookups: No

ACCOM: Mon. night thru Thurs. night rates for winterized (check if this is critical) rooms w/o
meals unless otherwise indicated.

Cabin; Max. Pers: Over 5; Bedding incl ?: $3 surcharge; Bath: Shared; A/C: No:
Rate for: Person; $35; Rate for additional persons "varies" per request of Ligonier mgmt.
Child Rate: 50% off under 12 yrs; free under 6. Includes kitchenette

Dorm; Max. Pers: 5; Bedding incl ?: $3 surcharge; Bath: Shared; A/C: No
Rate for: Person: $35; Rate for additional persons "varies" per request of Ligonier mgmt. Child
Rate: 50% off under 12 yrs; free under 6. Includes full kitchen

Motel; Max. Pers: 5; Bedding incl ?: $3 surcharge; Bath: Private; A/C: Yes:
Rate for: Person: $25; Rate for additional persons "varies" per request of Ligonier mgmt. Child
Rate: 50% off under 12 yrs; free under 6.

Main amenities available: Volleyball; Basketball; Hiking
Meals are served in dining room for transients only when other groups are present. Dinner price varies.

NAME OF CENTER: Mt. Chestnut Nazarene Center   Listing ID #: 300

Telephone: 724-287-4397; Fax: 724-287-4397; E-mail: pghctrmgr@aol.com
Address: 177 North Rd; Butler; PA; 16001
Nearest Interstate: I-79, Exit 8 miles; Nearest State/US Hwy: Rte 422; 1 miles.

Restrictions: Age: None; Pets: Not permitted; Alcohol: Not permitted; Smoking: Outdoors only;
Reservation Req'd: 1 mo; Max. Adv. Reser.: Open; Seasonal closing: None

RV/Campers overnight hookups: Yes; Water: Yes; Electric: Yes; Septic: n/a
Basic Rate/Night: $9.00/ veh

ACCOM: Mon. night thru Thurs. night rates for winterized (check if this is critical) rooms w/o
meals unless otherwise indicated.

Bunkroom; Max. Pers: Over 5; Bedding incl ?: $1.50 surcharge; Bath: Shared; A/C: No:
Rate for: Person; $6-10; Rate for #2 pers: $6-10; Rate for #3 pers: $6-10; Child Rate: n/a

Motel; Max. Pers: 5; Bedding incl ?: $1.50 surcharge; Bath: Private; A/C: No
Rate for: Person: $10; Rate for #2 pers: $10; Rate for #3 pers: $10; Child Rate: n/a

Main amenities available: Incidentals store; Volleyball; Basketball; Laundry machine; Ball field; Hiking
Meals are served in dining room for transients only when other groups are present. Dinner price: $3.50-6.00.

NAME OF CENTER: Pendle Hill Quaker Center   Listing ID #: 301

Telephone: 800-742-3150; Fax: 610-566-3679; E-mail: heather@pendlehill.org
Address: 338 Plush Mill Rd.; Wallingford; PA; 19086
Nearest Interstate: I-95, Exit 3 miles; Nearest State/US Hwy: Rte 476; 0.5 miles.

Restrictions: Age: None; Pets: Not permitted; Alcohol: Not permitted; Smoking: Outdoors only;
Reservation Req'd: None; Max. Adv. Reser.: 1 yr; Seasonal closing: Last 2 wks of Aug.

RV/Campers overnight hookups: No

ACCOM: Mon. night thru Thurs. night rates for winterized (check if this is critical) rooms w/o
meals unless otherwise indicated.

Motel; Max. Pers: 5; Bedding incl ?: **Yes; Bath: Private; A/C: Y/N:
Rate for: Person; $55; Rate for #2 pers: $25; Rate for #3 pers: $25; Child Rate: n/a
Both private & shared baths w and w/o A/C. ** w/notice

Main amenities available: Laundry machine; Volleyball; Basketball; Bookstore; Library; Hiking
Meals are served in dining room for transients only when other groups are present. Dinner price: $7.50.

REMEMBER TO CALL AHEAD

NAME OF CENTER: Pine Springs Camp, Inc.   Listing ID #: 302

Telephone: 814-629-9834; Fax: 814-629-6520; E-mail: dir@pinesprings.org
Address: 371 Pine Springs Camp Rd.; Jennerstown; PA; 15547
Nearest Interstate: I-76/70 (PA Tpke), Exit 10 (Somerset); 10 miles; Nearest State/US
Hwy: Rte 30; 0.5 miles.

Restrictions: Age: None; Pets: Not permitted; Alcohol: Not permitted; Smoking: Outdoors only;
Reservation Req'd: 1 day; Max. Adv. Reser.: Open; Seasonal closing: June - Aug

RV/Campers overnight hookups: No

ACCOM: Mon. night thru Thurs. night rates for winterized (check if this is critical) rooms w/o
meals unless otherwise indicated.

Cabin; Max. Pers: Over 4; Bedding incl ?: No; Bath: Shared; A/C: No:
Rate for: Person; $10; Rate for #2 pers: $10; Rate for #3 pers: $10; Child Rate: 50% off under
13 yrs; free under 4

Bunkroom; Max. Pers: Over 5; Bedding incl ?: No; Bath: Shared; A/C: No
Rate for: Person: $15; Rate for #2 pers: $15; Rate for #3 pers: $15; Child Rate: 50% off under
13 yrs; free under 4
Includes kitchenette

Main amenities available: Swimming; V-ball; Bsk ball; VCR-TV; Incidentals store (close); Ball field; Hiking
Meals are not served in dining room for transients .

NAME OF CENTER: Refreshing Mountain Camp, Inc.   Listing ID #: 303

Telephone: 717-738-1490; Fax: 717-733-6929; E-mail:
Address: 455 Camp Rd.; Stevens; PA; 17578
Nearest Interstate: I-76 (PA Tpke), Exit 10 miles; Nearest State/US Hwy: Rte 322; 3
miles.

Restrictions: Age: None; Pets: Permitted in RV area; Alcohol: Not permitted; Smoking:
Outdoors only; Reservation Req'd: None; Max. Adv. Reser.: Open; Seasonal closing: None

RV/Campers overnight hookups: Yes; Water: Yes; Electric: Yes; Septic: No
Basic Rate/Night: $19.00/ veh

ACCOM: Mon. night thru Thurs. night rates for winterized (check if this is critical) rooms w/o
meals unless otherwise indicated.

Motel; Max. Pers: 8; Bedding incl ?: Yes; Bath: Private; A/C: Yes:
Rate for: Person; $28; Rate for #2 pers: $28; Rate for #3 pers: $28; Child Rate: $3 for child
w/parents

Main amenities available: Swimming pool; Incidentals store; Shuffle board; Bookstore; V-ball; Bsk ball;
Recreation room
Meals are served in dining room for transients only when other groups are present. Dinner price: $7.05.

NAME OF CENTER: St. **Paul of the Cross Retreat Center**   Listing ID #: 304

Telephone: 412-381-7676; Fax: 412-431-3044; E-mail:
Address: 148 Monastery Ave.; Pittsburgh; PA; 15203
Nearest Interstate: I-76, Exit 15 miles; Nearest State/US Hwy: Rte 79; 12 miles.

Restrictions: Age: 12; Pets: Not permitted; Alcohol: Not permitted; Smoking: Designated interior smoking areas; Reservation Req'd: 5 days; Max. Adv. Reser.: 14 days; Seasonal closing: None

RV/Campers overnight hookups: No

ACCOM: Mon. night thru Thurs. night rates for winterized (check if this is critical) rooms w/o meals unless otherwise indicated.

Motel; Max. Pers: 4; Bedding incl ?: Yes; Bath: ** Private; A/C: Yes:
Rate for: Person; $25-30; Rate for #2 pers: $25-30; Rate for #3 pers: $25-30;   Child Rate: n/a
** Arrangements incl: private bath; shared bath; room w/sink

Main amenities available: Extensive gardens; Bookstore; Gift shop; VCR-TV; Quiet areas; Hiking
Meals are served in dining room for transients only when other groups are present. Dinner price: Many restaurants nearby.

NAME OF CENTER: **Sequanota Lutheran Conf. Ctr & Camp**   Listing ID #: 305

Telephone: 814-629-6627; Fax: 814-629-0128; E-mail: sequanota1@aol.com
Address: PO Box 245; Jennerstown; PA; 15547
Nearest Interstate: I-70, Exit 15 miles; Nearest State/US Hwy: Rte 30; 2 miles.

Restrictions: Age: None; Pets: Not permitted; Alcohol: Not permitted; Smoking: Outdoors only; Reservation Req'd: 1 day; Max. Adv. Reser.: 14 days; Seasonal closing: None

RV/Campers overnight hookups: No

ACCOM: Mon. night thru Thurs. night rates for winterized (check if this is critical) rooms w/o meals unless otherwise indicated.

Log cabin; Max. Pers: 4; Bedding incl ?: $5 surcharge; Bath: Private; A/C: No:
Rate for: Entire cabin; $50
Includes kitchen

Bunkroom; Max. Pers: Over 5; Bedding incl ?: $5 surcharge; Bath: Shared; A/C: No
Rate for: Person: $10; Rate for #2 pers: $10; Rate for #3 pers: $10; Child Rate: $5.00

Main amenities available: Swimming; Volleyball; Basketball; Boats; Bookstore; Hiking
Meals are not served in dining room for transients .

NAME OF CENTER: Spruce Lake Retreat   Listing ID #: 306

Telephone: 717-595-7505; Fax: 717-595-0328; E-mail: spruce.lake@juno.com
Address: RR #1; Box 605; Canadensis; PA; 18325
Nearest Interstate: I-80/I-84, Exit 15 miles; Nearest State/US Hwy: Rte 447; 0 miles.

Restrictions: Age: None; Pets: Not permitted; Alcohol: Not permitted; Smoking: Nowhere;
Reservation Req'd: 1 day; Max. Adv. Reser.: Open; Seasonal closing: None

RV/Campers overnight hookups: Yes; Water: Yes; Electric: Yes; Septic: No
Basic Rate/Night: $8.50/adult; $1.50 each for water & elect.; minimum $17/veh.

ACCOM: Mon. night thru Thurs. night rates for winterized (check if this is critical) rooms w/o
meals unless otherwise indicated.

Motel; Max. Pers: 4; Bedding incl ?: Yes; Bath: Private; A/C: No:
Rate for: Person; $28; Rate for #2 pers: $28; Rate for #3 pers: $28; Child Rate: $7 under 12
yrs; free under 6

Main amenities available: Virtually everything !; Swimming; V-ball; Bsk-ball; Ping-pong; Pool table; Winter
sports
Meals are served in dining room for transients only when other groups are present. Dinner price: $8.50; 50%
off under 12 yrs; free under 6.

NAME OF CENTER: Streamside Camp & Conference Ctr   Listing ID #: 307

Telephone: 570-629-1902; Fax: 570-629-9650; E-mail: streamsidecamp@juno.com
Address: RR #3; Box 3307; Stroudsburg; PA; 18360
Nearest Interstate: I-80, Exit 1 miles; Nearest State/US Hwy: Rte 715; 0.5 miles.

Restrictions: Age: None; Pets: Not permitted; Alcohol: Not permitted; Smoking: Outdoors only;
Reservation Req'd: 3 days; Max. Adv. Reser.: 1 yr; Seasonal closing: July-Aug

RV/Campers overnight hookups: No

ACCOM: Mon. night thru Thurs. night rates for winterized (check if this is critical) rooms w/o
meals unless otherwise indicated.

Dorm; Max. Pers: 5; Bedding incl ?: $5 surcharge; Bath: Shared; A/C: No:
Rate for: Person; $30; Rate for #2 pers: $30; Rate for #3 pers: $30; Child Rate: 50% off under
13 yrs; free under 2

Bunkroom; Max. Pers: Over 5; Bedding incl ?: $5 surcharge; Bath: Shared; A/C: No
Rate for: Person: $30; Rate for #2 pers: $30; Rate for #3 pers: $30; Child Rate: 50% off under
13 yrs; free under 2

Main amenities available: Swimming; V-ball; Bsk ball; Incidentals store; Laundry machine; Boat/canoeing;
Bookstore
Meals are served in dining room for transients only when other groups are present. Dinner price: $6-8.00.

NAME OF CENTER: **Tuscarora Inn & Conference Center**   Listing ID #: 308

Telephone: 570-897-6000; Fax: 570-897-5883; E-mail: tuscarinn@aol.com
Address: 3300 River Rd.; Mt. Bethel; PA; 18343
Nearest Interstate: I-80, Exit 4 miles; Nearest State/US Hwy: Rte 611; 4 miles.

Restrictions: Age: None; Pets: Not permitted; Alcohol: Not permitted; Smoking: Outdoors only;
Reservation Req'd: 5 PM of day; Max. Adv. Reser.: 14 days; Seasonal closing: None

RV/Campers overnight hookups: No

ACCOM: Mon. night thru Thurs. night rates for winterized (check if this is critical) rooms w/o
meals unless otherwise indicated.

Motel; Max. Pers: 3; Bedding incl ?: Yes; Bath: Private; A/C: Yes:
Rate for: Room; $45-55; Child Rate: n/a
$5/pers over 3 persons

Main amenities available: Swimming; V-ball; Bsk ball; Laundry machine; Bookstore; Canoeing;
VCR-TV/Tennis
Meals are served in dining room for transients only when other groups are present. Dinner price: $9.75.

NAME OF CENTER: **Wesley Woods Christian Edu. Ctr.**   Listing ID #: 309

Telephone: 800-295-0420; Fax: 814-436-7669; E-mail: hwest87245@aol.com
Address: RR #1 Box 155A; Grand Valley; PA; 16420
Nearest Interstate: I-80, Exit 35 miles; Nearest State/US Hwy: Rte 27; 2 miles.

Restrictions: Age: None; Pets: Not permitted; Alcohol: Not permitted; Smoking: Outdoors only;
Reservation Req'd: 1 day; Max. Adv. Reser.: Open; Seasonal closing: Closed to travelers June 1
- Sept 1 except for RV Park

RV/Campers overnight hookups: Yes; Water: n/a; Electric: n/a; Septic: n/a
Basic Rate/Night: $9.00/ veh

ACCOM: Mon. night thru Thurs. night rates for winterized (check if this is critical) rooms w/o
meals unless otherwise indicated.

Motel; Max. Pers: 4; Bedding incl ?: Yes; Bath: Private; A/C: No:
Rate for: Person; $19; Rate for #2 pers: $19; Rate for #3 pers: $19; Child Rate: $9.50 for
children

Dorm; Max. Pers: 4; Bedding incl ?: Yes; Bath: Shared; A/C: No
Rate for: Person: $19; Rate for #2 pers: $19; Rate for #3 pers: $19; Child Rate: $9.50 for
children

Bunkroom; Max. Pers: Over 4; Bedding incl ?: No; Bath: shared; A/C: No:
Rate for: Person: $16; Rate for #2 pers: $16; Rate for #3 pers: $16; Child Rate: $8 for children

Main amenities available: Awimming; Volleyball; Basketball; Ping-pong VCR-TV; Ball field; Hiking
Meals are served in dining room for transients only when other groups are present. Dinner price: $4.50-6.50.

194

NAME OF CENTER: YMCA - Bethlehem Listing ID: 310

Telephone: 610-867-7588   Fax: 610-867-8295
Address: 430 E. Broad St.; Bethlehem, PA 18018

Restrictions:
Accommodations offered to (M/F/Families): M. If M/F then must be over 18 yrs.
Pets: Not permitted; Alcohol: Not permitted; Smoking: Outdoors only
Reservation requirements: None
Reservations are accepted up to 14 days in advance. Seasonal closing: None

ACCOMMODATIONS:
Single room: Bedding included ?: Yes; Bath: Shared
Rate for 1 day: $13; Rate for 1 week: $82
YMCA guest membership $10 includes pol,gym, racquet ball

Main amenities: TV lounge;
Meals are not offered in their own cafeteria.

NAME OF CENTER: YMCA - Harrisburg - East Shore Br. Listing ID: 311

Telephone: 717-232-9622   Fax: 717-234-5859
Address: 701 N. Front St.; Harrisburg, PA 17101

Restrictions:
Accommodations offered to (M/F/Families): M. If M/F then must be over 18 yrs.
Pets: Not permitted; Alcohol: Not permitted; Smoking: Outdoors only
Reservation requirements: None
Reservations are accepted up to 0 days in advance. Seasonal closing: None

ACCOMMODATIONS:
Single room: Bedding included ?: Yes; Bath: Shared
Rate for 1 day: ** $55 for 2 nights; Rate for 1 week: **$61-65
** Includes membership in Y

Main amenities: Swimming; Gym; TV lounge
Meals are not offered in their own cafeteria.

NAME OF CENTER: YMCA - Pittsburgh - **Allegheny** Listing ID: 312

Telephone: 412-321-8594   Fax: 412-321-7818
Address: 600 W. North Ave.; Pittsburgh, PA 15212

Restrictions:
Accommodations offered to (M/F/Families): M. If M/F then must be over 18 yrs.
Pets: Not permitted; Alcohol: Not permitted; Smoking: Bedroom only
Reservation requirements: None
Reservations are accepted up to 0 days in advance. Seasonal closing: None

ACCOMMODATIONS:
Single room: Bedding included ?: Yes; Bath: Shared
Rate for 1 day: **$23+$5 dep; Rate for 1 week: **$63+$5 dep
** Includes membership in Y

Main amenities: Swimming; Gym; Laundry machine
Meals are not offered in their own cafeteria.

NAME OF CENTER: YMCA - Pittsburgh - **Centre Ave Br.** Listing ID: 313

Telephone: 412-621-1762   Fax: 412-681-4428
Address: 2621 Centre Ave; Pittsburgh, PA 15219

Restrictions:
Accommodations offered to (M/F/Families): M. If M/F then must be over 18 yrs.
Pets: Not permitted; Alcohol: Not permitted; Smoking: Bedroom only
Reservation requirements: 2-3 wk waiting list
Reservations are accepted up to 1 mo in advance. Seasonal closing: None

ACCOMMODATIONS:
Single room: Bedding included ?: Yes; Bath: Shared
Rate for 1 day: not offered; Rate for 1 week: $90 (incl dep)

Main amenities: TV lounge; Laundry machine
Meals are not offered in their own cafeteria.

NAME OF CENTER: YMCA - Reading Listing ID: 314

Telephone: 610-378-4700   Fax: 610-378-4780
Address: Reed & Washington Sts; PO Box 1622; Reading, PA 19603

Restrictions:
Accommodations offered to (M/F/Families): M & F. If M/F then must be over 18 yrs.
Pets: Not permitted; Alcohol: Not permitted; Smoking: Bedroom only
Reservation requirements: Application req'd
Reservations are accepted up to 8 days in advance. Seasonal closing: None

ACCOMMODATIONS:
Single room: Bedding included ?: Yes; Bath: Shared
Rate for 1 day: not offered; Rate for 1 week: ** $52+$72 dep
** Includes membership in Y

Main amenities: Swimming; Gym; TV lounge; Laundry machine
Meals are offered in their own cafeteria.

NAME OF CENTER: YWCA - Lancaster Listing ID: 315

Telephone: 717-393-1735   Fax: 717-396-0513
Address: 110 N. Lime St.; Lancaster, PA 17602

Restrictions:
Accommodations offered to (M/F/Families): F & M under 8 yrs. If M/F then must be over
None yrs.
Pets: Not permitted; Alcohol: Not permitted; Smoking: Outdoors only
Reservation requirements: None
Reservations are accepted up to 7 days in advance. Seasonal closing: None

ACCOMMODATIONS:
Single room: Bedding included ?: Yes; Bath: Shared
Rate for 1 day: $16+$16 dep; Rate for 1 week: $80+$16 dep

Main amenities: Laundry machine
Meals are not offered in their own cafeteria.

REMEMBER TO CALL AHEAD

RHODE ISLAND

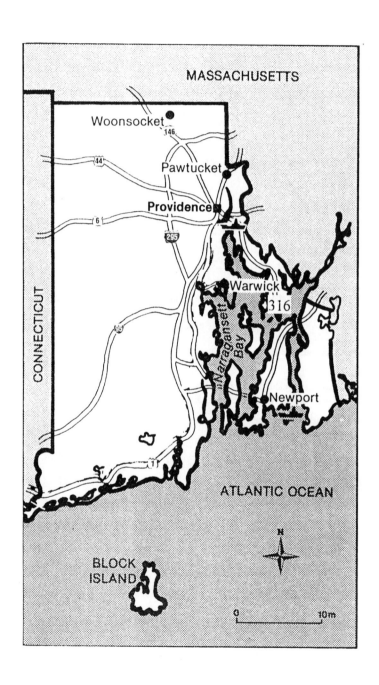

NAME OF CENTER: Mt. St. Joseph Spiritual Life Center   Listing ID #: 316

Telephone: 401-253-5434; Fax: ; E-mail:
Address: 13 Monkey Wrench Lane; Bristol; RI; 02809
Nearest Interstate: I-95, Exit 10 miles.

Restrictions: Age: 12; Pets: Not permitted; Alcohol: Permitted; Smoking: Outdoors only;
Reservation Req'd: 7 days w/dep; Max. Adv. Reser.: Open; Seasonal closing: June 15 - Sept. 15

RV/Campers overnight hookups: No

ACCOM: Mon. night thru Thurs. night rates for winterized (check if this is critical) rooms w/o
meals unless otherwise indicated.

House; Max. Pers: 10; Bedding incl ?: Yes; Bath: Semi-private; A/C: No:
Rate for: Person; $40; Rate for #2 pers: $40; Rate for #3 pers: $40; Child Rate: n/a
7 bedrooms w/1-2 beds each; 2 baths; kitchen; living rm; dining rm

Main amenities available: Near ocean; Quiet areas
Meals are not served in dining room for transients .

SOUTH CAROLINA

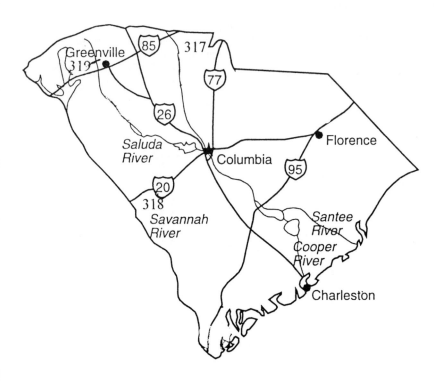

Greenville
85
317
319
77
26
Saluda
River
Florence
Columbia
95
20
318
Savannah
River
Santee
River
Cooper
River
Charleston

NAME OF CENTER: Bethelwoods   Listing ID #: 317

Telephone: 803-366-3722; Fax: 803-366-3722; E-mail: paulfogg@partynet.com
Address: 922 W. Mount Gallant Rd.; York; SC; 29745
Nearest Interstate: I-77, Exit 14 miles; Nearest State/US Hwy: Rte 161; 2 miles.

Restrictions: Age: None; Pets: Not permitted; Alcohol: Not permitted; Smoking: Outdoors only; Reservation Req'd: 7 days; Max. Adv. Reser.: 1 yr; Seasonal closing: None

RV/Campers overnight hookups: No

ACCOM: Mon. night thru Thurs. night rates for winterized (check if this is critical) rooms w/o meals unless otherwise indicated.

Motel; Max. Pers: 5; Bedding incl ?: $5 surcharge; Bath: Private; A/C: Yes:
Rate for: Person; $21; Rate for #2 pers: $21; Rate for #3 pers: $21; Child Rate: n/a

Main amenities available: Swimming; V-ball; Bsk-ball; Laundry machine; Bookstore; Ball field; Hiking
Meals are served in dining room for transients only when other groups are present. Dinner price: $4.25.

NAME OF CENTER: Bishop Gravatt Center   Listing ID #: 318

Telephone: 803-648-1817; Fax: 803-648-7453; E-mail: gravatt@groupz.net
Address: 1006 Camp Gravatt Rd.; Aiken; SC; 29805
Nearest Interstate: I-26, Exit 3 miles; Nearest State/US Hwy: Rte 49; 2 miles.

Restrictions: Age: None; Pets: Not permitted; Alcohol: Hard liquor not permitted; Smoking: Designated outdoor area; Reservation Req'd: Noon of day; Max. Adv. Reser.: 1 mo; Seasonal closing: Late December

RV/Campers overnight hookups: No

ACCOM: Mon. night thru Thurs. night rates for winterized (check if this is critical) rooms w/o meals unless otherwise indicated.

Dorm; Max. Pers: 5; Bedding incl ?: Yes; Bath: Semi-private; A/C: Yes:
Rate for: Person; ** $50; Rate for #2 pers: ** $50; Rate for #3 pers: ** $50; Child Rate: 50% off under 13 yrs; free under 3
** Includes 3 meals

Cabin; Max. Pers: Over 5; Bedding incl ?: Yes; Bath: Shared; A/C: Yes
Rate for: Person: ** $55; Rate for #2 pers: ** $55; Rate for #3 pers: ** $55; Child Rate: 50% off under 13 yrs; free under 3
** Includes 3 meals

Main amenities available: Lake swimming; VCR-TV; Tennis; Canoeing; Hiking
Meals are served in dining room for transients. Dinner price varies.

NAME OF CENTER: **Look-up Lodge**   Listing ID #: 319

Telephone: 864-836-6392; Fax: 864-836-4160; E-mail: www.lookuplodge.com
Address: 100 Look-up Lodge Rd.; Travelers Rest; SC; 29690
Nearest Interstate: I-26, Exit 22 miles; Nearest State/US Hwy: Us 25; 2 miles.

Restrictions: Age: None; Pets: Not permitted; Alcohol: Not permitted; Smoking: Outdoors only;
Reservation Req'd: Required w/dep; Max. Adv. Reser.: Open; Seasonal closing: None

RV/Campers overnight hookups: No

ACCOM: Mon. night thru Thurs. night rates for winterized (check if this is critical) rooms w/o
meals unless otherwise indicated.

Motel; Max. Pers: 6; Bedding incl ?: $5 surcharge; Bath: Private; A/C: Yes:
Rate for: Person; ** 45; Rate for #2 pers: ** $45; Rate for #3 pers: ** $45; Child Rate: 50%
off under 8 yrs; free under 4
** Includes 3 meals

Main amenities available: Volleyball; Basketball; Hiking
Meals are not served in dining room for transients . Dinner price varies.

SOUTH DAKOTA

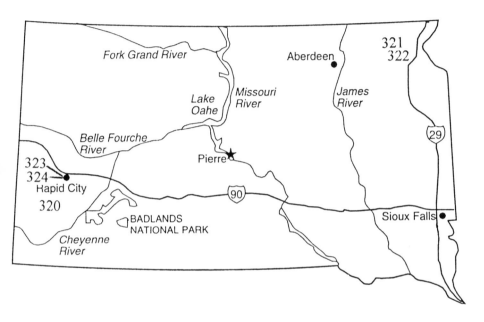

Fork Grand River

Aberdeen

321
322

Lake
Oahe

Missouri
River

James
River

Belle Fourche
River

29

323
324

Pierre

Hapid City

90

320

BADLANDS
NATIONAL PARK

Sioux Falls

Cheyenne
River

NAME OF CENTER: Baptist Camp Judson   Listing ID #: 320

Telephone: 605-574-2314; Fax: 605-574-2314; E-mail:
Address: 12965 Old Hill Cty Rd.; Keystone; SD; 57751
Nearest Interstate: I-90, Exit; 25 miles; Nearest State/US Hwy: Rte 16; 3 miles.

Restrictions: Age: None; Pets: Not permitted; Alcohol: Not permitted; Smoking: Designated outdoor area; Reservation Req'd: None; Max. Adv. Reser.: 7 days; Seasonal closing: Dec 16 - Jan 2

RV/Campers overnight hookups: Yes; Water: Yes; Electric: Yes; Septic: No
Basic Rate/Night: $15 + $2/pers/ veh

ACCOM: Mon. night thru Thurs. night rates for winterized (check if this is critical) rooms w/o meals unless otherwise indicated.

Cabin; Max. Pers: Over 5; Bedding incl ?: No; Bath: Toilet in cabin; shower hse ; A/C: No:
Rate for: **;   Child Rate: n/a
** $30 min.plus $5/pers over 4 persons

Dormitory; Max. Pers: 5; Bedding incl ?: No; Bath: Shared; A/C: No
Rate for: **;   Child Rate: n/a
** $35 min. plus $5/pers for over 4 persons.

Main amenities available: Incidentals store; V-ball; Bsk-ball; Canoe/boat; Swimming; Laundry machine; Near Mt Rushmore
Meals are not served in dining room for transients . Dinner price varies.

NAME OF CENTER: Klein Ranch   Listing ID #: 321

Telephone: 605-947-4440; Fax: 605-947-4379; E-mail: nsdlo@itctel.com
Address: RR #1; Box 85; Waubay; SD; 57273
Nearest Interstate: I-94, Exit 120 miles; Nearest State/US Hwy: Rte 65; 0 miles.

Restrictions: Age: None; Pets: Not permitted; Alcohol: Not permitted; Smoking: Outdoors only; Reservation Req'd: 7 days; Max. Adv. Reser.: Open; Seasonal closing: None

RV/Campers overnight hookups: No

ACCOM: Mon. night thru Thurs. night rates for winterized (check if this is critical) rooms w/o meals unless otherwise indicated.

Bunkroom; Max. Pers: 10; Bedding incl ?: No; Bath: Shared; A/C: No:
Rate for: Person; $11; Rate for #2 pers: $11; Rate for #3 pers: $11; Child Rate: $10 under 11 yrs; free under 4
Requested to "tidy" room and help w/meal cleanup

Main amenities available: Hiking; Volleyball; Horseback riding
Meals are served in dining room for transients only when other groups are present. Dinner price: $6.00.

NAME OF CENTER: Nesodak Bible Camp   Listing ID #: 322

Telephone: 605-947-4440; Fax: 605-947-4370; E-mail: nsdlo@itctel.com
Address: RR #1; Box 85; Waubay; SD; 57273
Nearest Interstate: I-29, Exit 20 miles; Nearest State/US Hwy: Rte 12; 7 miles.

Restrictions: Age: None; Pets: Not permitted; Alcohol: Not permitted; Smoking: Outdoors only;
Reservation Req'd: 7 days; Max. Adv. Reser.: Open; Seasonal closing: None

RV/Campers overnight hookups: Yes; Water: No; Electric: Yes; Septic: No
Basic Rate/Night: State Park Rate/ veh

ACCOM: Mon. night thru Thurs. night rates for winterized (check if this is critical) rooms w/o
meals unless otherwise indicated.

Bunkroom; Max. Pers: 12; Bedding incl ?: No; Bath: Shared; A/C: No:
Rate for: Person; $11; Rate for #2 pers: $11; Rate for #3 pers: $11; Child Rate: $10 under 11
yrs; free under 4
Requested to "tidy" room and help w/meal cleanup

Dorm; Max. Pers: 3; Bedding incl ?: No; Bath: Shared; A/C: No
Rate for: Person: $14; Rate for #2 pers: $14; Rate for #3 pers: $14; Child Rate: $13 under 12
yrs; free under 4

Main amenities available: Swimming; Volleyball; Basketball; Sauna; Canoe/boat; Hiking
Meals are served in dining room for transients only when other groups are present. Dinner price: $6.00.

NAME OF CENTER: Rimrock   Listing ID #: 323

Telephone: 605-339-1912; Fax: 605-339-1729; E-mail:
Address: 23125 Thunderhead Falls Rd; Rapid City; SD; 57702
Nearest Interstate: I-90, Exit 57; 10 miles; Nearest State/US Hwy: Rte 44; 1 miles.

Restrictions: Age: None; Pets: Permitted on leash; Alcohol: Not permitted; Smoking:
Designated outdoor area; Reservation Req'd: 5 days; Max. Adv. Reser.: 6 mo; Seasonal closing:
None

RV/Campers overnight hookups: Yes; Water: No; Electric: Yes; Septic: No
Basic Rate/Night: $11.00/ veh

ACCOM: Mon. night thru Thurs. night rates for winterized (check if this is critical) rooms w/o
meals unless otherwise indicated.

Cabin; Max. Pers: Over 5; Bedding incl ?: No; Bath: Separate bldg; A/C: No:
Rate for: Person; $12; Rate for #2 pers: $12; Rate for #3 pers: $12; Child Rate: $6 under 12
yrs; free under 5 yrs
Available only June - Aug.

Dorm; Max. Pers: 5; Bedding incl ?: No; Bath: Shared; A/C: No
Rate for: Person: $12; Rate for #2 pers: $12; Rate for #3 pers: $12; Child Rate: $13 under 12
yrs; free under 4
$40 min.; NOT available June - Aug.

Main amenities available: Swimming; V-ball; Bsk-ball; VCR-TV; Tether ball; Ping pong; Hiking
Meals are served in dining room for transients only when other groups are present. Dinner price: $6.00; $5
under 12 yrs; free under 5.

NAME OF CENTER: **Storm Mtn. Center**   Listing ID #: 324

Telephone: 605-343-4391; Fax: 605-343-0154; E-mail:
Address: 23740 Storm Mtn Rd; Rapid City; SD; 57702
Nearest Interstate: I-90, Exit 57; 14 miles; Nearest State/US Hwy: Rte 16; 2 miles.

Restrictions: Age: None; Pets: Not permitted; Alcohol: Not permitted; Smoking: Designated
outdoor area; Reservation Req'd: None; Max. Adv. Reser.: 14 days; Seasonal closing: None

RV/Campers overnight hookups: No

ACCOM: Mon. night thru Thurs. night rates for winterized (check if this is critical) rooms w/o
meals unless otherwise indicated.

Cabin; Max. Pers: 10-26; Bedding incl ?: No; Bath: Shared; A/C: No:
Rate for: Person; $22; Rate for #2 pers: $22; Rate for #3 pers: $22; Child Rate: $19 under 15
yrs; $16 under 10; free under 4

Dorm; Max. Pers: 7; Bedding incl ?: No; Bath: Shared; A/C: No
Rate for: Person: $24; Rate for #2 pers: $24; Rate for #3 pers: $24; Child Rate: $21 under 15
yrs; $18 under 10; free under 4

Main amenities available:Volleyball; Basketball; Hiking
Meals are served in dining room for transients only when other groups are present. Dinner price varies.

TENNESSEE

NAME OF CENTER: Camp Buffalo Mountain   Listing ID #: 325

Telephone: 423-753-6678; Fax: 423-753-6499; E-mail:
Address: 241 Methodist Camp Rd.; Jonesborough; TN; 37659
Nearest Interstate: I-181, Exit 15 miles; Nearest State/US Hwy: Rte 63; 7 miles.

Restrictions: Age: None; Pets: Not permitted; Alcohol: Not permitted; Smoking: Outdoors only (Smoke free in Summer); Reservation Req'd: 1 day; Max. Adv. Reser.: 14 days; Seasonal closing: None

RV/Campers overnight hookups: No

ACCOM: Mon. night thru Thurs. night rates for winterized (check if this is critical) rooms w/o meals unless otherwise indicated.

Motel; Max. Pers: 3; Bedding incl ?: Yes; Bath: Private; A/C: Yes:
Rate for: Person; $32; Rate for #2 pers: $0; Rate for #3 pers: $13; Child Rate: n/a

Dorm; Max. Pers: 3; Bedding incl ?: Yes; Bath: Shared; A/C: Yes
Rate for: Person: $27; Rate for #2 pers: $0; Rate for #3 pers: $3; Child Rate: n/a

Main amenities available: Creek & waterfall; Volleyball; Laundry machine; Game field; Hiking
Meals are not served in dining room for transients .

NAME OF CENTER: Cedar Lake Camp   Listing ID #: 326

Telephone: 615-823-5655; Fax: ; E-mail:
Address: 235 Conatser Lane; Livingston; TN; 38570
Nearest Interstate: I-40, Exit 21 miles; Nearest State/US Hwy: Rte 52; 0 miles.

Restrictions: Age: None; Pets: Outside only; Alcohol: Not permitted; Smoking: Outdoors only; Reservation Req'd: None; Max. Adv. Reser.: 7 days; Seasonal closing: None

RV/Campers overnight hookups: Yes; Water: Yes; Electric: Yes; Septic: No
Basic Rate/Night: $10.00/ veh

ACCOM: Mon. night thru Thurs. night rates for winterized (check if this is critical) rooms w/o meals unless otherwise indicated.

Dorm; Max. Pers: 3; Bedding incl ?: Yes; Bath: Shared; A/C: No:
Rate for: Person; $15; Rate for #2 pers: $15; Rate for #3 pers: $15; Child Rate: n/a

Main amenities available: Lake swimming; V-ball; Bsk-ball; Ball field; Canoeing; VCR-TV; Hiking
Meals are served in dining room for transients only when other groups are present. Dinner price: $6-7.00.

NAME OF CENTER: Coker Creek Village   Listing ID #: 327

Telephone: 423-261-2310; Fax: ; E-mail:
Address: 12528 Highway 68 (PO Box 98); Coker Creek; TN; 37314
Nearest Interstate: I-75, Exit Highway 68; 35 miles; Nearest State/US Hwy: Rte 68; 0 miles.

Restrictions: Age: None; Pets: Unk; Alcohol: Unk; Smoking: Unk; Reservation Req'd: None; Max. Adv. Reser.: Open; Seasonal closing: None

RV/Campers overnight hookups: Yes; Water: Yes; Electric: Yes; Septic: Yes
Basic Rate/Night: $12.00/ veh

ACCOM: Mon. night thru Thurs. night rates for winterized (check if this is critical) rooms w/o meals unless otherwise indicated.

Bunkroom; Max. Pers: Over 5; Bedding incl ?: No; Bath: Separate bldg; A/C: No:
Rate for: Person; $8; Rate for #2 pers: $8; Rate for #3 pers: $8; Child Rate: n/a

Main amenities available: 200 acres; Mountain biking; Rafting; Waterfall hikes; Horseback riding
Meals are served in dining room for transients . Dinner price: Price varies.

NAME OF CENTER: Lighthouse Christian Camp   Listing ID #: 328

Telephone: 615-597-1264; Fax: 615-597-1264; E-mail:
Address: 205 Serenity Place; Smithville; TN; 37166
Nearest Interstate: I-40, Exit Smithville; 15 miles; Nearest State/US Hwy: Rte. 70 E.; 3 miles.

Restrictions: Age: None; Pets: Not permitted; Alcohol: Not permitted; Smoking: Nowhere; Reservation Req'd: None; Max. Adv. Reser.: Open; Seasonal closing: None

RV/Campers overnight hookups: Yes; Water: Yes; Electric: Yes; Septic: Yes
Basic Rate/Night: $12.00/ veh

ACCOM: Mon. night thru Thurs. night rates for winterized (check if this is critical) rooms w/o meals unless otherwise indicated.

Cabin; Max. Pers: 8; Bedding incl ?: Yes; Bath: Shared; A/C: Yes:
Rate for: Entire cabin; $64
$64 min. covers 4 pers; each additional pers is $8.; fully furnished w/fireplace

Main amenities available: Swimming in Center Hill lake; Laundry machine; VCR-TV; Ping-pong; Fishing; Hiking
Meals are served in dining room for transients only in June - Aug. when campers are present.. Dinner price: $4.00.

REMEMBER TO CALL AHEAD

NAME OF CENTER: Mtn Lake Ranch Christian Retreat   Listing ID #: 329

Telephone: 423-397-1000; Fax: 423-397-4208; E-mail: mlranch@juno.com
Address: 2865 Mountain Ranch Dr.; Dandridge; TN; 37725
Nearest Interstate: I-40, Exit 407 (E); 412 (W); 5 miles; Nearest State/US Hwy: Rte 139; 0 miles.

Restrictions: Age: None; Pets: Permitted; Alcohol: Not permitted; Smoking: Outdoors only; Reservation Req'd: Yes w/dep; Max. Adv. Reser.: Open; Seasonal closing: None

RV/Campers overnight hookups: Yes; Water: Yes; Electric: Yes; Septic: Yes
Basic Rate/Night: $10.50/ veh

ACCOM: Mon. night thru Thurs. night rates for winterized (check if this is critical) rooms w/o meals unless otherwise indicated.

Chalet; Max. Pers: 4; Bedding incl ?: No; Bath: Private; A/C: Yes:
Rate for: Entire chalet; ** $60
** Fee covers 2 adults & 2 children. Incl 2 bedrooms, 2 baths, kitchen, living & dining rooms

Chalet; Max. Pers: 4; Bedding incl ?: No; Bath: Private; A/C: Yes
Rate for: Entire chalet: ** $80
** Fee covers 4 adults. Incl 2 bedrooms, 2 baths, kitchen, living & dining rooms

Main amenities available: Swimming; Volleyball; Basketball; Fishing (must release); Pontoon boats; Hiking
Meals are served in dining room for transients only when other groups are present. Dinner price varies.

NAME OF CENTER: Wesley Woods   Listing ID #: 330

Telephone: 423-448-2246; Fax: 423-448-3904; E-mail:
Address: 329 Wesley Wods Rd; Townsend; TN; 37882
Nearest Interstate: I-40, Exit 50 miles; Nearest State/US Hwy: Rte 321; 5 miles.

Restrictions: Age: None; Pets: Not permitted; Alcohol: Not permitted; Smoking: Outdoors only; Reservation Req'd: 7 days; Max. Adv. Reser.: Open; Seasonal closing: None

RV/Campers overnight hookups: No

ACCOM: Mon. night thru Thurs. night rates for winterized (check if this is critical) rooms w/o meals unless otherwise indicated.

Rustic Bunkroom; Max. Pers: 12; Bedding incl ?: No; Bath: Separate bldg; A/C: No:
Rate for: Person; $10; Rate for #2 pers: $10; Rate for #3 pers: $10; Child Rate: n/a

Main amenities available: Hiking; Ball field; Basketball
Meals are served in dining room for transients only when other groups are present. Dinner price: $5.00.

NAME OF CENTER: YMCA - Memphis - Mason Br. Listing ID: 331

Telephone: 901-323-4505   Fax: 901-327-7545
Address: 3548 walker Branch; Memphis, TN 38111

Restrictions:
Accommodations offered to (M/F/Families): M. If M/F then must be over 18 yrs.
Pets: Not Permitted; Alcohol: Not permitted; Smoking: Outdoors only
Reservation requirements: Requires application
Reservations are accepted up to an indefinite time in advance. Seasonal closing: None

ACCOMMODATIONS:
Single room: Bedding included ?: No; Bath: Shared
Rate for 1 day: not offered; Rate for 1 week: $79+$30 dep

Main amenities: Swimming; Gym; TV lounge
Meals are not offered in their own cafeteria.

NAME OF CENTER: YWCA - Knoxville Listing ID: 332

Telephone: 423-523-6126   Fax: 423-637-5263
Address: 420 W. Clinch Ave.; Knoxville, TN 37902

Restrictions:
Accommodations offered to (M/F/Families): F. If M/F then must be over 18 yrs.
Pets: Not permitted; Alcohol: Not permitted; Smoking: Outdoors only
Reservation requirements: Requires application
Reservations are accepted up to 1 mo in advance. Seasonal closing: None

ACCOMMODATIONS:
Single room: Bedding included ?: Yes; Bath: Shared
Rate for 1 day: $12; Rate for 1 week: $38
Overnight Y membership available for fee. Includes kitchen privileges

Main amenities: Laundry machine; TV lounge
Meals are not offered in their own cafeteria.

TEXAS

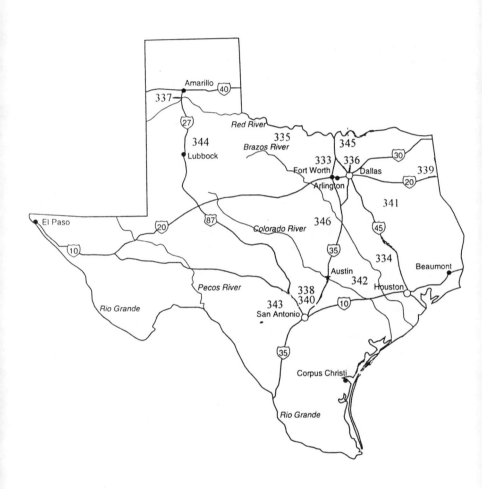

Amarillo
337
40
27
Red River
335
344
Brazos River
Lubbock
333 336
345
30
Fort Worth
Dallas
339
Arlington
20
341
El Paso
20
87
Colorado River
346
45
10
35
334
Austin
Beaumont
Pecos River
338
342
Houston
Rio Grande
343
340
10
San Antonio
35
Corpus Christi
Rio Grande

NAME OF CENTER: Briarwood Retreat Center   Listing ID #: 333

Telephone: 940-455-7002; Fax: 940-455-2157; E-mail: bw@lorms.com
Address: 670 Copper Canyon Rd.; Argyle; TX; 76226
Nearest Interstate: I-35, Exit 7 miles; Nearest State/US Hwy: Rte 407; 1 miles.

Restrictions: Age: None; Pets: Not permitted; Alcohol: Permitted w/restrictions; Smoking: Outdoors only; Reservation Req'd: 1 day; Max. Adv. Reser.: n/a; Seasonal closing: None

RV/Campers overnight hookups: Yes; Water: Yes; Electric: Yes; Septic: unk
Basic Rate/Night: $15.00/ veh

ACCOM: Mon. night thru Thurs. night rates for winterized (check if this is critical) rooms w/o meals unless otherwise indicated.

Bunkroom; Max. Pers: 16; Bedding incl ?: Yes (w/notice); Bath: Shared; A/C: Yes: Rate for: Person; $26; Rate for #2 pers: $26; Rate for #3 pers: $26; Child Rate: n/a

Cabin; Max. Pers: 8; Bedding incl ?: Yes (w/notice); Bath: In bldg, shared; A/C: Yes Rate for: Person: $39; Rate for #2 pers: $39; Rate for #3 pers: $39; Child Rate: n/a

Motel; Max. Pers: 4; Bedding incl ?: Yes (w/notice); Bath: Private; A/C: Yes: Rate for: Person: $62; Rate for #2 pers: $32; Rate for #3 pers: $32; Child Rate: n/a

Main amenities available: Library; Volleyball; Basketball; Softball; Swimming; Hiking
Meals are served in dining room for transients only when other groups are present. Dinner price: $6.50.

NAME OF CENTER: Camp Allen   Listing ID #: 334

Telephone: 409-825-7175; Fax: 409-825-8495; E-mail:
Address: Rte 1; Box 426; Navasota; TX; 77868
Nearest Interstate: I-45, Exit 30 miles; Nearest State/US Hwy: Rte 6; 15 miles.

Restrictions: Age: None; Pets: Not permitted; Alcohol: n/a; Smoking: Designated outdoor areas; Reservation Req'd: 10 days; Max. Adv. Reser.: 3 mo w/dep; Seasonal closing: None

RV/Campers overnight hookups: No

ACCOM: Mon. night thru Thurs. night rates for winterized (check if this is critical) rooms w/o meals unless otherwise indicated.

Motel; Max. Pers: 4; Bedding incl ?: Yes; Bath: Private; A/C: Yes: Rate for: Person; **$83; Rate for #2 pers: **$60; Rate for #3 pers: **$55; Child Rate: 25% off under 10 yr; free under 2
**Rates include three meals.

Main amenities available: Hot tub; sauna; Volleyball; Basketball; Swimming; Laundry machine; Many others
Meals are served in dining room for transients . Dinner price varies.

NAME OF CENTER: Camp Chaparral   Listing ID #: 335

Telephone: 940-855-4182; Fax: 940-855-4187; E-mail: cbc@cyberstation.net
Address: 3784 Church Camp Rd; Iowa Park; TX; 76367
Nearest State/US Hwy: FM 367; 3 miles.

Restrictions: Age: None; Pets: Not permitted; Alcohol: Not permitted; Smoking: Outdoors only; Reservation Req'd: 2 days; Max. Adv. Reser.: ; Seasonal closing: None

RV/Campers overnight hookups: Yes; Water: n/a; Electric: n/a; Septic: n/a
Basic Rate/Night: $7.50/ veh

ACCOM: Mon. night thru Thurs. night rates for winterized (check if this is critical) rooms w/o meals unless otherwise indicated.

Motel; Max. Pers: 4; Bedding incl ?: Yes; Bath: Private; A/C: Yes:
Rate for: Person; $45; Rate for #2 pers: $9; Rate for #3 pers: $21; Child Rate: n/a

Suite Room; Max. Pers: 11; Bedding incl ?: No; Bath: Shared; A/C: Yes
Rate for: Person: **$16; Rate for #2 pers: **$16; Rate for #3 pers: **$16; Child Rate: n/a
**$96 minimum; kitchen privileges

Main amenities available: Children playground; Volleyball; Basketball; Swimming; Ping pong; Boating
Meals are served in dining room for transients . Dinner price: $5.00.

NAME OF CENTER: Catholic Conf. & Formation Center   Listing ID #: 336

Telephone: 214-943-6585; Fax: 214-943-6587; E-mail:
Address: 901 S. Madison; Dallas; TX; 75208
Nearest Interstate: I-35, Exit ; 0 miles.

Restrictions: Age: None; Pets: Not permitted; Alcohol: Not permitted; Smoking: Outdoors only; Reservation Req'd: 1 day; Max. Adv. Reser.: Open; Seasonal closing: None

RV/Campers overnight hookups: No

ACCOM: Mon. night thru Thurs. night rates for winterized (check if this is critical) rooms w/o meals unless otherwise indicated.

Dorm; Max. Pers: 5; Bedding incl ?: Yes; Bath: Shared; A/C: Yes:
Rate for: Person; $18; Rate for #2 pers: $18; Rate for #3 pers: $18; Child Rate: "Very young - free"

Main amenities available: Reading room; Laundry machine; Hiking; Softball field; Bookstore
Meals are served in dining room for transients only when other groups are present. Dinner price: $7.00.

NAME OF CENTER: Ceta Canyon Meth. **Camp & Ret Ctr**   Listing ID #: 337

Telephone: 806-488-2268; Fax: 806-488-2594; E-mail: cetacan@arn.net
Address: HCR 1, Box 31; Happy; TX; 79042
Nearest Interstate: I-27, Exit 10 miles; Nearest State/US Hwy: Rte 285; 3 miles.

Restrictions: Age: None; Pets: Not permitted; Alcohol: Not permitted; Smoking: Outdoors only; Reservation Req'd: Noon of day; Max. Adv. Reser.: 6 mo; Seasonal closing: None

RV/Campers overnight hookups: Yes; Water: Yes; Electric: Yes; Septic: unk
Basic Rate/Night: $12.00/ veh

ACCOM: Mon. night thru Thurs. night rates for winterized (check if this is critical) rooms w/o meals unless otherwise indicated.

Bunkroom; Max. Pers: Over 5; Bedding incl ?: $5 surcharge; Bath: Shared; A/C: Yes:
Rate for: Person; $21; Rate for #2 pers: $21; Rate for #3 pers: $21; Child Rate: $17 under 12 yr, free under 3

Motel; Max. Pers: 5; Bedding incl ?: $5 surcharge; Bath: Private; A/C: Yes
Rate for: Person: $26; Rate for #2 pers: $21; Rate for #3 pers: $21; Child Rate: $17 under 12 yr, free under 3

Main amenities available: Swimming; Volleyball; Basketball; Hiking
Meals are served in dining room for transients only when other groups are present. Dinner price: $4.00-8.00.

NAME OF CENTER: **Christ of the Hills Monastery**   Listing ID #: 338

Telephone: 830-833-5363; Fax: 830-833-5813; E-mail:
Address: New Sarov; Blanco; TX; 78606
Nearest Interstate: I-35, Exit 30 miles; Nearest State/US Hwy: US 281; 5 miles.

Restrictions: Age: None; Pets: Not permitted; Alcohol: Hard liquor not permitted; Smoking: Nowhere; Reservation Req'd: None; Max. Adv. Reser.: 1 yr; Seasonal closing: None

RV/Campers overnight hookups: No

ACCOM: Mon. night thru Thurs. night rates for winterized (check if this is critical) rooms w/o meals unless otherwise indicated.

Monastery; Max. Pers: Many; Bedding incl ?: Yes; Bath: Shared; A/C: Yes:
Free will offering. All men in monastery and women in convent. Children as appropriate

Main amenities available: Library; Bookstore; Hiking
Meals are served in dining room for transients .
** Russian Orthodox Monastery. Free will offering for lodging and meals.

NAME OF CENTER: Gilmont Program Center   Listing ID #: 339

Telephone: 800-737-0001; Fax: 903-797-6400; E-mail: campgilmont@juno.com
Address: Rte 6; Box 254; Gilmer; TX; 75644
Nearest Interstate: I-20 & I-30, Exit 30 miles; Nearest State/US Hwy: Rte 271; 6 miles.

Restrictions: Age: None; Pets: Not permitted; Alcohol: Not permitted; Smoking: Outdoors only; Reservation Req'd: Required w/dep; Max. Adv. Reser.: ; Seasonal closing: None

RV/Campers overnight hookups: Yes; Water: Yes; Electric: Yes; Septic: Yes
Basic Rate/Night: $10.00/ veh

ACCOM: Mon. night thru Thurs. night rates for winterized (check if this is critical) rooms w/o meals unless otherwise indicated.

Cabin; Max. Pers: 16; Bedding incl ?: $2 surcharge; Bath: Shared; A/C: Yes:
Rate for: Person; $23; Rate for #2 pers: $23; Rate for #3 pers: $23; Child Rate: 50% off under 10 yr; free under 4

Motel; Max. Pers: 2; Bedding incl ?: Yes; Bath: Private; A/C: Yes
Rate for: Person: $26; Rate for #2 pers: $26; Child Rate: 50% off under 10 yr; free under 4

Main amenities available: Volleyball; Basketball; Hiking
Meals are served in dining room for transients only when other groups are present. Dinner price: $5.75.

NAME OF CENTER: John Knox Ranch   Listing ID #: 340

Telephone: 830-935-4568; Fax: 830-935-4189; E-mail: JOHNKNOX@GUTC.COM
Address: 1661 John Knox Road; Fischer; TX; 78623
Nearest Interstate: I-35, Exit 21 miles; Nearest State/US Hwy: Rte 32; 3 miles.

Restrictions: Age: None; Pets: Not permitted; Alcohol: Not permitted; Smoking: Outdoors only; Reservation Req'd: None; Max. Adv. Reser.: Open; Seasonal closing: None

RV/Campers overnight hookups: Yes; Water: Yes; Electric: Yes; Septic: n/a
Basic Rate/Night: $17.00/ veh

ACCOM: Mon. night thru Thurs. night rates for winterized (check if this is critical) rooms w/o meals unless otherwise indicated.

Bunkroom; Max. Pers: 8; Bedding incl ?: $3 surcharge; Bath: Shared; A/C: Yes:
Rate for: Person; $12; Rate for #2 pers: $12; Rate for #3 pers: $12; Child Rate: n/a

Cabin; Max. Pers: 6; Bedding incl ?: Yes; Bath: Private; A/C: Yes
Rate for: Two persons: $36; Rate for #2 pers: n/a; Rate for #3 pers: $6; Child Rate: n/a

Main amenities available: Swimming; Volleyball; Basketball; Laundry machine; Canoeing; Hiking
Meals are served in dining room for transients only when other groups are present. Dinner price: $4.50-6.50.

NAME OF CENTER: Lakeview Methodist Conf. Center   Listing ID #: 341

Telephone: 903-538-2711; Fax: 903-538-2797; E-mail:
Address: Box 5586; Palestine; TX; 75801
Nearest Interstate: I-46, Exit 35 miles; Nearest State/US Hwy: Rte 294; 0 miles.

Restrictions: Age: None; Pets: Not permitted; Alcohol: Not permitted; Smoking: Outdoors only; Reservation Req'd: 11AM of day; Max. Adv. Reser.: 1 yr; Seasonal closing: Dec 10 - Jan 2

RV/Campers overnight hookups: Yes; Water: Yes Yes; Electric: ; Septic: Yes
Basic Rate/Night: $14.00/ veh

ACCOM: Mon. night thru Thurs. night rates for winterized (check if this is critical) rooms w/o meals unless otherwise indicated.

Bunkroom; Max. Pers: 6-12; Bedding incl ?: No; Bath: Private; A/C: Yes:
Rate for: Person; $18; Rate for #2 pers: $18; Rate for #3 pers: $18; Child Rate: n/a
Family rate $40 max

Cabin; Max. Pers: 4-6; Bedding incl ?: Yes; Bath: Private; A/C: Yes
Rate for: Person: $26; Rate for #2 pers: $26; Rate for #3 pers: $26; Child Rate: n/a
Family rate $56 max.; fireplace

Motel; Max. Pers: 4; Bedding incl ?: Yes; Bath: Private; A/C: Yes:
Rate for: Person: $26; Rate for #2 pers: $26; Rate for #3 pers: $26; Child Rate: n/a
Family rate $56 max.

Main amenities available: Lake swimming; Volleyball; Basketball; Tennis; Incidentals store; Paddle boats
Meals are served in dining room for transients only when other groups are present. Dinner price: $5.00; $3 under 10 yrs.

NAME OF CENTER: Lutherhill Camp & Retreat Ctr   Listing ID #: 342

Telephone: 409-249-3232; Fax: 409-249-4032; E-mail: kathy-haueisen@ecunet.org
Address: PO Box 99; LaGrange; TX; 78945
Nearest Interstate: I-10, Exit 25 miles; Nearest State/US Hwy: Rte 77; 4 miles.

Restrictions: Age: None; Pets: Permitted on leash/carrier; Alcohol: Permitted in designated area; Smoking: Outdoors only; Reservation Req'd: 3 days; Max. Adv. Reser.: 1 mo; Seasonal closing: June - August 7

RV/Campers overnight hookups: No

ACCOM: Mon. night thru Thurs. night rates for winterized (check if this is critical) rooms w/o meals unless otherwise indicated.

Bunkroom; Max. Pers: 10; Bedding incl ?: $2 surcharge; Bath: Private; A/C: Yes:
Rate for: Person; $25; Rate for #2 pers: $5; Rate for #3 pers: $5; Child Rate: $2.50 under 12 yr; free under 3

Cabin; Max. Pers: ; Bedding incl ?: $2 surcharge; Bath: Shared; A/C: Yes
Rate for: Person: $25; Rate for #2 pers: $6; Rate for #3 pers: $6; Child Rate: $2.50 under 12 yrs; free under 3

Dorm; Max. Pers: 5; Bedding incl ?: $2 surcharge; Bath: Shared; A/C: Yes:
Rate for: Person: $35; Rate for #2 pers: $6; Rate for #3 pers: $6; Child Rate: $3 under 12 yrs, free under 3

Main amenities available: n/a
Meals are not served in dining room for transients .

NAME OF CENTER: Mo Ranch   Listing ID #: 343

Telephone: 800-460-4401; Fax: 830-238-4202; E-mail: www.moranch.com
Address: HC1; Box 158; Hunt; TX; 78024
Nearest Interstate: I-10, Exit 23 miles; Nearest State/US Hwy: Rte 41; 11 miles.

Restrictions: Age: None; Pets: Not permitted; Alcohol: Permitted in bedroom; Smoking:
Outdoors only; Reservation Req'd: 1 day; Max. Adv. Reser.: ; Seasonal closing: None

RV/Campers overnight hookups: No

ACCOM: Mon. night thru Thurs. night rates for winterized (check if this is critical) rooms w/o
meals unless otherwise indicated.

Cabin; Max. Pers: 8; Bedding incl ?: By request; Bath: Shared; A/C: No:
Rate for: Cabin; $49

Motel; Max. Pers: 2; Bedding incl ?: Yes; Bath: Private; A/C: Yes
Rate for: Room: $72; Child Rate: n/a
"Call long ahead in summer"

Main amenities available: Swimming; Volleyball; Basketball; Laundry machine; Bookstore; Many others
Meals are served in dining room for transients only when other groups are present. Dinner price: $8.00; $5.50
for children; free under 4 yrs.

NAME OF CENTER: Plains Baptist Camp   Listing ID #: 344

Telephone: 806-983-3954; Fax: 806-983-2008; E-mail:
Address: Rte 3; Box 162; Floydada; TX; 79235
Nearest Interstate: I-27, Exit 30 miles; Nearest State/US Hwy: Rte 62/207; 2 miles.

Restrictions: Age: None; Pets: Not permitted; Alcohol: Not permitted; Smoking: Outdoors only;
Reservation Req'd: None; Max. Adv. Reser.: ; Seasonal closing: None

RV/Campers overnight hookups: Yes; Water: Yes; Electric: Yes; Septic: unk
Basic Rate/Night: RV hookup $11 for 2 people; $3/add'l over 2 yrs

ACCOM: Mon. night thru Thurs. night rates for winterized (check if this is critical) rooms w/o
meals unless otherwise indicated.

Bunkroom; Max. Pers: Over 9; Bedding incl ?: Yes; Bath: Shared; A/C: Yes:
Rate for: Person; $18; Rate for #2 pers: $17; Rate for #3 pers: $16; Child Rate: n/a

Motel; Max. Pers: 10; Bedding incl ?: Yes; Bath: Private; A/C: Yes
Rate for: Two persons: $56; Child Rate: n/a

Main amenities available: Swimming; Volleyball; Basketball; Bookstore; Ping pong; Hiking
Meals are served in dining room for transients only when other groups are present. Dinner price: $5.00.

NAME OF CENTER: Texoma Lutheran Camp   Listing ID #: 345

Telephone: 888-886-6198; Fax: 903-786-8883; E-mail: lomtexoma.texoma.net
Address: 418 Lutheran Dr.; Pottsboro; TX; 75076
Nearest Interstate: I-35, Exit 45 miles; Nearest State/US Hwy: Rte 75; 20 miles.

Restrictions: Age: None; Pets: Not permitted; Alcohol: Permitted; Smoking: Outdoors only; Reservation Req'd: 1 day; Max. Adv. Reser.: 1 yr; Seasonal closing: None

RV/Campers overnight hookups: Yes; Water: n/a; Electric: Yes; Septic: unk
Basic Rate/Night: $5 per person

ACCOM: Mon. night thru Thurs. night rates for winterized (check if this is critical) rooms w/o meals unless otherwise indicated.

Bunkroom; Max. Pers: 20; Bedding incl ?: No; Bath: Shared; A/C: Yes:
Rate for: Person; $14; Rate for #2 pers: $14; Rate for #3 pers: $14; Child Rate: n/a

Dorm; Max. Pers: 5; Bedding incl ?: Yes; Bath: Shared; A/C: Yes
Rate for: Person: $20; Rate for #2 pers: $20; Rate for #3 pers: $20; Child Rate: 1/2 price under 12; free under 6

Main amenities available: Lake swimming; Volleyball; Laundry machine; Canoeing; Archery; Hiking
Meals are served in dining room for transients only when other groups are present. Dinner price: $6.80.

NAME OF CENTER: **Three Mountain Retreat**   Listing ID #: 346

Telephone: 254-675-3188; Fax: 254-675-3188; E-mail:
Address: Intersection of Rte 219 & Highway 182; Clifton; TX; 76634
Nearest Interstate: I-35, Exit 40 miles; Nearest State/US Hwy: Rte 6; 7 miles.

Restrictions: Age: None; Pets: Permitted; Alcohol: Not permitted; Smoking: Outdoors only; Reservation Req'd: None; Max. Adv. Reser.: 2 days; Seasonal closing: None

RV/Campers overnight hookups: No

ACCOM: Mon. night thru Thurs. night rates for winterized (check if this is critical) rooms w/o meals unless otherwise indicated.

Bunkroom; Max. Pers: 12; Bedding incl ?: No; Bath: Shared; A/C: Yes:
Rate for: Bunkroom; $75; Child Rate: n/a

Duplex Motel; Max. Pers: 4; Bedding incl ?: Yes; Bath: Private; A/C: Yes
Rate for: Room: $75; Child Rate: n/a
2 adjoining rooms each w/bath - 8 total

Main amenities available: Laundry machine; Volleyball; Basketball; Hiking
Meals are served in dining room for transients only when other groups are present. Dinner price: $5.00.

REMEMBER TO CALL AHEAD

NAME OF CENTER: YMCA - Houston, Cossaboom Branch Listing ID: 347

Telephone: 713-643-2804   Fax:
Address: 7903 South Loop East; Houston, TX 77012

Restrictions:
Accommodations offered to (M/F/Families): M. If M/F then must be over 18 yrs.
Pets: Not permitted; Alcohol: Not permitted; Smoking: Bedroom only
Reservation requirements: None
Reservations are accepted up to 0 days in advance. Seasonal closing: None

ACCOMMODATIONS:
Single room: Bedding included ?: Yes; Bath: Shared
Rate for 1 day: $18.45+$10 dep; Rate for 1 week: $85.75+$10 dep
Room fee includes membership in Y

Main amenities: Laundry machine; Sauna
Meals are not offered in their own cafeteria.

NAME OF CENTER: YMCA - Houston, Downtown Listing ID: 348

Telephone: 713-659-8501   Fax: 713-659-4314
Address: 1600 Louisiana St.; PO Box 3007; Houston, TX 77002

Restrictions:
Accommodations offered to (M/F/Families): M&F. If M/F then must be over 18 yrs.
Pets: Not permitted; Alcohol: Not permitted; Smoking: Bedroom only
Reservation requirements: None
Reservations are accepted up to 0 days in advance. Seasonal closing: None

ACCOMMODATIONS:
Single room: Bedding included ?: Yes; Bath: Shared
Rate for 1 day: $19.43+$12.50 dep; Rate for 1 week: $89.36+$12.50 dep
$5/visit charge for use of Y pool, gym etc. Facility closed to transients 12/31/99

Main amenities: Volleyball; Basketball
Meals are not offered in their own cafeteria.

NAME OF CENTER: YMCA - Houston, South Central Branch Listing ID: 349

Telephone: 713-748-5405   Fax: 713-748-5415
Address: 3531 Wheeler St.; Houston, TX 77004

Restrictions:
Accommodations offered to (M/F/Families): M. If M/F then must be over 18 yrs.
Pets: Not permitted; Alcohol: Not permitted; Smoking: Bedrooms only
Reservation requirements: None
Reservations are accepted up to 0 days in advance. Seasonal closing: None

ACCOMMODATIONS:
Single room: Bedding included ?: Yes; Bath: Shared
Rate for 1 day: $17.76+$10 dep; Rate for 1 week: $77.70+$10 dep
Room fee includes membership in Y.

Main amenities: Laundry machine; Pool; Gym
Meals are not offered in their own cafeteria.

UTAH

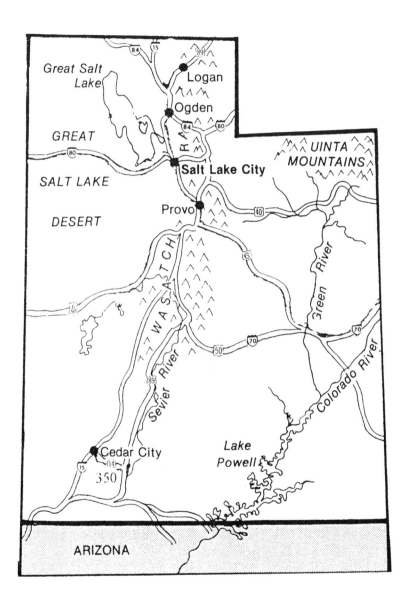

NAME OF CENTER: Lutherwood   Listing ID #: 350

Telephone: 435-635-7708; Fax: 702-263-9890; E-mail:
Address: Mail: PO Box 16034; Las Vegas; NV; 89101
Nearest Interstate: I-15, Exit 43 miles; Nearest State/US Hwy: Junct US 89 & Rte 14; 2 miles.
Camp is in Utah mid-way between Orderville & Hatch in Long Valley Junction

Restrictions: Age: None; Pets: Permitted on leash; Alcohol: Permitted; Smoking: Outdoors only; Reservation Req'd: None; Max. Adv. Reser.: 1 tr; Seasonal closing: Nov 1 - May 1

RV/Campers overnight hookups: Yes; Water: Yes; Electric: Yes; Septic: No
Basic Rate/Night: $9 + $2 w/elect/ veh

ACCOM: Mon. night thru Thurs. night rates for winterized (check if this is critical) rooms w/o meals unless otherwise indicated.

Bunk trailer; Max. Pers: 10; Bedding incl ?: No; Bath: Shared; A/C: No:
Rate for: Person; ** $5; Rate for #2 pers: ** $5; Rate for #3 pers: ** $5; Child Rate: n/a
** Lodging fees are donations.

Family trailer; Max. Pers: 3; Bedding incl ?: PrivateNo; Bath: Private; A/C: No
Rate for: Trailer: ** $20; Rate for #2 pers: n/a; Rate for #3 pers: n/a; Child Rate: n/a
** Lodging fees are donations.

Main amenities available: 1400 acres at 7500' ; Volleyball; Horse shoes; Hiking; Ball field
Meals are served in dining room for transients totally at the discretion of the retreat gp.. Dinner price varies.

VERMONT

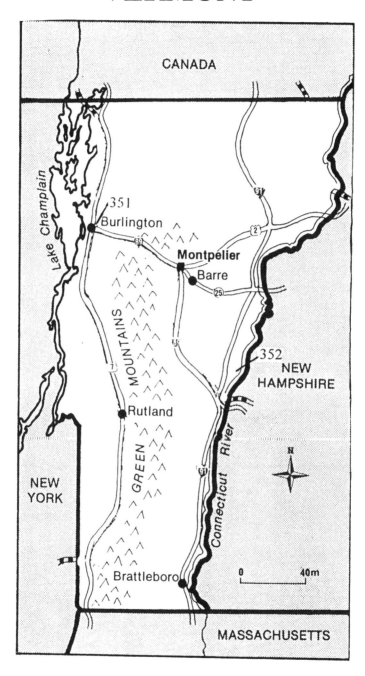

CANADA

Lake Champlain

351
Burlington

89

2

Montpelier
Barre

25

MOUNTAINS

7

GREEN

Rutland

352
NEW
HAMPSHIRE

Connecticut River

91

N

NEW
YORK

Brattleboro

0   40m

MASSACHUSETTS

NAME OF CENTER: Bishop Booth Conference Center   Listing ID #: 351

Telephone: 802-658-6233; Fax: 802-658-8836; E-mail: bbcc3@aol.com
Address: 20 Rock Point Circle; Burlington; VT; 05821
Nearest Interstate: I-89, Exit 6 miles; Nearest State/US Hwy: Rte 127; 0.5 miles.

Restrictions: Age: None; Pets: Not permitted; Alcohol: Permitted; Smoking: Outdoors only;
Reservation Req'd: 3 days; Max. Adv. Reser.: 2 mo; Seasonal closing: mid June - mid Aug.

RV/Campers overnight hookups: No

ACCOM: Mon. night thru Thurs. night rates for winterized (check if this is critical) rooms w/o
meals unless otherwise indicated.

Dorm; Max. Pers: 5; Bedding incl ?: Yes; Bath: Semi-private; A/C: No:
Rate for: Person; ** $22; Rate for #2 pers: ** $22; Rate for #3 pers: ** $22; Child Rate: n/a
** Max: $70 per room. Do not accept credit cards

Cabin; Max. Pers: Over 5; Bedding incl ?: No; Bath: Shared; A/C: No
Rate for: Person: $10; Rate for #2 pers: $10; Rate for #3 pers: $10; Child Rate: n/a

Main amenities available: Library; Volleyball; Basketball; VCR-TV; Hiking
Meals are served in dining room for transients only when other groups are present. Dinner price: $9.50.

NAME OF CENTER: Gove Hill Camp & Conference Ctr.   Listing ID #: 352

Telephone: 802-785-4000; Fax: 802-785-4000; E-mail: govehill@juno.com
Address: 1646 Gove Hill Road; Thetford; VT; 05075
Nearest Interstate: I-91, Exit 14; 6 miles; Nearest State/US Hwy: Rte 132; 2 miles.

Restrictions: Age: None; Pets: Permitted on leash; Alcohol: Not permitted; Smoking: Outdoors
only; Reservation Req'd: 1 day; Max. Adv. Reser.: 1 yr; Seasonal closing: Dec. - March

RV/Campers overnight hookups: Yes; Water: No; Electric: Yes; Septic: No
Basic Rate/Night: $10.00/ veh

ACCOM: Mon. night thru Thurs. night rates for winterized (check if this is critical) rooms w/o
meals unless otherwise indicated.

A - Frame; Max. Pers: 6-8; Bedding incl ?: $5 surcharge; Bath: Shared; A/C: No:
Rate for: Entire A-Frame; $40
Includes 3 bedrooms; kitchen; dinette; living room

Main amenities available: Pond at A-Frame; Paddle boat; Canoe; TV ; Hiking
Meals are not served in dining room for transients .

VIRGINIA

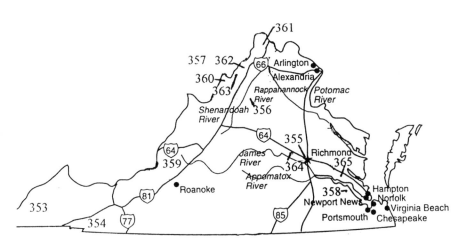

361

357 362   66   Arlington

360   Alexandria

363   Rappahannock River   Potomac River

Shenandoah River   356

64   355

64   Richmond

359   James River   364   365

Appomatox River

81   Roanoke   358   Hampton

Norfolk

353   Newport News   Virginia Beach

354   77   85   Portsmouth   Chesapeake

NAME OF CENTER: **Camp Bethel**   Listing ID #: 353

Telephone: 540-328-6876; Fax: 540-328-6877; E-mail:
Address: PO Box 390; Wise; VA; 24293
Nearest Interstate: I-81, Exit 50 miles; Nearest State/US Hwy: Rte 23; 2 miles.

Restrictions: Age: None; Pets: Permitted on leash; Alcohol: Not permitted; Smoking: Outdoors
only; Reservation Req'd: None; Max. Adv. Reser.: Open; Seasonal closing: None

RV/Campers overnight hookups: Yes; Water: Yes; Electric: Yes; Septic: No
Basic Rate/Night: $10; $12 for A/C/ veh

ACCOM: Mon. night thru Thurs. night rates for winterized (check if this is critical) rooms w/o
meals unless otherwise indicated.

Main amenities available: Swimming; Ping-pong; Boating; Canoeing; Hiking
Meals are not served in dining room for transients .

NAME OF CENTER: **Camp Dickenson**   Listing ID #: 354

Telephone: 540-744-7241; Fax: 540-744-7241; E-mail:
Address: 801 Camp Dickenson Lane; Fries; VA; 24333
Nearest Interstate: I-57, Exit 17 miles; Nearest State/US Hwy: Rte 638; 1 miles.

Restrictions: Age: None; Pets: Permitted on leash; Alcohol: Not permitted; Smoking: Permitted
in RV area; Reservation Req'd: None; Max. Adv. Reser.: Open; Seasonal closing: Closed
weekdays June - July

RV/Campers overnight hookups: Yes; Water: Yes; Electric: Yes; Septic: Yes
Basic Rate/Night: $14 ($12 "pop-ups")/ veh

ACCOM: Mon. night thru Thurs. night rates for winterized (check if this is critical) rooms w/o
meals unless otherwise indicated.

Main amenities available: Swimming (weekends); Volleyball; Basketball; Located on New River
Meals are not served in dining room for transients .

NAME OF CENTER: Camp Hanover   Listing ID #: 355

Telephone: 804-779-2811; Fax: 804-779-3056; E-mail: chanover@erols.com
Address: 3163 Parsleys Mill Rd.; Mechanicsville; VA; 23111
Nearest Interstate: I-295, Exit 13 miles; Nearest State/US Hwy: I-64; 10 miles.

Restrictions: Age: None; Pets: Not permitted; Alcohol: Not permitted; Smoking: Outdoors only; Reservation Req'd: 7 days; Max. Adv. Reser.: Open; Seasonal closing: None

RV/Campers overnight hookups: No

ACCOM: Mon. night thru Thurs. night rates for winterized (check if this is critical) rooms w/o meals unless otherwise indicated.

Motel; Max. Pers: 4; Bedding incl ?: Yes (w/notice); Bath: Private; A/C: No:
Rate for: Person; $13; Rate for #2 pers: $13; Rate for #3 pers: $13; Child Rate: 50% off under 12 yrs; free under 4

Dorm; Max. Pers: 4; Bedding incl ?: Yes (w/notice); Bath: Shared; A/C: No
Rate for: Person: $13; Rate for #2 pers: $13; Rate for #3 pers: $13; Child Rate: 50% off under 12 yrs; free under 4

Bunkroom; Max. Pers: Over 5; Bedding incl ?: Yes (w/notice); Bath: Shared; A/C: No:
Rate for: Person: $11; Rate for #2 pers: $11; Rate for #3 pers: $11; Child Rate: 50% off under 12 yrs; free under 4

Main amenities available: Swimming; Volleyball; Climbing wall; Fishing/Boating lake; Hiking
Meals are served in dining room for transients only when other groups are present. Dinner price: $5.50.

NAME OF CENTER: Camp Shenandoah Springs   Listing ID #: 356

Telephone: 540-923-4300; Fax: 540-923-4109; E-mail:
Address: PO Box 770; Madison; VA; 22727
Nearest Interstate: I-64, Exit 55 miles; Nearest State/US Hwy: Rte 29; 6 miles.

Restrictions: Age: None; Pets: Not permitted; Alcohol: Not permitted; Smoking: Outdoors only; Reservation Req'd: None; Max. Adv. Reser.: Open; Seasonal closing: None

RV/Campers overnight hookups: No

ACCOM: Mon. night thru Thurs. night rates for winterized (check if this is critical) rooms w/o meals unless otherwise indicated.

Motel; Max. Pers: 4; Bedding incl ?: Yes; Bath: Private; A/C: No:
Rate for: Person; $100; Rate for #2 pers: $0; Rate for #3 pers: $20; Child Rate: n/a
Includes breakfast

Cottage; Max. Pers: 11; Bedding incl ?: Yes; Bath: Shared; A/C: No
Rate for: Person: $100; Rate for #2 pers: $0; Rate for #3 pers: $20; Child Rate: n/a
Includes breakfast

Main amenities available: Swimming; Volleyball; Bookstore; Horseback riding; Boating; Canoeing
Meals are served in dining room for transients only when other groups are present. Dinner price: $5.95.

NAME OF CENTER: Caroline Furnace Lutheran Camp   Listing ID #: 357

Telephone: 540-933-6266; Fax: 540-933-6971; E-mail: cfcamp@shentel.net
Address: 2239 Camp Roosevelt Rd; Fort Valley; VA; 22652
Nearest Interstate: I-81, Exit 20 miles; Nearest State/US Hwy: Rte 675; 0 miles.

Restrictions: Age: None; Pets: Not permitted; Alcohol: Not permitted; Smoking: Permitted everywhere; Reservation Req'd: None; Max. Adv. Reser.: 14 daya; Seasonal closing: Christmas week

RV/Campers overnight hookups: No

ACCOM: Mon. night thru Thurs. night rates for winterized (check if this is critical) rooms w/o meals unless otherwise indicated.

Cabin; Max. Pers: 12; Bedding incl ?: No; Bath: Shared; A/C: No:
Rate for: Person; $18; Rate for #2 pers: $18; Rate for #3 pers: $18; Child Rate: 50% off under 13 yrs; free under 2
For two nights $20.50

House; Max. Pers: 5; Bedding incl ?: No; Bath: Shared; A/C: No
Rate for: Person: $20; Rate for #2 pers: $20; Rate for #3 pers: $20; Child Rate: 50% off under 13 yrs; free under 2
For two nights $25

Main amenities available: Lake swimming; Volleyball; Basketball; Canoeing; Ball field; Hiking
Meals are served in dining room for transients only when other groups are present. Dinner price: $7; 50% off under 13 yrs; free under 2.

NAME OF CENTER: Chanco Camp & Conference Ctr.   Listing ID #: 358

Telephone: 757-294-3126; Fax: 757-294-0727; E-mail:
Address: 394 Floods Dr.; PO Box 378; Surry; VA; 23883
Nearest Interstate: I-95, Exit Hopewell Rte 10; 35 miles; Nearest State/US Hwy: Rte 610; 0 miles.

Restrictions: Age: None; Pets: Not permitted; Alcohol: Permitted; Smoking: Outdoors only; Reservation Req'd: None; Max. Adv. Reser.: 14 days; Seasonal closing: None

RV/Campers overnight hookups: No

ACCOM: Mon. night thru Thurs. night rates for winterized (check if this is critical) rooms w/o meals unless otherwise indicated.

Motel; Max. Pers: 2; Bedding incl ?: Yes; Bath: Private; A/C: Yes:
Rate for: Person; $41; Rate for #2 pers: $41; Child Rate: $26 under 12 yrs; free under 3; $10 "on the floor"

Main amenities available: swimming in pool & river; Volleyball; VCR-TV; Laundry machine; Hiking;
Meals are served in dining room for transients only when other groups are present. Dinner price: $9.00.

NAME OF CENTER: Grace Bible Camp   Listing ID #: 359

Telephone: 540-997-9316; Fax: 540-997-0073; E-mail:
Address: 111 Bible Camp Lane; Goshen; VA; 24439
Nearest Interstate: I-64, Exit 43; 4 miles; Nearest State/US Hwy: Rte 780; 0.5 miles.

Restrictions: Age: None; Pets: Not permitted; Alcohol: Not permitted; Smoking: Outdoors only;
Reservation Req'd: None; Max. Adv. Reser.: Open; Seasonal closing: None

RV/Campers overnight hookups: Yes; Water: Yes; Electric: Yes; Septic: No
Basic Rate/Night: $10.00/ veh

ACCOM: Mon. night thru Thurs. night rates for winterized (check if this is critical) rooms w/o
meals unless otherwise indicated.

Main amenities available: n/a
Meals are served in dining room for transients only when other groups are present. Dinner price varies.

NAME OF CENTER: Highland Retreat   Listing ID #: 360

Telephone: 540-852-3226; Fax: 540-852-9272; E-mail:
Address: 14783 Upper Highland Dr.; Bergton; VA; 22811
Nearest Interstate: I-81, Exit 21 miles; Nearest State/US Hwy: Rte 259; 0 miles.

Restrictions: Age: None; Pets: Not permitted; Alcohol: Not permitted; Smoking: Outdoors only;
Reservation Req'd: 1 day; Max. Adv. Reser.: Open; Seasonal closing: None

RV/Campers overnight hookups: Yes; Water: Yes; Electric: Yes; Septic: No
Basic Rate/Night: $17.00/ veh

ACCOM: Mon. night thru Thurs. night rates for winterized (check if this is critical) rooms w/o
meals unless otherwise indicated.

Motel; Max. Pers: Over 4; Bedding incl ?: $2.50 surcharge; Bath: Private; A/C: Yes:
Rate for: Room; $30/4 pers.; Child Rate: n/a
For over 4 pers. add $7.50/pers.

Main amenities available: Swimming; Volleyball; Basketball; Ping-pong; Ball field; Hiking
Meals are not served in dining room for transients .

REMEMBER TO CALL AHEAD

NAME OF CENTER: Hunting Ridge Retreat   Listing ID #: 361

Telephone: 540-662-9004; Fax: 540-678-4781; E-mail: hrr@visuallink.com
Address: 1011 Hunting Ridge Rd.; Winchester; VA; 22603
Nearest Interstate: I-81, Exit 8 miles; Nearest State/US Hwy: Rte 522; 2 miles.

Restrictions: Age: None; Pets: Not permitted; Alcohol: Not permitted; Smoking: Outdoors only; Reservation Req'd: 1 day; Max. Adv. Reser.: Open; Seasonal closing: None

RV/Campers overnight hookups: No

ACCOM: Mon. night thru Thurs. night rates for winterized (check if this is critical) rooms w/o meals unless otherwise indicated.

Motel; Max. Pers: 4; Bedding incl ?: No; Bath: Private; A/C: No:
Rate for: Person; $18; Rate for #2 pers: $18; Rate for #3 pers: $18; Child Rate: $9 under 10 yrs.

Bunkroom; Max. Pers: Over 5; Bedding incl ?: No; Bath: Shared; A/C: No
Rate for: Person: $9; Rate for #2 pers: $9; Rate for #3 pers: $9; Child Rate: $9 under 10 yrs

Main amenities available: Swimming; V-ball; Bsk-ball; Ball field; Ping-pong; Tennis; Hiking
Meals are served in dining room for transients . Dinner price: $7.00.

NAME OF CENTER: Shenandoah Meadows   Listing ID #: 362

Telephone: 888-933-6650; Fax: ; E-mail:
Address: PO Box 124; Fort Valley; VA; 22652
Nearest Interstate: I-81, Exit 20 miles; Nearest State/US Hwy: Rte 678; 1 miles.

Restrictions: Age: None; Pets: Not permitted; Alcohol: Permitted; Smoking: Outdoors only; Reservation Req'd: None; Max. Adv. Reser.: 7 days; Seasonal closing: None

RV/Campers overnight hookups: No

ACCOM: Mon. night thru Thurs. night rates for winterized (check if this is critical) rooms w/o meals unless otherwise indicated.

House; Max. Pers: 6; Bedding incl ?: Yes; Bath: Semi-private; A/C: Yes:
Rate for: Entire house; $110
Capacity ~15 pers. Inquire for rates over 6 pers. Includes living rm & kitchen & 3 baths.

Main amenities available: Swimming; Volleyball; Basketball; VCR-TV; Hiking
Meals are not served in dining room for transients .

NAME OF CENTER: Shrine Mont   Listing ID #: 363

Telephone: 540-856-2141; Fax: 540-856-8520; E-mail:
Address: 221 Shrine Mont Circle; Orkney; VA; 22845
Nearest Interstate: I-81, Exit 15 miles; Nearest State/US Hwy: Rte 263; 0 miles.

Restrictions: Age: None; Pets: Not permitted; Alcohol: Hard liquor not permitted; Smoking: Designated outdoor area; Reservation Req'd: 14 days (for weekends); Max. Adv. Reser.: 1 yr; Seasonal closing: Dec. - March

RV/Campers overnight hookups: No

ACCOM: Mon. night thru Thurs. night rates for winterized (check if this is critical) rooms w/o meals unless otherwise indicated.

Motel; Max. Pers: 2; Bedding incl ?: Yes; Bath: Private; A/C: No:
Rate for: Person; ** $55; Rate for #2 pers: ** $55; Rate for #3 pers: n/a; Child Rate: 50% off under 13 yrs; free under 4
** Includes 3 meals

Cottage; Max. Pers: Over 4; Bedding incl ?: Yes; Bath: Shared; A/C: No
Rate for: Person: ** $55; Rate for #2 pers: ** $55; Rate for #3 pers: **$55; Child Rate: 50% off under 13 yrs; free under 4
** Includes 3 meals.

Main amenities available: Two outdoor pools; V-ball; Bsk-ball; Laundry machine; VCR-TV; Children's playground; Tennis/Horse shoes
Meals are served in dining room for transients . Dinner price varies.

NAME OF CENTER: West View on the James   Listing ID #: 364

Telephone: 804-457-4210; Fax: 804-457-2178; E-mail:
Address: 1231 West View Rd.; Goochland; VA; 23063
Nearest Interstate: I-64, Exit Goochland/Oilville; 16 miles; Nearest State/US Hwy: Rte 600/Rte 643; 0 miles.

Restrictions: Age: None; Pets: Permitted on leash; Alcohol: Not permitted; Smoking: Designated outdoor area; Reservation Req'd: None; Max. Adv. Reser.: 6 mo; Seasonal closing: Dec. 15 - Jan 1

RV/Campers overnight hookups: Yes; Water: Yes; Electric: Yes; Septic: Yes
Basic Rate/Night: $14/2 pers; $2/addtl/ veh

ACCOM: Mon. night thru Thurs. night rates for winterized (check if this is critical) rooms w/o meals unless otherwise indicated.

Dorm; Max. Pers: 5; Bedding incl ?: No; Bath: Shared; A/C: Yes:
Rate for: Person; $12; Rate for #2 pers: $12; Rate for #3 pers: $12; Child Rate: Free under 5 yrs

Cabin; Max. Pers: Over 5; Bedding incl ?: No; Bath: Separate bldg; A/C: No
Rate for: Person: $7; Rate for #2 pers: $7; Rate for #3 pers: $7; Child Rate: n/a

Main amenities available: Pool swimming; V-ball; Bsk-ball; Incidentals store; Laundry machine; VCR-TV; Boating/Fishing
Meals are served in dining room for transients only when other groups are present. Dinner price: $6.00.

NAME OF CENTER: **Williamsburg Christian Retreat Center**   Listing ID #: 365

Telephone: 757-566-2256; Fax: 757-566-4875; E-mail: wcrc@visi.net
Address: 9275 Barnes Rd.; Toano; VA; 23168
Nearest Interstate: I-64, Exit 2 miles; Nearest State/US Hwy: Rte 30; 1 miles.

Restrictions: Age: None; Pets: Permitted w/adv notice; Alcohol: Not permitted; Smoking: Outdoors only; Reservation Req'd: Noon of day; Max. Adv. Reser.: Open; Seasonal closing: None

RV/Campers overnight hookups: Yes; Water: Yes; Electric: Yes; Septic: Yes
Basic Rate/Night: $20 ($15 primitive)/ veh

ACCOM: Mon. night thru Thurs. night rates for winterized (check if this is critical) rooms w/o meals unless otherwise indicated.

Motel; Max. Pers: 4; Bedding incl ?: Yes; Bath: Private; A/C: Yes:
Rate for: Person; ******; Child Rate: n/a
** $45 - 2 person room; $55 - 4 person room

Main amenities available: Swimming; V-ball; Bsk-ball; Bookstore; Ping-pong; Tennis; Hiking
Meals are served in dining room for transients only when other groups are present. Dinner price: $4.95-7.95.

WASHINGTON

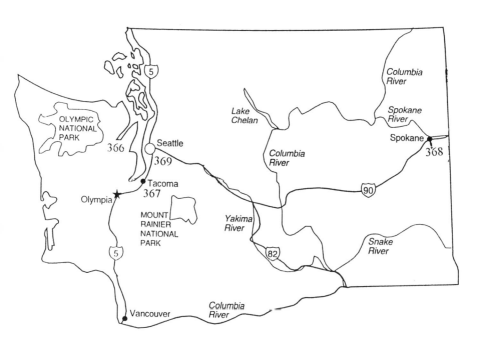

NAME OF CENTER: Alderbrook Inn   Listing ID #: 366

Telephone: 800-622-9370; Fax: 360-898-4610; E-mail:
registration@alderbrookinn.com
Address: 7101 E. State Route 106; Union; WA; 98592
Nearest Interstate: I-5, Exit 60 miles; Nearest State/US Hwy: Rte 101; 12 miles.

Restrictions: Age: None; Pets: Not permitted; Alcohol: Not permitted; Smoking: Outdoors only;
Reservation Req'd: None; Max. Adv. Reser.: 6 mo; Seasonal closing: None

RV/Campers overnight hookups: No

ACCOM: Mon. night thru Thurs. night rates for winterized (check if this is critical) rooms w/o
meals unless otherwise indicated.

Deluxe cottage; Two bedrooms (3 rms); Bedding incl ?: Yes; Bath: Private; A/C: No:
Rate for: Cottage; $129-209; Rate for #2 pers: n/a; Rate for #3 pers: n/a; Child Rate: Free
under 12 yrs.
Kitchenette included

Motel; Max. Pers: 5; Bedding incl ?: Yes; Bath: Private; A/C: No
Rate for: Room: $72-139; Rate for #2 pers: $10; Rate for #3 pers: $10; Child Rate: Free under
12 yrs.

Main amenities available: Swimming; Volleyball; Boating; Golf; TV; Tennis
Full service restaurant and cafe'. Dinner price: $8.00-25.00.

NAME OF CENTER: Benbow Campground   Listing ID #: 367

Telephone: 360-879-5426; Fax: 360-879-5270; E-mail:
Address: 32919 Benbow Drive East; Graham; WA; 98338
Nearest Interstate: I-512, Exit 20 miles; Nearest State/US Hwy: Rte 151; 5 miles.

Restrictions: Age: None; Pets: Not permitted; Alcohol: Not permitted; Smoking: Outdoors only;
Reservation Req'd: None; Max. Adv. Reser.: 6 mo; Seasonal closing: None

RV/Campers overnight hookups: Yes; Water: Yes; Electric: Yes; Septic: Yes
Basic Rate/Night: $16 + $2 w/septic/ veh

ACCOM: Mon. night thru Thurs. night rates for winterized (check if this is critical) rooms w/o
meals unless otherwise indicated.

Cabin; Max. Pers: 7; Bedding incl ?: Yes; Bath: Shared; A/C: No:
Rate for: Cabin; $100
One bedroom, kitchen, bath

Cabin; Max. Pers: 7; Bedding incl ?: Yes; Bath: Shared; A/C: No
Rate for: Cabin: $125
Two bedrooms, kitchen, bath

Main amenities available: Laundry machine; Volleyball; Basketball; Swimmiong; Incidentals store; Hiking
Meals are not served in dining room for transients .

NAME OF CENTER: Immaculate Heart Retreat Center   Listing ID #: 368

Telephone: 509-448-1224; Fax: 509-448-1623; E-mail:
Address: 6910 S. Ben Burr Rd.; Spokane; WA; 99223
Nearest Interstate: I-90, Exit 5 miles; Nearest State/US Hwy: Palouse Hwy; 2 miles.

Restrictions: Age: None; Pets: Not permitted; Alcohol: Hard liquor not permitted; Smoking:
Outdoors only; Reservation Req'd: 2 days; Max. Adv. Reser.: Open; Seasonal closing: n/a

RV/Campers overnight hookups: No

ACCOM: Mon. night thru Thurs. night rates for winterized (check if this is critical) rooms w/o
meals unless otherwise indicated.

Bunkroom; Max. Pers: 2; Bedding incl ?: Yes (w/notice); Bath: Shared; A/C: No:
Rate for: Person; $30; Rate for #2 pers: $10; Child Rate: n/a
Guests must make bed.

Motel; Max. Pers: 2; Bedding incl ?: Yes; Bath: Private; A/C: No
Rate for: Person: $30; Rate for #2 pers: $10; Child Rate: n/a
Guest must make bed.

Main amenities available: Library/bookstore; TV; Hiking
Meals are served in dining room for transients . Dinner price: $6.00-10.00.

NAME OF CENTER: LOMA Center for Renewal   Listing ID #: 369

Telephone: 425-392-1871; Fax: 425-391-7451; E-mail: LOMACenter@ad.com
Address: 3212 218th Ave. SE; Issaquah; WA; 98029
Nearest Interstate: I-90, Exit 5 miles.

Restrictions: Age: 14; Pets: Not permitted; Alcohol: Hard liquor not permitted; Smoking:
Outdoors only; Reservation Req'd: 8 AM of day; Max. Adv. Reser.: 1 mo; Seasonal closing:
None

RV/Campers overnight hookups: Yes; Water: No; Electric: Yes; Septic: unk
Basic Rate/Night: $10.00/ veh

ACCOM: Mon. night thru Thurs. night rates for winterized (check if this is critical) rooms w/o
meals unless otherwise indicated.

Dorm; Max. Pers: 2; Bedding incl ?: Yes; Bath: Shared; A/C: No:
Rate for: Person; $35; Rate for #2 pers: $30; Child Rate: n/a
Guests must put clean sheets on bed.

Main amenities available: Laundry machine; Volleyball; Hot tub; Billards ; Bookstore/library; Lawn games
Meals are served in dining room for transients only when other groups are present. Dinner price: $9.50.

NAME OF CENTER: YWCA - Seattle Listing ID: 370

Telephone: 206-461-4851   Fax: 206-461-4860
Address: 1118 Fifth Ave.; Seattle, WA 98101

Restrictions:
Accommodations offered to (M/F/Families): F. If M/F then must be over 18 yrs.
Pets: Not permitted; Alcohol: Not permitted; Smoking: Bedroom only
Reservation requirements: None
Reservations are accepted up to 6 mo in advance. Seasonal closing: None

ACCOMMODATIONS:
Single room: Bedding included ?: Yes; Bath: Shared
Rate for 1 day: $33; Rate for 1 week: $198

Single room: Bedding included ?: Yes; Bath: Private
Rate for 1 day: $38; Rate for 1 week: $228

Main amenities: Laundry machine
Meals are not offered in their own cafeteria.

WEST VIRGINIA

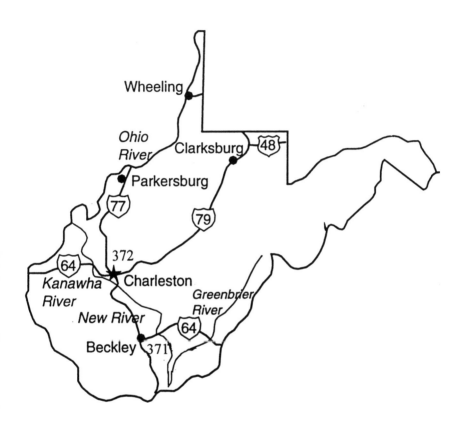

NAME OF CENTER: **Bluestone Conference Center**   Listing ID #: 371

Telephone: 304-466-0660; Fax: 304-466-0660; E-mail:
Address: HC 77; Box 44; Hinton; WV; 25951
Nearest Interstate: I-64, Exit 139; 20 miles; Nearest State/US Hwy: Rte 460; 24
miles.

Restrictions: Age: None; Pets: Not permitted; Alcohol: Not permitted; Smoking: Outdoors only;
Reservation Req'd: None; Max. Adv. Reser.: 1 mo; Seasonal closing: Thanksgiving thru Easter

RV/Campers overnight hookups: No

ACCOM: Mon. night thru Thurs. night rates for winterized (check if this is critical) rooms w/o
meals unless otherwise indicated.

Cabin; Max. Pers: Over 5; Bedding incl ?: No; Bath: Shared; A/C: No:
Rate for: Person; $18; Rate for #2 pers: $18; Rate for #3 pers: $18; Child Rate: 50% off under
12 yrs; free under 7

Main amenities available: Swimming; V-ball; Bsk-ball; Horse shoes; VCR-TV; Library; Hiking
Meals are served in dining room for transients only when other groups are present. Dinner price: $7; 50% off
under 12 yrs; free under 7.

NAME OF CENTER: **Claymont Society**   Listing ID #: 372

Telephone: 304-725-5990; Fax: ; E-mail: peter@claymont.org
Address: Huyett Rd. (mail: Rt 1; Box 279); Charlestown; WV; 25414
Nearest Interstate: I-81/I-70/I-270, Exit 30 miles; Nearest State/US Hwy: Rte 340; 2
miles.

Restrictions: Age: None; Pets: Not permitted inside; Alcohol: Permitted; Smoking: Outdoors
only; Reservation Req'd: 2 days; Max. Adv. Reser.: 6 mo; Seasonal closing: None

RV/Campers overnight hookups: No

ACCOM: Mon. night thru Thurs. night rates for winterized (check if this is critical) rooms w/o
meals unless otherwise indicated.

**Historic Hse; Max. Pers: 5 rooms; Bedding incl ?: Yes; Bath: Private/semi-private; A/C:
Yes:
Rate for: Person; ** $65-110; Rate for #2 pers: $0; Rate for #3 pers: $10; Child Rate: n/a
**Bldg in Historic Register; 2 rms w/private bath; 3 w/semi-private; Largest holds 6 pers.

Claymont is an ecumenical retreat hse; not specifically Christian. Call ahead if this is a
concern.

Main amenities available: Children's playground; Llama petting ; 360 acre organic farm; Hiking
Meals are not served in dining room for transients . Dinner price: Breakfast is included in room fee..

WISCONSIN

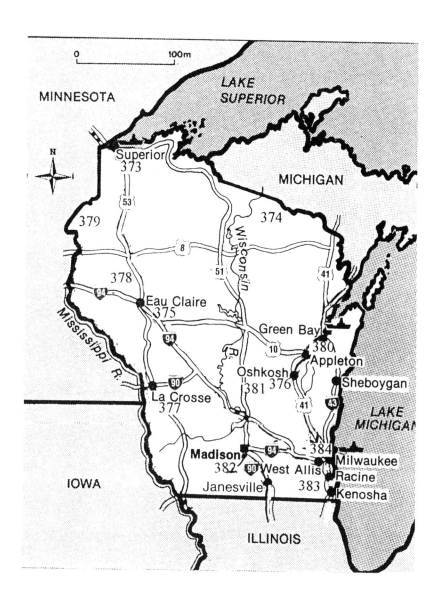

NAME OF CENTER: Camp Amnicon   Listing ID #: 373

Telephone: 715-364-2606; Fax: 715-364-2652; E-mail: www.amnicon.org
Address: 8450 E. Camp Amnicon Rd.; South Range; WI; 54874
Nearest Interstate: I-35, Exit 20 miles; Nearest State/US Hwy: Rte 13; 5 miles.

Restrictions: Age: None; Pets: Not permitted; Alcohol: Permitted in cabin; Smoking: Outdoors only; Reservation Req'd: Yes; Max. Adv. Reser.: Open; Seasonal closing: None

RV/Campers overnight hookups: No

ACCOM: Mon. night thru Thurs. night rates for winterized (check if this is critical) rooms w/o meals unless otherwise indicated.

Cabin; Max. Pers: 2; Bedding incl ?: Yes; Bath: Separate bldg; A/C: No:
Rate for: Person; $31; Rate for #2 pers: $6; Child Rate: n/a
Includes kitchenette

Main amenities available: Swimming; Sauna; Volleyball; Canoeing; X-Ctry skiing; Hiking
Meals are served in dining room for transients . Dinner price: $7.00.

NAME OF CENTER: Camp Luther   Listing ID #: 374

Telephone: 715-546-3647; Fax: 715-546-2396; E-mail:
Address: 1889 Koubenic Rd; Three Lakes; WI; 54562
Nearest Interstate: I-39, Exit 60 miles; Nearest State/US Hwy: Rte 45; 0.5 miles.

Restrictions: Age: None; Pets: Not permitted; Alcohol: Permitted; Smoking: Outdoors only; Reservation Req'd: 1 mo summer (1day other); Max. Adv. Reser.: 1 yr, Seasonal closing: None

RV/Campers overnight hookups: No

ACCOM: Mon. night thru Thurs. night rates for winterized (check if this is critical) rooms w/o meals unless otherwise indicated.

Cottages; Max. Pers: 8; Bedding incl ?: $4 surcharge; Bath: Shared; A/C: No:
Rate for: Entire cottage; ** $85-95
** Avail. only on wkly basis June 1 - Sept 1 for $485-555. Includes kitchen

Main amenities available: Lake swimming; Rowboat w/cottage; V-ball; Bsk-ball; Laundry mach. in summer; Children's playground; Hiking
Meals are not served in dining room for transients . Dinner price varies.

REMEMBER TO CALL AHEAD

NAME OF CENTER: Christine Ctr for Unitive Spirituality   Listing ID #: 375

Telephone: 715-267-7507; Fax: 715-267-7512; E-mail: weareone@christinecenter.org
Address: W. 8291 Mann Rd; Willard; WI; 54493
Nearest Interstate: I-94, Exit 35 miles; Nearest State/US Hwy: Rte 10; 10 miles.

Restrictions: Age: None; Pets: Not permitted; Alcohol: Not permitted; Smoking: Outdoors only; Reservation Req'd: 2 days; Max. Adv. Reser.: Open; Seasonal closing: None

RV/Campers overnight hookups: Yes; Water: Yes; Electric: Yes; Septic: No
Basic Rate/Night: $20.00/ veh

ACCOM: Mon. night thru Thurs. night rates for winterized (check if this is critical) rooms w/o meals unless otherwise indicated.

Dorm; Max. Pers: 5; Bedding incl ?: Yes; Bath: Shared; A/C: No:
Rate for: Person; **$50; Rate for #2 pers: **$20; Rate for #3 pers: **$20; Child Rate: **$10
** Includes 3 meals

Cabin; Max. Pers: Over 5; Bedding incl ?: Yes; Bath: Shared; A/C: No
Rate for: Person: ** $60; Rate for #2 pers: ** $10; Rate for #3 pers: ** $10; Child Rate: Free under 6 yrs
** Includes 3 meals

Bunkrooms; Max. Pers: Over 5; Bedding incl ?: Yes; Bath: Shared; A/C: No:
Rate for: Person: ** $40; Rate for #2 pers: ** $15; Rate for #3 pers: ** $15; Child Rate: ** $10
** Includes 3 meals

Main amenities available: Sauna; VCR-TV; Library; Bookstore; Hiking
Meals are served in dining room for transients only when other groups are present. Dinner price varies.

NAME OF CENTER: Lake Lucerne Camp & Retreat Ctr.   Listing ID #: 376

Telephone: 920-293-4488; Fax: 920-293-4361; E-mail: lucerne@wirural.net
Address: W 6460 County YY; Neshkoro; WI; 54960
Nearest Interstate: I-39, Exit 20 miles; Nearest State/US Hwy: Rte 41; 30 miles.

Restrictions: Age: None; Pets: Not permitted; Alcohol: Not permitted; Smoking: Outdoors only; Reservation Req'd: None; Max. Adv. Reser.: 1 yr; Seasonal closing: mid June - mid Aug

RV/Campers overnight hookups: No

ACCOM: Mon. night thru Thurs. night rates for winterized (check if this is critical) rooms w/o meals unless otherwise indicated.

Bunkroom; Max. Pers: Over 5; Bedding incl ?: No; Bath: Shared; A/C: No:
Rate for: Person; $13; Rate for #2 pers: $13; Rate for #3 pers: $13; Child Rate: $7.25 for children

Dorm; Max. Pers: 5; Bedding incl ?: Yes; Bath: Shared; A/C: No
Rate for: Person: $18; Rate for #2 pers: $18; Rate for #3 pers: $18; Child Rate: $10.75 for children

Main amenities available: Incidentals store; V-ball; Bsk-ball; Canoeing/sailing; Swimming; Tennis; Hike on 535 acres
Meals are served in dining room for transients only when other groups are present. Dinner price: $5.50.

NAME OF CENTER: Living Waters Bible Camp   Listing ID #: 377

Telephone: 608-634-4373; Fax: 608-634-3570; E-mail: lwbc@mwt.net
Address: Rt #1; Box 86A; Westby; WI; 54667
Nearest Interstate: I-90, Exit 20 miles; Nearest State/US Hwy: Rte 27; 2 miles.

Restrictions: Age: None; Pets: Not permitted; Alcohol: Not permitted; Smoking: Outdoors only;
Reservation Req'd: 7 days; Max. Adv. Reser.: 2 mo; Seasonal closing: June 11 - Aug. 20

RV/Campers overnight hookups: Yes; Water: Yes; Electric: Yes; Septic: No
Basic Rate/Night: $20.00/ veh

ACCOM: Mon. night thru Thurs. night rates for winterized (check if this is critical) rooms w/o
meals unless otherwise indicated.

Dorm; Max. Pers: 2; Bedding incl ?: No; Bath: Shared; A/C: No:
Rate for: Room; $25; Rate for #2 pers: $0; Child Rate: n/a

Cabin; Max. Pers: 4; Bedding incl ?: No; Bath: Shared; A/C: No
Rate for: Person: $25; Rate for #2 pers: $0; Rate for #3 pers: $8; Child Rate: n/a
Max: $40

Main amenities available: Laundry machine; Volleyball; Basketball; Bookstore; Ball field; Hiking
Meals are served in dining room for transients only when other groups are present. Dinner price: $7-10.00.

NAME OF CENTER: Luther Park   Listing ID #: 378

Telephone: 715-859-2215; Fax: 715-859-6474; E-mail: lutherpark@ecunet.org
Address: 944 24 1/4 st; Luther Park Rd; Chetek; WI; 54728
Nearest Interstate: I-94, Exit 75 miles; Nearest State/US Hwy: Rte 53; 3 miles.

Restrictions: Age: None; Pets: Not permitted; Alcohol: Not permitted; Smoking: Outdoors only;
Reservation Req'd: None; Max. Adv. Reser.: 13 mo; Seasonal closing: None

RV/Campers overnight hookups: Yes; Water: No; Electric: Yes; Septic: No
Basic Rate/Night: $7.50/ veh

ACCOM: Mon. night thru Thurs. night rates for winterized (check if this is critical) rooms w/o
meals unless otherwise indicated.

Dorm; Max. Pers: 3; Bedding incl ?: No; Bath: Shared; A/C: No:
Rate for: Room; $25; Child Rate: n/a

Half cabin; Max. Pers: 10; Bedding incl ?: No; Bath: Shared; A/C: No
Rate for: Half cabin: $75
Each half cabin has own bath.

Main amenities available: Swim in lake or pool; Volleyball; Basketball; Canoeing; Hiking
Meals are served in dining room for transients only when other groups are present. Dinner price: $6.00.

NAME OF CENTER: Luther Point Bible Camp   Listing ID #: 379

Telephone: 715-689-2347; Fax: 715-689-2348; E-mail:
Address: 11525 Luther Point Rd.; Grantsburg; WI; 54840
Nearest Interstate: I-35, Exit 25 miles; Nearest State/US Hwy: Rte 70; 3 miles.

Restrictions: Age: None; Pets: Not permitted; Alcohol: Not permitted; Smoking: Designated outdoor area; Reservation Req'd: None; Max. Adv. Reser.: Open; Seasonal closing: None

RV/Campers overnight hookups: Yes; Water: No; Electric: Yes; Septic: No
Basic Rate/Night: $9-10/ veh

ACCOM: Mon. night thru Thurs. night rates for winterized (check if this is critical) rooms w/o meals unless otherwise indicated.

Rustic Family Cabins; Max. Pers: 5; Bedding incl ?: No; Bath: Private; A/C: No:
Rate for: Entire cabin; $30
1 or 2 bedrooms; kitchenette; available late spring to early fall; space heater

Main amenities available: Incidentals store; Volleyball; Basketball
Meals are served in dining room for transients only when other groups are present. Dinner price: $5.50.

NAME OF CENTER: Norbertine Center for Spirituality   Listing ID #: 380

Telephone: 920-337-4315; Fax: 920-337-4328; E-mail: ncs@sncac.edu
Address: 1016 N. Broadway; DePere; WI; 54115
Nearest Interstate: I-72, Exit 1 miles; Nearest State/US Hwy: ; miles.

Restrictions: Age: 16; Pets: Not permitted; Alcohol: Not permitted; Smoking: Outdoors only; Reservation Req'd: 1 day; Max. Adv. Reser.: Open; Seasonal closing: None

RV/Campers overnight hookups: No

ACCOM: Mon. night thru Thurs. night rates for winterized (check if this is critical) rooms w/o meals unless otherwise indicated.

Dorm; Max. Pers: 5; Bedding incl ?: Yes; Bath: Shared; A/C: No:
Rate for: Person; $20; Rate for #2 pers: $20; Rate for #3 pers: $20; Child Rate: n/a
Guests are requested to remake beds w/clean linens

Main amenities available: Indoor pool; Sauna; Bookstore; Laundry machine; Incidentals store; VCR-TV
Meals are served in dining room for transients only when other groups are present. Dinner price: $6.50.

NAME OF CENTER: Pine Lake United Methodist Camp   Listing ID #: 381

Telephone: 608-296-2720; Fax: 608-296-4188; E-mail: pinelake@maqs.net
Address: W8301 Cty Hwy M; Westfield; WI; 53964
Nearest Interstate: I-39, Exit 9 miles; Nearest State/US Hwy: Rte 21; 8 miles.

Restrictions: Age: None; Pets: Not permitted; Alcohol: Not permitted; Smoking: Outdoors only; Reservation Req'd: None; Max. Adv. Reser.: 1 yr; Seasonal closing: None

RV/Campers overnight hookups: Yes; Water: No; Electric: Yes; Septic: No
Basic Rate/Night: $11.00/ veh

ACCOM: Mon. night thru Thurs. night rates for winterized (check if this is critical) rooms w/o meals unless otherwise indicated.

Motel; Max. Pers: 5; Bedding incl ?: No; Bath: Private; A/C: No:
Rate for: Person; $9; Rate for #2 pers: $9; Rate for #3 pers: $9; Child Rate: $6

Dorm; Max. Pers: 5; Bedding incl ?: No; Bath: Shared; A/C: No
Rate for: Person: $9; Rate for #2 pers: $9; Rate for #3 pers: $9; Child Rate: $5.75

Cabin/Bunkroom; Max. Pers: Over 5; Bedding incl ?: No; Bath: Shared; A/C: No:
Rate for: Person: $11; Rate for #2 pers: $11; Rate for #3 pers: $11; Child Rate: $7

Main amenities available: Swimming; V-ball; Bsk-ball; Bookstore/Library; Boat/Canoeing; Ball field; Hiking
Meals are served in dining room for transients only when other groups are present. Dinner price: $6-6.50.

NAME OF CENTER: Saint Benedict Center   Listing ID #: 382

Telephone: 608-836-1631; Fax: 608-831-9312; E-mail: eschaaf@sbcenter.org
Address: 4200 Cty Hwy M; Middleton; WI; 53562
Nearest Interstate: I-90/94, Exit 10 miles; Nearest State/US Hwy: ; miles.

Restrictions: Age: None; Pets: Not permitted; Alcohol: Permitted; Smoking: Outdoors only; Reservation Req'd: None; Max. Adv. Reser.: 3 mo; Seasonal closing: None

RV/Campers overnight hookups: No

ACCOM: Mon. night thru Thurs. night rates for winterized (check if this is critical) rooms w/o meals unless otherwise indicated.

Dorm; Max. Pers: 6; Bedding incl ?: Yes; Bath: Shared; A/C: No:
Rate for: Person; $30; Rate for #2 pers: $10; Rate for #3 pers: $10; Child Rate: Free under 12 yrs; $10/pers over three presons.

Main amenities available: Incidentals store; Volleyball; Laundry machine; Children's playground; Library; Hike on 135 acres
Meals are served in dining room for transients only when other groups are present. Dinner price: $7; $5 under 12 yrs.

NAME OF CENTER: St. *Francis Retreat Center*   Listing ID #: 383

Telephone: 414-763-3600; Fax: 414-763-4229; E-mail:
Address: 503 S. Browns Lake Dr.; Burlington; WI; 53105
Nearest Interstate: I-94, Exit 18 miles; Nearest State/US Hwy: Rte 38; 0 miles.

Restrictions: Age: 12; Pets: Not permitted; Alcohol: Not permitted; Smoking: Not permitted in bedroom; Reservation Req'd: 7 days; Max. Adv. Reser.: 1 yr; Seasonal closing: None

RV/Campers overnight hookups: No

ACCOM: Mon. night thru Thurs. night rates for winterized (check if this is critical) rooms w/o meals unless otherwise indicated.

Motel; Max. Pers: 5; Bedding incl ?: Yes; Bath: Private; A/C: No**:
Rate for: Person; $29; Rate for #2 pers: $29; Rate for #3 pers: $29; Child Rate: n/a
** Lounges are air-conditioned. Room fee includes 3 meals.

Dorm; Max. Pers: 5; Bedding incl ?: Yes; Bath: Shared; A/C: **No
Rate for: Person: $29; Rate for #2 pers: $29; Rate for #3 pers: $29; Child Rate: n/a
** Lounges are air-conditioned. Room fee includes 3 meals.

Main amenities available: VCR-TV; V-ball; Bsk-ball; Bookstore/Library; Tennis; Ball field; Hiking
Meals are served in dining room for transients .

NAME OF CENTER: Schoenstatt Center   Listing ID #: 384

Telephone: 414-547-7733; Fax: 414-547-7749; E-mail:
schoenstattwaukesha@juno.com
Address: W284 N698 Cherry Lane; Waukesha; WI; 53188
Nearest Interstate: I-94, Exit 3 miles; Nearest State/US Hwy: Rte 18; 3 miles.

Restrictions: Age: None; Pets: Not permitted; Alcohol: Hard liquor not permitted; Smoking: Nowhere; Reservation Req'd: 7 days; Max. Adv. Reser.: 1 ye; Seasonal closing: None

RV/Campers overnight hookups: No

ACCOM: Mon. night thru Thurs. night rates for winterized (check if this is critical) rooms w/o meals unless otherwise indicated.

Motel; Max. Pers: 5; Bedding incl ?: $5 surcharge; Bath: Private; A/C: No:
Rate for: Person; ** $49; Rate for #2 pers: ** $43; Rate for #3 pers: ** $43; Child Rate: 20% off for children   ** Includes 3 meals

Bunkroom; Max. Pers: Over 5; Bedding incl ?: $5 surcharge; Bath: Shared; A/C: No
Rate for: Person: ** $49; Rate for #2 pers: ** $43; Rate for #3 pers: ** $43; Child Rate: 20% off for children   ** Includes 3 meals

Cabin; Max. Pers: 2; Bedding incl ?: $5 surcharge; Bath: Private; A/C: No:
Rate for: Person: ** $49; Rate for #2 pers: ** $43; Child Rate: 20% off for children
** Includes 3 meals

Main amenities available: Quiet areas; Chapel. **Meals** are served in dining room for transients.

WYOMING

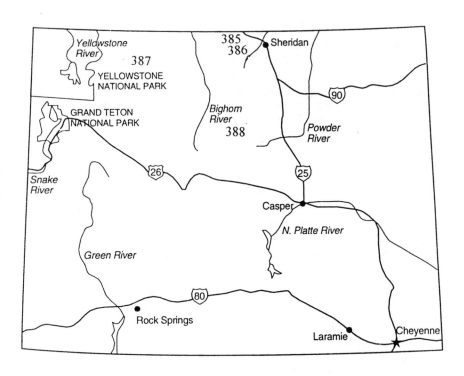

Yellowstone River

387

YELLOWSTONE NATIONAL PARK

385
386

Sheridan

90

GRAND TETON NATIONAL PARK

Bighorn River

388

Powder River

Snake River

26

25

Casper

N. Platte River

Green River

80

Rock Springs

Laramie

Cheyenne

NAME OF CENTER: Retreat of the Rockies   Listing ID #: 385

Telephone: 307-638-3322; Fax: 307-638-3322; E-mail:
Address: PO Box 1351; Cheyenne; WY; 82003
Nearest Interstate: I-80, Exit Harriman Rd; 8 miles; Nearest State/US Hwy: Cty Rd.
54; 1 miles.

Restrictions: Age: None; Pets: Not permitted; Alcohol: Not permitted; Smoking: Designated
outdoor area; Reservation Req'd: None; Max. Adv. Reser.: 6 mo; Seasonal closing: None

RV/Campers overnight hookups: No

ACCOM: Mon. night thru Thurs. night rates for winterized (check if this is critical) rooms w/o
meals unless otherwise indicated.

Duplex cabin; Max. Pers: 5; Bedding incl ?: Yes; Bath: Private; A/C: No:
Rate for: Entire duplex; $75
Incl: 2 bedrooms, bath, dining rm, living rm, kitchenette

Main amenities available: Tennis; Horse shoes; Basketball; Pond
Meals are not served in dining room for transients . Dinner price varies.

NAME OF CENTER: San Benito Monastery   Listing ID #: 386

Telephone: 307-655-9013; Fax: ; E-mail:
Address: 859 Main St; Dayton; WY; 82836
Nearest Interstate: I-90, Exit 6 miles.

Restrictions: Age: None; Pets: Not permitted; Alcohol: Not permitted; Smoking: Outdoors only;
Reservation Req'd: 3 days; Max. Adv. Reser.: 1 yr (must reconfirm); Seasonal closing: None

RV/Campers overnight hookups: No

ACCOM: Mon. night thru Thurs. night rates for winterized (check if this is critical) rooms w/o
meals unless otherwise indicated.

Mobile home; Max. Pers: Over 3; Bedding incl ?: Yes; Bath: Private; A/C: No:
Rate for: Person; $30; Rate for #2 pers: $30; Rate for #3 pers: $30; Child Rate: n/a
Incl: Kitchenette, breakfast food (you prepare it)

Main amenities available:Peace and quiet in the Mountains
Meals are not served in dining room for transients .

NAME OF CENTER: Thomas the Apostle Center   Listing ID #: 387

Telephone: 307-587-4400; Fax: 307-587-4400; E-mail: thomap@wave.park.wy.us
Address: 45 Road 3 CX-S; Cody; WY; 82414
Nearest State/US Hwy: Rte 20; 0 miles.

Restrictions: Age: None; Pets: Not permitted; Alcohol: Hard liquor not permitted; Smoking: Nowhere; Reservation Req'd: 1 mo; Max. Adv. Reser.: 3 mo; Seasonal closing: January

RV/Campers overnight hookups: No

ACCOM: Mon. night thru Thurs. night rates for winterized (check if this is critical) rooms w/o meals unless otherwise indicated.

Dorm; Max. Pers: 5; Bedding incl ?: Yes (w/notice); Bath: Shared; A/C: No:
Rate for: Person; $30; Rate for #2 pers: $30; Rate for #3 pers: $30; Child Rate: $15 w/parents

Motel; Max. Pers: 2; Bedding incl ?: Yes (w/notice); Bath: Private; A/C: No
Rate for: Person: $30; Rate for #2 pers: $30; Child Rate: n/a
All room fees are donations.

Main amenities available: Even more peace and quiet in the Mountains.
Meals are not served in dining room for transients .

NAME OF CENTER: United Methodist Circle J Ranch   Listing ID #: 388

Telephone: 307-366-2241; Fax: ; E-mail:
Address: HC 30; Box 2220; Ten Sleep; WY; 82442
Nearest Interstate: I-25, Exit 50 miles; Nearest State/US Hwy: Rte 16; 0 miles.

Restrictions: Age: None; Pets: Not permitted; Alcohol: Not permitted; Smoking: Outdoors only; Reservation Req'd: 2 mo; Max. Adv. Reser.: 1 yr; Seasonal closing: None

RV/Campers overnight hookups: Yes; Water: No; Electric: Yes; Septic: No
Basic Rate/Night: **/ veh

ACCOM: Mon. night thru Thurs. night rates for winterized (check if this is critical) rooms w/o meals unless otherwise indicated.

Bunkroom; Max. Pers: Over 5; Bedding incl ?: No; Bath: Shared; A/C: No:
Rate for: Person; $13; Rate for #2 pers: $13; Rate for #3 pers: $13; Child Rate: $12.50 under 12 yrs; $9 under 7; free under 3
Requested to: Sweep & mop floor; clean bath room before leaving

Dormitory; Max. Pers: 5; Bedding incl ?: No; Bath: Shared; A/C: No
Rate for: Person: $13; Rate for #2 pers: $13; Rate for #3 pers: $13; Child Rate: $12.50 under 12 yrs; $9 under 7; free under 3

Main amenities available: ; Volleyball; Basketball
Meals are not served in dining room for transients.

INTERSTATE HIGHWAY CROSS-INDEX

IS	State	ID #	Page	State	ID #	Page	State	ID #	Page
I-101	CA	37	23	CA	38	24	CA	39	24
I-4	FL	67	42						
I-5	CA	18	14	CA	19	14	CA	21	15
	CA	29	19	CA	30	20	CA	33	21
	CA	35	22	OR	283	180	OR	284	180
	OR	285	181	WA	366	234			
I-805	CA	27	18						
I-8	CA	23	16	CA	28	19			
I-10	CA	17	13	CA	20	15	CA	22	16
	CA	25	17	FL	68	42	FL	76	46
	MS	186	116	MS	187	116	TX	342	217
	TX	343	218						
I-210	CA	36	23						
I-512	WA	367	234						
I-14	CA	32	21						
I-15	CA	40	25	MT	197	124	NV	207	132
	UT	350	222						
I-17	AZ	7	7	AZ	8	7	AZ	9	8
	AZ	10	8	AZ	11	9	AZ	12	9
I-20	LA	137	85	TX	339	216			
I-25	CO	44	28	CO	45	28	CO	47	29
	CO	48	30	CO	49	30	CO	50	31
	CO	51	31	CO	53	32	CO	54	33
	NM	218	141	NM	219	142	WY	388	248
I-26	SC	318	201	SC	319	202			
I-27	TX	337	215	TX	344	218			
I-29	IA	114	70	KS	124	76			
	ND	265	167	SD	322	205			
I-30	TX	339	216						
I-430	AR	4	5						
I-131	MI	164	105						

INTERSTATE HIGHWAY CROSS-INDEX

IS	State	ID #	Page	State	ID #	Page	State	ID #	Page
I-35	IA	118	72	IA	120	73	IA	121	74
	KS	126	77	MN	182	113	MO	191	119
	MO	194	121	OK	280	177	OK	281	177
	TX	333	213	TX	336	214	TX	338	215
	TX	340	216	TX	345	219	TX	346	219
	WI	373	240	WI	379	243			
I-39	WI	374	240	WI	376	241	WI	381	244
I-40	AR	6	5	AZ	13	10	NC	255	161
	NC	256	161	NC	258	162	NC	259	163
	NC	260	163	NC	261	164	TN	326	208
	TN	328	209	TN	329	210	TN	330	210
I-44	AR	5	5	MO	190	119	MO	192	120
	MO	196	122	NM	220	142			
I-45	TX	334	213						
I-46	TX	341	217						
I-55	IL	91	58	MS	185	115	MO	189	118
I-255	IL	93	59						
I-57	VA	354	226						
I-59	AL	2	2						
I-64	IN	104	65	IN	108	67	KY	127	79
	KY	129	80	VA	356	227	VA	359	229
	VA	364	231	VA	365	232	WV	371	238
I-65	AL	1	2	IN	100	63	KY	128	79
I-265	KY	131	81						
I-465	IN	103	64						
I-67	MO	188	118	MO	193	120			
I-69	MI	164	103						
I-70	CA	46	29	CO	52	32	IN	107	66
	KS	123	76	KS	125	77	MD	147	92
	MD	148	92	MO	195	121	OH	270	171
	OH	273	172	PA	296	188	PA	299	189
	PA	302	191	PA	305	192	WV	372	238

INTERSTATE HIGHWAY CROSS-INDEX

IS	State	ID #	Page	State	ID #	Page	State	ID #	Page
I-71	OH	266	169	OH	268	170	OH	269	170
I-72	WI	380	243						
I-74	IL	94	59	IN	102	64			
I-75	FL	66	41	FL	71	44	FL	74	45
	FL	75	46	GA	80	50	GA	86	53
	KY	130	80	KY	134	82	KY	135	83
	MI	164	103	MI	166	104	MI	168	105
	327	209	TN						
I-275	FL	78	47	OH	275	173			
I-76	PA	291	185	PA	294	187	PA	296	188
	PA	299	189	PA	302	191	PA	303	191
	PA	304	192						
I-77	OH	267	169	OH	271	171	SC	317	201
I-78	PA	297	188						
I-79	PA	300	190						
I-80	CA	16	13	CA	26	18	CT	56	35
	IL	92	58	IN	98	62	IN	99	62
	IN	101	63	IN	106	66	IA	113	69
	IA	112	69	IA	117	72	MI	161	102
	NE	200	127	NE	201	127	NE	202	128
	NE	203	128	NE	204	129	NE	205	129
	NV	208	132	NJ	212	137	NJ	214	138
	NJ	215	138	OH	274	173	PA	292	186
	PA	298	189	PA	306	193	PA	307	193
	PA	308	194	PA	309	194	WY	385	247
I-680	CA	24	17						
I-880	CA	34	22						
I-81	NY	254	160	PA	286	183	PA	288	184
	PA	289	184	VA	353	226	VA	357	228
	VA	360	229	VA	361	230	VA	362	230
	VA	363	231	WV	372	238			
I-181	TN	325	208						

INTERSTATE HIGHWAY CROSS-INDEX

IS	State	ID #	Page	State	ID #	Page	State	ID #	Page
I-83	PA	293	186						
I-84	CT	57	35	NY	232	149	NY	235	151
	NY	239	153	PA	306	193			
I-85	GA	81	50	NC	257	162			
I-285	GA	85	52						
I-86	ID	88	55						
I-87	NY	223	145	NY	228	147	NY	229	148
	NY	236	151	NY	237	152			
I-287	NJ	213	137	NY	238	152			
I-89	NH	211	135	VT	351	224			
I-90	ID	87	55	ID	89	56	ID	90	56
	IN	98	62	IN	99	62	IN	101	63
	IN	106	66	IA	113	70	IA	115	71
	IA	116	71	IA	119	73	MA	152	96
	MA	153	96	MA	155	97	MA	156	98
	MN	178	111	MT	199	125	NY	224	145
	NY	225	146	NY	227	147	NY	230	148
	NY	231	149	NY	233	150	NY	234	150
	PA	287	183	PA	290	185	PA	295	187
	SD	320	204	SD	323	205	SD	324	206
	WA	368	235	WA	369	235	WI	377	242
	WI	382	244	WY	386	247			
I-190	NY	226	146						
I-91	MA	156	98	MA	158	99			
	NH	210	134	VT	352	224			
I-93	NH	209	134						
I-94	MI	167	105	MI	169	106	MI	171	107
	MN	179	111	MN	180	112	MN	181	112
	MN	183	113	MN	184	115	ND	264	167
	SD	321	204	WI	375	241	WI	378	242
	WI	382	244	WI	383	245	WI	384	245

INTERSTATE HIGHWAY CROSS-INDEX

IS	State	ID #	Page	State	ID #	Page	State	ID #	Page
I-95	FL	70	43	FL	72	44	FL	73	45
	GA	82	51	GA	83	51	GA	84	52
	ME	139	87	ME	140	87	ME	141	88
	ME	142	88	MD	149	93	MD	150	93
	MA	154	97	PA	301	190	RI	316	199
	VA	358	228						
I-295	VA	355	227						
I-96	MI	165	104						
I-196	MI	170	106						
FL T'pke		65	41						
KY T'pke		132	81						
Pennyril Pkwy		133	82						